DESIRES FOR REALITY

DESIRES FOR REALITY

RADICALISM AND REVOLUTION IN WESTERN EUROPEAN FILM

BY
BENJAMIN HALLIGAN

Published in 2016 by
Berghahn Books
www.berghahnbooks.com

© 2016 Benjamin Halligan

Library of Congress Cataloging-in-Publication Data
A C.I.P. cataloging record is available from the Library of Congress

British Library Cataloguing in Publication Data
A catalogue record for this book is available from the British Library

ISBN 978-1-78533-110-7 hardback
ISBN 978-1-78533-111-4 ebook

Contents

Illustrations

Acknowledgements

My sincere thanks to those associates of this research, who offered company and conversation, and advice and sympathy, across several countries: Jacques Baratier, Chiara Barbo, Bifo, Peter Brunette, Ian Christie, Ray Durgnat, Sergio Germani, Olaf Möller, Toni Negri, Bulle Ogier, Gerald Raunig, Jackie Raynal, Werner Schroeter, Mike Shaw, Iain Sinclair, Pete Tombs, David Walsh, Bill Van Wert, Slavoj Žižek. I gratefully acknowledge the support of the universities of Aberystwyth, York St John and Salford, and Stonyhurst College, over the many too many years of this research. And I wish to note my appreciation of the work of the programmers and denizens of the Leeds International Film Festival, the International Short Film Festival in Oberhausen, and I Mille Occhi in Trieste.

Ioan Willians and John Hefin together made this work possible. This book is dedicated to them.

Benjamin Halligan
Manchester, Easter Sunday 2014

CHAPTER ONE

'All All All'

'I take my desires for reality, for I believe in the reality of my desires'.

— 1968 slogan

'We are still the contemporaries of May '68'.

— Alain Badiou, *The Communist Hypothesis* (2010)

Periodising the 1960s in Cinema

What was the progressive cinema of the 1960s? In the absence of any generally agreed definitions, differing ideas abound, originating from two areas: firstly, the critical/academic histories of 1960s cinema, and secondly the conception of a 'progressive cinema' that is apparent in a number of 1960s films. The initial point of departure for this study is the conflict that arises between these two areas: the progressive cinema of the 1960s, as articulated in its own artefacts, does not always fully support, verify or validate the idea of a progressive cinema of the 1960s to be found in critical/academic histories. This disparity will be used to orientate this study as it seeks to expand the parameters of the critical/academic histories in order to identify and conceptualise, in a sustained way, the progressive cinema of the 1960s.

The first of these overall groupings, the critical/academic histories of 1960s cinema, is always localised and mostly operates within the framework of 'national cinemas' as a methodological structuring device; there are no serious pan-European studies of progressive film of this period. Such an absence is particularly arresting, since the '1960s phase' of European film, in its look and feel, preoccupations and recurring themes, even colour palettes and sound mixes, could be said to be particularly distinctive. The strength of the identity of a '1960s phase' is such that the term 'period' seems inadequate; more than the terminology of temporal measurements is required. 'Era' – especially in the popular imagination – captures something of the self-contained nature of those years; the exercise of new freedoms within newly expanded limits of artistic expression, often in relation to experimentation and confrontation, a time defined by the results of a paradigm shift – a newness to things that automatically breaks with the old order. The 1960s era remains prominently visible – as much for those elements since assimilated within the language and practices of contemporary culture (the legacy of the era) as those elements that have stubbornly resisted this process (the dated – to be pastiched or satirised, or forgotten).

The strong boundaries of the 1960s era delineate this area, as a whole, as appropriate for critical scrutiny. The era begins decisively with a modernist phase in the arts in metropolitan centres in the late 1950s (particularly popular music, fashion and photography – totemic of the dividend of the end of post-war scarcity; such breakthroughs in theatre and literature can be placed in the mid 1950s) and ends spectacularly with the events of 1968. Questions flowing from the aftermath of 1968 were to define and preoccupy the subsequent period. Cinema was intrinsic to the cultural scene of the 1960s, and often central to the reinvention and reimagining of other art forms at that time. As with many other 1960s artistic endeavours, the 'expanded cinema', to use Gene Youngblood's description (1970), came to be characterised by interdisciplinism. Thus the popular vernacular associated with the reception of artistic endeavours towards the end of the decade (as 'progressive' increasingly turned to 'radical') effectively collapses formal differences between art forms in favour of a totalising subjective expression of the encounter: it would be a 'happening', 'a trip', an 'epiphany', the 'be-in' or 'love-in' as a fusion of music, media and social gathering; it was 'far out', something one would 'dig'. The plundering of the terminology of Eastern traditions of mysticism – a lexicon of 'oneness', 'togetherness', 'karma' and the 'cool', and the mantra of 'tune in, turn on, and drop out' – allowed for an articulation of a sense of art that went way beyond an appreciation qualified by an acknowledgment of the limitations of individual art forms. Artistic expression had edged towards the collective: 'of' all (a mass ownership and mass creation of the 'happening'), with all (the shared experiences of such a 'happening') and for all (experiences as freely available for participants, even as defining their lifestyles). Such a conceptual expansion, once applied to the idea of cinema, wrested it away – even fancifully – from previous imaginings of individuals positioned in front of a cinema screen, comparatively assessing their individual experiences of the film afterwards. Now the psychologically 'expanded cinema'[1] broke its banks and intermingled with other art forms before, during and after projection. Film, in this respect, comes to be considered as akin to a psychedelic liquid light show – a highly collective experience. This conceptual expansion of cinema substantially complicates critical scrutiny of 1960s-era cinema.

The critical/academic history invariably acknowledges the self-contained nature of the era and the intrinsic position of cinema in relation to this, but fails to find a viewpoint from which the full range of characteristics may be seen in relation to each other. Such a viewpoint cannot be achieved when its subject remains uncertain. That is, the critical/academic history of progressive cinema of the 1960s has not attempted an explicit answer to the question 'what was the progressive cinema of the 1960s?' Clusters of similarities (shared concerns, shared methodological approaches to film, a commonality of preoccupations) can be discerned or even observed, compiled or tabulated, but an underlying structure – the grid of connections upon which the expansion of the idea of cinema is built – remains frustratingly 'just beyond' the reach of these histories.

An earlier period, the Popular Front of the 1930s, presents no such problem. The grid of connections can be found in the overarching anti-fascist concern of a united and inclusive artistic scene of that time. It is possible, when speaking of 'Popular Front-ism', to include the artistic endeavours – such as Jean Renoir's – fashioned to cast the shadow of ascendant European fascism over everyday reality. These connections are 'overground' and represent the essential terrain to be scrutinised in discussing the purposes of the artistic artefacts of this period. The identification of a comparable essential terrain in relation to the 1960s era is not so readily achieved. Often the terrain is manifest only obliquely in its countering of a variety of hegemonic positions (Stalinism, Western consumerism, a countering of the dominant cultural practices) across a wide spectrum (from formal politics and political militancy to individualised, 'biopolitical' concerns).[2] What do the screaming hordes of fans of A Hard Day's Night (Richard Lester, 1964) say about the particular dynamic of the times, and/or of the reception of The Beatles? The behaviour, and rapture, of the fans suggests a series of oblique, even unconscious, positions 'for' (this music, their shouting, youth itself) and against (the establishment, its behavioural codes for young people). Clearly there is an agenda of sorts animating this activity – and the film's concentration on such activity underlines as much – but the agenda escapes hard definition, and even focuses (on individuals, or the collective fans; on the masses, or even the often absent Beatles themselves), and so 'baffled cultural commentators and alarmed moral guardians' (Goddard, Halligan, Spelman 2013: 3). Such sequences could be said to be about an exuberant non-specificity; but is this activity, as presented, the agenda itself, or evidence of an agenda elsewhere, 'off camera'? Thus the grid of connections is difficult to pin down, and the essential terrain to be scrutinised is seemingly everywhere, in evidence, and nowhere, in detail. Whereas, when an essential terrain is manifest directly in the 1960s – which is often perceived to be the case in semi-totalitarian countries , or police or barrack states – while no less complex in its strategy, a purpose is visible and the oppositionism qualified mostly to that end alone.[3] So in *Lásky Jedné Plavovlásky* (*Loves of a Blonde*, Miloš Forman, (1965)), youth, also in mild rebellion and with such rebellion also finessed by popular music, presents an entirely different proposition – now the connections are unavoidable. Thus this youth is 'a generation', to borrow Wajda's term, and one that comes to figure – even in the idle strumming of a guitar or talk of Picasso – in the liberalism of its time and place (Czechoslovakia's aspirant 'socialism with a human face').

This ability of metamorphosis in the essential terrain, in the former 'oblique' instance, points to a grid of 'deeper' connections, in an underlying, subterranean area. And while critical/academic scrutiny of a structuralist or post-structuralist approach would tend to dismiss the actualité of such a quality, or place it in the area of reception/audience studies for further empirical investigation, many artefacts of the time do not hesitate to present this quality as the foundation for their praxis, despite the obscurity of quality's nature. Julian Beck, of the Living Theatre, resorts to the term 'vibrations' to name such a grid of connections in his 1968 poem 'Paradise Now'. He finds these vibrations running directly from the nodes of social upheaval to his Artaudian-Dionysian theatre work. Beck writes, 'i am a magic realist / i see the adorers of che / i see the black man / forced to accept / violence / i see the pacifists / despair / and accept violence / i see all all all / corrupted / by the vibrations / vibrations of violence of civilization'. The poem then moves to the proposed response: 'we want/ to zap them / with holiness', and 'we want / to levitate them / with joy'. Thereafter 'we want / to make the land and its cities glow / with creation / we want to make it / irresistible / even to racists / we want to change / the demonic character of our opponents / into productive glory' (quoted in Roszek 1971: 150–151).

Figure 1.1 Paradisiac aphrodisiacs: the piled up and writhing bodies of the Living Theatre cleanse the 'vibrations of violence of civilization' (*Paradise Now*, Topp, 1968)

The battle over, or for, these vibrations – whether to be turned to good ends (joy, holiness, creation – the 'paradise now' of the poem's title, and of one of Beck's most celebrated countercultural theatre events) – or bad ones (despairing pacifists turning to violence in the face of their demonic opponents, the state and its repressive apparatus) – is for the 'all all all' protesting on the streets, both pacifists and militants. The artist's expanded role, to be of all, with all and for all, is to raise consciousness via and 'along' such vibrations – running the energy from the streets into the good karma zone of the theatre, to the betterment of the streets, the theatre and the masses. At this rarefied level, 'art' and 'revolution', as both in and of the streets, are to become interchangeable, complimentary – or even the same. By 1968 Beck's consciousness-raising ideas were falling out of favour, but this expansive, all-encompassing conception of a 'magic' (and in that respect 'realist') theatre – the area of the meeting and melding of politics and love, hedonism and militant agitation for change; the theatre event as the agent of renewal for a collapsing society – is entirely emblematic of the radical-progressive understanding of the role of art in the latter half of the 1960s. (And 'Paradise Now' was published in *International Times*, aka *IT* – the paper of the radical-progressive counterculture in the United Kingdom.)

The assumed expanded reach of the subterranean grid of connections is apparent in a further facet of interdisciplinism: the ways in which the arts were able to 'speak to' the times, and the times to 'speak to' the arts – indeed, in Beck's case, this interaction was a necessity for the existence of meaningful or positive art. But the identification of such assumed processes, with more specificity than 'vibrations', remains. So while there is a general tendency to posit an ill-defined but uniquely close relationship between the 1960s artefacts and their era (accepting Beck's 'vibrations' in the then modus operandi of art), a close relationship apparent even now (the artefact, as seen or experienced now, is 'very much of' its time), there remains a reluctance to outline the 'hardwiring' between the artefact and its era, or to identify the osmosis-like processes between the artefact and its era. (And, along with interdisciplinism, or even as part of an interdisciplinism, this close relationship also characterises the arts of this era.) It remains a largely unknown quality.

For example, to return to the question of theatre and a zeitgeist, Lacey questions why George Devine, often identified as the father of the 'Angry Young Man' period, writing in 1959, had been 'evasive' in elucidating exactly how a 'true expression of, or a revelation about, certain deep feelings in a particular society' had, as Devine had claimed, been achieved in various theatres. The explanation Lacey gives is that the acknowledged intention to achieve often rendered unnecessary its actual achievement: it becomes sufficient for work to be solely platitudinal. Two roughly contemporary commentators of the Royal Court of the 'Angry Young Man' phase are used to illustrate this: 'That the house was made to twitter at some titbit of dialectical reasoning was taken as evidence that the wedding of art and social commitment had in fact taken place. That Marx in the process had been made into a bourgeois humorist was either missed or ignored'; 'one only has to go up on a public platform . . . for nine-tenths of the audience immediately to assume that one believes that novels should be simple tracts about factories or strikes or economic injustice' (Lacey 1995: 39). Lacey concludes at the close of his first chapter, in relation to his own methodology: 'With the idea of politics contaminated by its associations with communism and the consensus, and with committed theatre identified with propaganda, it was in the discourse of realism that the project of creating a contemporary and anti-hegemonic theatre was pursued' (Lacey 1995: 39). Such an approach is well-suited to a history mostly determined by a 'soft' and non-aligned left, one for which a system of strategic dissent (rather than a heightened realism) would be perceived to be irrelevant. And Lacey's study covers 1956–1965, a period of innovation of form. Comparable phenomena are apparent in European film of this time too – from 1958/59, and the beginnings of the European New Waves, to circa 1963 and the end of a phase chiefly characterised by experiments with form, as shall be argued.

Where histories of progressive film of the 1960s exhibit a general trend of premature curtailment, then, the suspicion is that it is a resonation of this 'unknown quality', at the very heart of their conceptualisations of 1960s film, that blocks the way. So, in the shying away from this problematic, in premature curtailments, a completeness of approach and scope in the histories comes to be eclipsed by a sole or exaggerated concentration on the beginnings. This 'era', in the critical/academic histories, now fails to reach its, or a, climax. This results in a concern with revolutionary means, but rarely their projected revolutionary ends.

This curtailing in critical/academic histories is particularly acute in relation to New Wave films. These are easily grouped into a movement or school at the moment of their inception, especially when considered en masse, and represent the most outwardly experimental of progressive films of this period, not least because of the influence exerted on them by 'Brechtian' methods. There is disagreement over the end date of the New Waves; circa 1963 is generally given. The formal beginnings of the New Waves, however, can be incontrovertibly placed as 1958/59, when looking to their arrival in the public consciousness.[4] Yet these films as representative of a new movement or school seem harder to place; it raises a question typically avoided in the critical/academic history: the full identification cannot occur without first specifying what it is that is being identified. Thus Kline notes, of the French cycle of New Wave films: 'I use the term Nouvelle Vague with the usual precautions. By now, most historians have agreed that there was no movement per se, in the sense of a program, but rather a temporal coincidence of reaction' (Kline 1992: 227, footnote 8). The same may be said of Italy, and the films that Lino Miccichè terms 'l'operazione "Nouvelle Vague" italiana' (Viano 1993: 50), which: 'failed as an attempt to create a unitary movement with a stylistic and theoretical identity of its own. [Yet] nevertheless launched the autori who, together with the triad of mature auteurs from the previous generation (Antonioni, Visconti, and Fellini) and Bellocchio, who debuted in 1966, contributed to the "decisive decade" of Italian cinema' (Viano 1993: 50–51). This lack of a common agenda is illustrated by the way in which some critics even perceived the Nouvelle Vague to be a 'movement of the right' (Marie 2003: 34), despite a prehistory closely associated with leftist concerns. Douchet finds this possible in the concentration on the images of prosperity over poverty (Douchet 1999: 23). But this reading was achieved by latching on to select comments from Godard and Truffaut (Benayoun does this, for example, in the 1962 *Positif* article 'The King is Naked'; see Benayoun 1968: 174), so that they were seemingly claiming for the disparate results of this 'temporal coincidence' a common goal: attacking the 'poetic realism' of the better films of the 'tradition of quality' on the grounds of their soft leftism and humanism. This attack was mounted so as to reform French film-making, which could do without such wistful sentiments. In this way, such critics (of the time, but the reading still persists) found no quarrel with the association Chabrol makes with the Nouvelle Vague and regeneration under de Gaulle (Nicholls 1993: 10), converging with the way in which 'A certain French chauvinism sees its own cinema at the root of this international revolution [of the New Waves]' (Marie 2003: 128).[5] And Kline himself lumps Bresson in with the Nouvelle Vague film-makers, indicating that Kline's definition of the Nouvelle Vague is entirely one of 'temporal coincidence'; Bresson's refined, minimalist film form was the very opposite of the messy and cluttered radicalisation of form typical of Nouvelle Vague film.

It is difficult to avoid the impression that in these approaches apparent in this brief review of tendencies in critical literature on the period the films are not comprehended on the biggest of scales (whether they are 'left' or 'right'), or on the smallest (their aesthetic commonalities – Bresson as rubbing shoulders with Varda). From this a conclusion can be made: the New Wave film remains, in essence, unidentified from the point of its inception. And the need for a pseudo-identification in the critical/academic history comes to rest on a discussion of aesthetic innovations – the very visible surface of the wave, not the currents beneath it.

As to the cut-off date of this movement, Neupert's study gives an end date of 1964 (Neupert 2002: xviii, xxix), while Williams's delineation of the Nouvelle Vague, one in which 'French filmmaking after roughly 1962 should be called post-New Wave cinema' (Williams 1992: 328), is more accurate for the British New Wave – the moment at which it abandoned its 'Northern' concerns. Such premature endings are only possible if the Nouvelle Vague is exclusively considered as a period of aesthetic innovation, with any sense of the creation of a wider discourse as tangential – if not accidental. Graham, in his 1968 study *The New Wave*, identified the centrality of the idea of ideology and linked this to the radicalisation of form arising from 'production' methods – the way in which the films were made and why, and the praxis or methodology that had arisen (which itself was a notable aspect of the New Wave 'look'): 'the phenomenon of the Nouvelle Vague was not purely a question of cinematic ideology. It was above all a revolution in *production*, in the attitude of the public and, in particular, producers' (Graham 1968: 8, his italics). Removing this element of ideology from a consideration of the results of this praxis would suggest that the Nouvelle Vague, as a period of aesthetic experimentation, did indeed grind to a halt in the early/mid

'60s, after all the major aesthetic innovations had been achieved. Graham's consideration of ideology in relation to the 'revolution in production' makes sense when confronted by the unavoidable fact of the 'new look' of Nouvelle Vague films. The production – how this look was achieved – is the foremost characteristic only, and is the element that caused such a stir in 1958/59. But the idea of an evolution fired by a certain ideological attitude towards the question of film and film-making persisted well beyond the mid 1960s. So, if one is to see the aesthetic surface as merely a prelude to the real unification of a variety of films into a wave, with such a unification as occurring in relation to the reinvention of film with the creation of a progressive/radical cinema in the 1960s, then the New Wave history is suddenly elongated. After all, after the period of experimentation with form, where is film to go? One does not master a language so as to never speak the language again, safe in the knowledge that it has been mastered. Indeed, many of the speakers of that language (the European auteurs associated with progressive film), active in the early 1960s, remained active through the mid 1960s; even where their films changed, a set of underlying assumptions remained constant – as shall be argued.

A straight empirical history of these figures and their times would find, in the 1960s, an elongation of the New Wave as possible in relation to a shared ideological project then running its course: dissenting, agitational, and allied with leftist Western intellectuals. Even with such a basic methodological approach, the Western European New Waves can be seen to stretch until 1968/69 – or, more precisely, the New Waves ended as a consequence of the failure and fallout of the upheavals of 1968, the culmination of the ideological and agitational activities of leftist Western intellectuals, workers and students.

In the critical/academic histories, the aporia of curtailments, in relation to identification and periodisation, may be said to be a symptom of a canonical impulse: the assembly of a series of texts that illustrate a successful measure of innovation, and the overlooking of texts that extend such innovations and illustrate their logical conclusions at these extended limits. And those films outside the canon fade from view. They remain unseen, their prints ragged or in copyright limbo, or lost altogether, with their restoration – in the physical sense – as offering little or no hope of emotional or intellectual, or indeed financial, recompense.

However, in looking to the conception of a progressive cinema evident in a number of 1960s films (the latter of the two groups mentioned at the outset of this section) two answers to the otherwise shirked question ('what was the progressive cinema of the 1960s?') are apparent. In a number of 1960s films, the possibility of an identification of this 'unknown quality' is raised.

In the first instance, the 'progressive' element arises from a dialectic with previous films. The end of post-war scarcity, with the reinvigoration of film culture, resulted in a realigning of the idea of the medium of film: it was now not only to be the exclusive preserve of the working classes – as a fillip for their leisure times – but also be of direct interest to white collar workers. (Again, the metropolitan centres figure, now as exerting a centrifugal force in this regard.) This phenomenon can be identified as an 'intellectualisation' of film culture. It is particularly apparent, in its embryonic stage, as a trend in the United Kingdom, arising from the coming together of a number of different artistic and class-based interests and concerns, and with the United Kingdom as a well-positioned optic for directions in wider European film culture. This study will briefly identify and review this intellectual phase as the first answer, arising 'in the field' itself, to the question of a progressive film of the 1960s. It will not be necessary to pass judgement on this area; the possibilities that arose rapidly became unstuck with the wilful sabotage of the project by those involved in it, resulting in a crisis of film culture and practice. This is identified as an impasse, and occurs from 1966.

In the second instance, questions of film culture and practice – purpose and method – were also to become central to another area associated with the 'progressive': a film culture alert to the traumas of fascism (historical and contemporary) and/or aligned with the drift of 'progressive' politics of the left. This drift begins in the mid 1950s, with a number of events that led to the exodus of members from Soviet Russia-affiliated Western European Communist parties (the Suez crisis, the failure of de-Stalinisation in the wake of Stalin's death, the Hungarian October), resulting in the maelstrom in which the New Left was formed and from which the attempts to reform East Bloc states grew.[6] Here the 'politics' ranged from dissenting and liberal, to militant and radical – from CND (Campaign for Nuclear Disarmament) and trade unionism to revolutionary Leninism and Maoism. The clearest expression of crisis – to put it in such a general way – was visible in those metropolitan centres, from May of 1968 onwards. And while an outline of the intellectualised progressive film culture can be promptly assembled (indeed, this strain represents the assimilatable of the era), it is a picture of the film culture aligned with the drift of 'progressive' politics of the left that is lacking in critical/academic histories (so that this strain represents the unassimilatable – the dated or forgotten – of the era). The critical/academic preoccupation has been with the beginnings of this phase – aesthetic innovations (often associated with European New Waves of film-making), the usurping of previous traditions of film-making and a reengagement with others for a recalibration of film's concerns in relation to the here and now. The high summer that inexorably follows this spring – the crisis phase, on the streets and on the screen, with both as a continuation of the leftist progressive impulses identified above – is passed over in critical/academic histories. This phase, then, requires more than the brief review to be afforded here to the intellectual phase. Its beginnings (the early New Wave years), discussed and analysed in detail elsewhere, are only relevant in this study in relation to the way in which they evolve and develop, holistically, into a revolutionary phase.

To be specific: a sustained study of film as self-reflexively akin to and a facet of the revolutionary sensibility and activity on the streets of this period, rather than just coinciding with and being 'like' such activity, has not been published. In the periodisation of a progressive 1960s cinema that relies on surface similarities and formal aesthetic innovations, there is a sleight of hand that obscures the usual methodological lacuna in respect to such studies. The absent element is a consideration of the relationship – rather than the shared concerns – between text (or artefact or film) and context (or time or sociopolitical background). In his own study of films specifically about 1968, Bates says as much, though in different words, when he writes: 'recent historical accounts have ordered the events of May [1968] in predictable ways, making a study such as this, which [Bates claims] correlates revolutionary and artistic insight, sound almost mystical' (Bates 1985: 28). The present study will attempt to remove the mystification of such a correlation through identifying the relationship between text and context.

Avoiding this sleight of hand presents a clear task in this regard: to attempt to uncover such subterranean connections rather than noting a simple 'likeness'. However, the attempt arises from more than simple housekeeping (that is, attempting to revise and expand the idea of a progressive 1960s cinema). It is also a matter of the recovery of this period of film history; many of the films, invariably those lost in the curtailment of the critical/academic histories, now appear, long after their time, as singular and peculiar – even nonsensical or cryptic – and their concerns archaic and obscure. This marginalised quarter of the progressive cinema of the 1960s illustrates the reason why a consideration of the 'hardwiring' between text and context, of this time, has remained unexplored. In assembling a canonical narrative of directions in film from this time, this marginalised quarter suggests the potential to problematise, or undermine, or even give the lie to, the scope of that narrative. The corollary of the avoidance of such a disruptive intrusion, then, is a limitation of the scope of the critical/academic narrative of this period. Small steps can be taken – following the way in which film-maker A reworked literary source B so as to make film C, where C represents a break with previous films drawn from literary sources (or autobiographies, or film genres, or specific locales, or film actors, and so on). Large steps, however, call into question the very parameters of this narrative. In film-maker X's methods, the possibility of film as existing outside conception Y is glimpsed – a direction that reaches fruition in film Z, where Z evidences the failure (or limitations, or misunderstandings, or degeneration) of such a direction in its entirety. In the final analysis, the marginalised body of work calls into question the veracity of the critical/academic history. From this vantage point, the critical/academic history seems to be revisionist, and effectively renders the artefacts innocuous (that is, depoliticising them) – unconsciously falling into that trope identified by Raymond Williams as the 'selective tradition' (Williams 1973: 9).

What, then, is the thread through progressive 1960s cinema, which runs from beginnings to fruitions, and so offers the possibility of an entry into, and full engagement with, the marginalised final stages of this period? My approach concerns a conception of film realism, its understood relationship with the world from which it is drawn (which presupposes a position on the nature of film itself), and its relationship with the reality film is then 'thrown back into'. If this is difficult to name, it is because this approach is coloured by the series of difficult outcomes noted above: the failures or limitations or misunderstandings or degenerations of this conception of film realism. And these difficult outcomes are only partially rooted in the more orthodox conceptions of film realism apparent at their beginnings. However, a body of original assumptions and understandings pertaining to film and film realism is prominent: the confluence of a tradition of realism in which the progressive films place themselves, as outlined and discussed by André Bazin. This represents the starting point of this study but it must be preceded, here, by a consideration of how best to approach this unifying conception.

Methodological Approach

Moving beyond a tendency of noting likenesses between text and context introduces a series of methodological questions. To ask where to look in searching for the 'unknown quality' – the subterranean 'hardwiring' between artefact and time – is also to ask how to look. While a straight post-structuralist approach will prove to be useful in so far as differentiating the various 'avant-gardisms' on display within the field at hand, such 'textual' readings of the artefacts potentially wrenches them from their specific contexts. The existence of the film culture to which they belonged and of which they were a part, in its interdisciplinarian leanings and revolutionary aspirations, requires a wider consideration if the analysis is to be more than partial. And it is just such a limited close textual analysis that – even though rarely enacted in critical/academic histories – tends to lock the considerations of progressive 1960s film into the 'beginnings' phase: a formalist consideration of aesthetic innovations in themselves.

To go to the other extreme: an approach allied with new historicism (reception theory, audience studies) offers the possibility of assessing how the artefacts were understood at the time, but in so doing overrides the artefacts' own assumed context (which can be identified through a textual consideration) as moments in the revolutionary struggle. Irrespective of reactions to film Z, film Z's ambitions historically remain unrealised. Films at the service of a revolution that did not occur exist as a lost vanguard, not as texts that fully demand a consideration of their reception at the time.

So there is an impetus to return to the texts themselves as the loci of their own revolutionary conceptions, and offer close aesthetic readings of the texts that draw on a contextualisation of gestures, concerns and images within the wider discourses of the 1960s. And there is an impetus to identify film form as the prime focus of this analysis – to move beyond the modishness and the noting of instances of 'likeness', and to see in the practices of film-making the conceptualisation of film itself as a newly revolutionary medium. This approach is one of a deconstructionist bent, where the system of original signification is drawn from that tradition of film realism outlined and discussed by Bazin. I do not wish to 'free' the texts of retrospectively imposed meanings, again via post-structural approaches – a methodology typical of a project to recover forgotten or marginalised periods of cultural history. A deconstructionist approach seeks to allow a wider consideration of the film language that is evident – a wider consideration that then extends into areas of revolutionary practice, linking film form directly with revolutionary practice; a locating of the language that united the two. This methodology offers the best path in the endeavour of exposing the subterranean connection, and so revealing something of the nature of the revolutionary phase of European 1960s film.

But the nature of the historical context demands another prerequisite for my approach. The study moves towards the revolution that failed, with its imaginings and calls to action, despite initial appearances, coming to little or no long-term achievement. This is the study, therefore, of oversight and overreach, wishful thinking and a lack of rigour in respect to the most important tactical and analytical questions made in the heat of the moment. Such retrospective thinking sheds a new light on the nature of any common language of revolutionary practice and film form. The osmosis-like connection actively sought by these films 'of' the revolution comes to be one in which the films come to function as a mirror to their revolutionary times rather than, or as much as, vehicles for the extension of the revolutionary struggle. Thus the condition of failure is as present in the artefacts as surely as in the times; it is immanent to both. Therefore the methodology must be one that seeks out and analyses what does not occur, the failure of their revolutionism, as founded on their blind spots and assumptions – the absences, or the state of absence, in the evolving revolutionary film form. The film texts can be said to be 'delicate' – therefore they may not survive deconstruction, so to speak; their cryptic nature is a token of their original lightness of touch, their obscure status is a returning of them to a precise moment in which their resonances and concerns spoke loudly, only to be rapidly silenced thereafter. The method of deepest, and most sympathetic, penetration into their workings is a deconstruction from an oblique angle: to examine the aporias (to use Derrida's term) of film form.

Brunette and Wills, in their importing of Derrida to film theory for their 1989 study, are hostile to Bazin's formulation of film realism. Through an analysis of the same Bazin texts discussed below, they diagnose an unthinking 'logocentric position' (Brunette and Wills 1989: 68), and so conclude 'the cinema . . . is no longer to be considered as the means by which a privileged visual medium controls and guarantees reality's "fall" into language and representation, with minimum loss of its original integrity . . . the screen becomes not the site of the consecration of that . . . metaphysically orientated or motivated operation but rather its marginal or liminal support' (Brunette and Wills 1989: 79). And so, thereafter, they can dismiss Bazin's reading of film realism as predicated on critically unsatisfactory assumptions – indeed, the dismissal is necessary to then enable their deconstruction of film language per se. A similarly forthright and totalising deconstruction is inappropriate for my subject matter, since the nature of the 'failure' mentioned above is clearly generative. I am not concerned with the discourse of film realism, but with the conception of film realism, as evident in the discourse of a precise period. Furthermore, as I shall argue, there is a discernible reconceptualisation of the progressive European film after 1968 – that is, I will suggest, the field eventually, and to a far-reaching degree, 'corrects' itself anyhow. So it is through an aporetic analysis that this study will attempt to isolate and interrogate the limit of the progressive European film before 1968. And this limit becomes visible at the moments of impasse or suspension: the aporias. I am not accusing Brunette and Wills of throwing the baby out with the bath water, but I am returning to a process in which the bath water had its use – a process that reveals the explanation for the eventual discarding of the bath water (as the field 'corrects' itself).

Such an aporetic analysis is one that looks to Derrida's use of the term 'aporia', the 'barred passage' as he puts it (Derrida and Attridge 1992: 399) – a term fully developed towards the latter half of his academic life. In a different context (roughly, the question of the possibility of one's own death, as the 'passage' of oneself from life to death), Derrida writes, when he first encounters the possibility of aporia:

> the difficult or the impracticable, here the impossible, passage, the refused, denied, or prohibited passage, indeed the nonpassage, which can in fact be something else, the event of a coming of a future advent [événement de venue ou d'avenir], which no longer has the form of the movement that consists in passing, traversing, or transiting. It would be the "coming to pass" of an event that would no longer have the form or the appearance of a pas: in sum, a coming without pas. (Derrida 1993: 8)

The aporetic analysis is applied by Derrida and by subsequent post-structuralists, and with a characteristic looseness (breaking with 'scientific' dogma of structuralism), to the fields of ethics, politics, law, and philosophy itself. The aporia highlights the point, or nodes, of the unqualified assumptions in such discourses, so corroding the total readings seemingly, or potentially, possible with structuralism (or earlier structuralism). The aporetic analysis prompts a search for the irreducible underpinnings of the argument, the area that remains in a state of being unaccounted for by – or within or, finally, as – the parameters of the argument.

The aporia is quite other to the structuring thought that determines the field – in Derridean terms, a ghost to the live text, or the uncanny to the canny; the impossible, uninvited, undesired agent that then casts doubt on the entire enterprise. And this other world is revealed through a close textual examination of that which is as often as not, in the text itself, fudged, circumnavigated, overlooked or dissolved into strategies of avoidance. In the aporetic analysis of Derrida's *Aporias*, the aporias multiply – auto-engender, so to speak – until a climax is reached; it is more apparent here than in Derrida's earlier writing that the aporia is not a minor or accidental appendage to the text. It is, rather, the very condition that engulfs the text – that enables it, in the sense of allowing it to be created, and then providing a motor or conceptual foundation for that creation. The aporia is the very condition of the text. In this respect, an aporetic analysis allows for a radical rereading of the text – a '*negative form*' (Derrida 1993: 19, Derrida's italics) that splits the text asunder and reveals the workings of the conceptual foundation.

To invoke Derrida at this early stage is to suggest that a dense post-structuralist encounter with the outer reaches of the extremes of progressive and countercultural film is to come. Certainly, post-structuralists of the late 1960s onwards favoured just such film-making; Films that flaunted their awareness of and undermining of the expectation to which they were to adhere (that is, that invited the viewer to deconstruct normative film language) achieved a progressive status in such circles. And, as Derrida insisted, aporia are ultimately the enabling factor in themselves, not, or not merely, the transgressing of norms: in the aporia is the ability to articulate, with the aporia as first presupposing and finally containing the existence of such articulations. And this enabling – the 'to' – leads me to the wider supposed revolutionary moment rather than the countering of non-revolutionary norms; the movement in and for which the films functioned. Thus an instinctive contention was, from the outset of this study, that the revolutionary cinema shared aporia with the revolutionary movement (or, rather, with 'revolutionism'): the revolutionary aesthetic strategies were built upon a foundation that itself was shaky to begin with – lacking, it later seemed, historical analysis and theoretical rigour. The sympathetic reading that would therefore be required necessitates creating a framework for an aporetic analysis rather than any 'Derridean' or Derrida-derived programmatic aporetic analysis (if, indeed, such a thing can be said to exist; Brunette and Wills, despite their explicitly Derridean analyses of film texts, go to great lengths to cast their attempt as anything other than 'an explicit model of how deconstructive analysis was to be "done"' (Brunette and Wills 1989:

139)). And such a framework for an aporetic analysis prompts a critical lexicon: the examination of film form compels me to reach for (or warmly recognise in other critical writing) terms such as 'blind spot', 'lacuna', 'impasse', 'suspension of meaning', 'cul-de-sac', 'problematisation', 'vacuum' and 'lack'.

Positing Post-Bazinian Realism

The impetus behind the revolutionary phase of European 1960s film is grounded in the nature of the films themselves at the point at which a common denominator can be seen to stretch across this period – a consistency, or thread, that can be tracked from the beginnings to the fruitions, linking the formal aesthetic innovations of the early years to the messy failures of the later years. This common denominator, the existence of which is already and most immediately suggested in the shared characteristics of the films of this era, is the 'unknown quality' particular to progressive European film of the 1960s. The characteristics derive from the praxis, and the praxis speaks of a shared belief in realism as the quality that validates the film as a potentially serious endeavour (film as a non-frivolous, non-trivial reflection of the world at large). Or, more precisely, that still validated film as a potentially serious endeavour; this was no new idea but the bolstering of an old one – a furthering of the tradition of European film realism. Film realism, and the elements of film realism, becomes the vehicle with which a connection with found reality can occur, and be reproduced as the film is then shown. That connection transfigures film; the technology of film-making is rendered as little more than utilitarian in enabling an encounter with 'the real' – and the consciousness-raising potential of that encounter for the film viewers once reproduced. This suggests a clear path through the first phase of the New Wave films – to put to one side all other considerations so as to follow the evolution of a specific form of film realism in these, as well as other, progressive films of the 1960s.

Such a conception of film realism can be found in Bazin's early writing. However, it would be ahistorical to claim that, despite some anecdotal evidence, Bazin was the progenitor of this idea, as it flourished after his death in 1958. Indeed, in this early writing, as shall be argued, Bazin was only observing, and putting shape to, observable trends in film culture. His role was that of journalist and theorist, not manifesto writer or guiding intelligence; he championed a tradition of film realism by importing conceptual frameworks with which to first identify and then – to put it at its simplest – 'tell the story' of the art of film. Elevating Bazin to the position of creator rather than chronicler would be erroneous. And any sense of a 'Bazin tradition' or 'Bazin school' is, in itself, inappropriate for the directions in film realism, as evident in progressive European film in the late 1960s; these directions were a far cry from the realism identified and championed by Bazin.

And yet the body of thought associated with Bazin sheds the most light on films from the 1960s. It reveals – that is, enables the identification of – the common denominator that stretches across the era in its entirety. Bazin's initial identification of film realism – which is done in religious and mystical terms – articulates a 'real connection' between found reality and reproduced reality. From this articulation arises an entire reading of the essence of film. And a sense of such a 'real connection', which may be called a Bazinian conception or understanding of film, remains as the basis of the development of revolutionary film in the 1960s. The milieu of this development was therefore 'Bazinian', and the development itself occurred within or against a heritage, with an orthodox and non-orthodox wing, of the Bazinian conception or understanding of film. For the purposes of this study, then, the period under scrutiny can best be revealed, examined and organised when identified as that of a post-Bazinian realism. The points of connection between Bazin and the films of this period remain loose, even tenuous at times, and so a post-Bazinian realism can be discerned as arising without adherence to an orthodoxy, and with Bazin's writing demoted to a mythical rather than prescriptive or programmatic theory of film realism. Therefore, following a brief consideration of Bazin's relevant writings, the situation in which a post-Bazinian realism could evolve, and the background of such an evolution, will be summarised.

It is more than an afterthought to note the scope of Bazin's own project, which MacCabe describes as the attempt at 'gaining control of a certain section of the French [film] industry' (MacCabe 2003: 60) through the cultivation of 'an educated taste' (MacCabe 2003: 72). 'This is a political programme in itself' notes MacCabe (MacCabe 2003: 72), and the merging of politics and aesthetics into one critical discourse occurs outside orthodox political affiliation, in the way in which Bazin's co-founded journal, *Cahiers du Cinéma,* 'was thus conceived as a project which rejected both the culture of the state and the culture of the Communist left' (MacCabe 2003: 71). In this way, Bazin saw himself as the forger of new traditions, and not as a lowly film reviewer. And the raison d'être for Bazin's activity might be said to be in his own political line – an anti-Stalinist of the left; that is, a Western intellectual outside an orthodox Communist party, radicalised by the events of the 1950s, and seeking to find a progressive path outside the Stalinist hegemony. Film, as a serious artistic endeavour, was to be a part of the building of that path (and it had its own Stalinist apologists 'in house'; figures such as Guido Aristarco and Georges Sadoul). In this respect, the progressive films of the 1960s, in their heady revolutionary phase, recall the scale of the cultural-political ambitions associated with the figure of Bazin.

Notes

1. For a brief summation of differing interpretations of the notion of 'expanded cinema' and/or 'expanded screen', a tendency of the late 1960s of 'projections and activities that exploded the framework of the cinema' (Michalka 2004: 10, note 4), see (Michalka 2004: 7 and ff, and 85 note 16).
2. For Hardt and Negri on the biopolitical, see Hardt and Negri (2001: 22 and ff).
3. For this reason, this book concentrates on national film cultures where auteurs had 'less' to complain about – predominantly Italy, France, West Germany and the United Kingdom. Radicalism in these film cultures was mostly unreconstructed and rarely tactical; the persistence of Stalinism was not detrimental to the physical or mental well-being of the populace (a sentiment forcibly driven home in the films of the Czech New Wave, and true too of the Yugoslav New Wave), and bureaucratic state censorship did not draw their fire in terms of liberalism and freedom of expression (as with Spain and the German Democratic Republic, where the film industries were monitored at the point of distribution as well as production). In short, this study engages with Western European left film culture. Indeed, this culture was rarely parochial and tended to consider its targets (either bourgeois or Communist-party affiliated) as European rather than specific to French, Italian, British or West German societies. Comparable studies to this that have tended to country-specific discussions and demarcations have often therefore imposed unhelpful categories that are bound up to nation states rather than classes, and local governance rather than ideology.

   This consideration of areas of concentration in this book is also made pragmatically in terms of the existence of a substantial, national film culture per se, which was not active in some Western European countries in the 1960s.
4. Truffaut's *Les Quatre Cents Coups* premiered in France on 3 June 1959 and Godard's *A Bout de Souffle* was released on 16 March 1960 (and in New York in February 1961). Chabrol's *Le Beau Serge* was released slightly earlier (11 February 1959; filming on it began in December 1957), as was his *Les Cousins* (11 March 1959), but these films

failed to generate the international attention soon afforded to Truffaut and Godard (despite their success; see Neupert 2002: 125, 129). Although the surrounding publicity saw in these two releases the 'arrival' of the Nouvelle Vague proper, Houston notes that in 1959 twenty-four film-makers presented debut features, and a further forty-three in 1960 (Houston and Roud 1968: 100). Perhaps Cannes 1959 is a more appropriate choice for the moment of arrival: Marcel Camus' *Orfeu Negro* was awarded the Grand Prix, *Les Quatre Cents Coups* the prize for direction and *Hiroshima, Mon Amour* (Alain Resnais, 1959) the International Critics' prize. Truffaut had gone from persona non grata at the festival (for his inflammatory journalism) to its toast. In 1959 Godard defiantly defined the new in relation to the old; the Nouvelle Vague was a breaking with the 'tradition of quality' and a filmic equivalent of the dissenting 'MacMahonist' sensibility:

> All we have to say to you is this. Your pan shots are ugly because your subjects are poor, your actors act badly because your dialogue is lousy; to sum up, you cannot shoot films because you do not know what cinema is. Today we have won the day. It is our films that will prove at Cannes that France looks good, cinematographically speaking. And next year it will be the same. Let there be no doubt about that! Fifteen new brave, sincere, lucid, beautiful films will again stand in the way of conventional productions. We may have won a battle, but the war is not yet over. (quoted in de Baecque 1997: 155)

In fact, Godard's estimations were conservative; French and Jacob tally 170 debut films from French film-makers between 1959 and 1963, the majority of which have long since been forgotten (French 1993: xii; Jacob 1964/65: 5). In more general terms, and with a number of exceptions, the term 'New Wave' films, in relation to 1960s European cinema, denotes films characterised by an 'immediacy' via their inclusion of contemporary reality and a 'freedom' of film form (unbound by the rules or norms of 'good' film grammar).

5. Chabrol notes a certain irony in the subsequent association of the term Nouvelle Vague with opposition to bourgeois society and mores:

> For, let there be no mistake about this, if the press talked about us so much, it was because they wished to establish the equation: de Gaulle equals Renewal. In the cinema as well as everything else. The General arrives, the Republic changes, France is reborn. Look at this flowering of talent. The intellect blossoms in the shadow of the cross of Lorraine. Make way for the young! (Nicholls 1993: 10)

Benayoun agreed and uses this as grounds for criticism; that the Nouvelle Vague was intrinsically Gaullist: 'it is quite clear that Gaullist France, with its raucous demagogy and its blindness to realities, was ideal ground for a school of ultra-bourgeois expression' (Benayoun 1968: 158), noting too the export of the films for the purposes of 'French propaganda' (Benayoun 1968: 157).

6. In this study the terms 'Left' and 'orthodox Left' denote the Communist parties, and their members, formally associated with the Communist Party of the Soviet Union (CPSU); 'radical', 'dissident', 'dissenting', 'progressive', 'non-orthodox Left' and 'left' denote leftists outside or critical of these parties. Radical, here, is often aspirational: to break with the conventions of political discourse and articulate a fuller and even subjective response to what was, as the 1960s progressed, an evermore unpredictable and vibrant political and cultural scene. But the radical critique, as discussed in this book, often stopped short of proposing or demanding a radical change. That step, promoting or even catalysing revolution, was also aspirational, or arose from a reading of the social situation as truly pre-revolutionary, and hence the deployment, here, of the term 'revolutionism'. That term denotes excising in a state of revolutionariness, or aspirant revolution, articulating in a revolutionary manner, but all without the existence of an actual revolution, in the classically understood sense.

    Years later, two film-makers who feature prominently in this study, Bernardo Bertolucci and Philippe Garrel, would revisit 1968. *The Dreamers* (2003) and *Les Amant Réguliers* (*Regular Lovers*, 2005), respectively, evoked the rich countercultural and revolutionary ambience of the times, even at the point of violent resistance to the provocations of the armed security forces of the state: just such a 'revolutionism'. By contrast, Chris Marker's *A Grin without a Cat* (1977,1993) would follow the trajectory from revolutionary aspirations of 1968 to one-issue matters and the early years of identity politics in the 1970s, tracing revolutionism back through radicalism and then to reformism.

CHAPTER TWO

Prehistory – from Late Neo-realism to the New Waves

Bazin's Ontology

Before outlining the evolution of a post-Bazinian realism, it is necessary to briefly review the Bazinian orthodoxy that informally underpins it. The concern in this respect is not with the coordinates of his particular approach to film and the practice of film-making, with the entirety of Bazin's writings then explained in relation to this. And the concern is only partially with the film culture associated with Bazin – this will be discussed in relation to the immediate Bazinian heritage, an outgrowth of that film culture, in the subsequent section. Rather, the chief relevance of Bazin's writings here is in relation to his philosophical conceptualisation of film. This philosophical conceptualisation resides in Bazin's making the 'real connection' between found reality and reproduced reality. The film-making practices that arise from, or were unconsciously in sympathy with, the idea of a 'real connection' were predicated on a shared understanding of the relationship between found reality and reproduced reality. This reading of the apparatus of cinema, which can be historically situated in relation to traditions of realism in European film,[1] and was articulated by Bazin in relation to the entire development of artistic practices, remained in the foundation of progressive and radical 1960s European film.

The tenets of Bazin's understanding of film can be located[2] in Bazin's reading of photographic reproduction in his essay 'The Ontology of the Photographic Image' (see Bazin 1967: 9–16). Here Bazin argues that, at base, 'we are forced to accept as real the existence of the object reproduced, actually *re*-presented, set before us, that is to say, in time and space. Photography enjoys a certain advantage in virtue of this transference of reality from the thing to its reproduction' (Bazin 1967: 13–14). Bazin's analogy for the image as photographed is the Shroud of Turin: a 'relic [i.e., a remnant of, or partly of, Christ's physical body] and photograph [i.e., a reproduction of his image]' (Bazin 1967: 14). In the myth of the Shroud, the difference between the two is collapsed; the reproduction is, miraculously, the remnant – to touch the image on the Shroud is to touch Christ's actual excretions, to touch the bodily material of Christ himself. And so the Shroud was, at that time, proclaimed as a material proof of his existence – not a reproduction, or not just a reproduction, but also a fingerprint or death mask (in fact, two analogies for film that Bazin also resorts to). Thus Bazin's analogy is not one of graphic exactitude (say Pre-Raphaelite painting or architectural drawing) but the ineffability of the processes of the image filmed and reproduced. So, to return to the consideration of the photographic image, there is therefore an element of photographed 'real' transferred via or during the act of photography to, or coming to reside in, the reproduction. This element is paradoxically both very visible (in the objective correctness of the image) and yet invisible (the metaphysical quality of 'the real' as transferred) – and Bazin further complicates this paradox through couching the process in terms of religious belief. And this process of transference, which is the crux of the conceptualisation, remains unqualified. In addition, as Henderson notes, Bazin does not define 'the real . . . nor [does he] develop any doctrine of the real whatever'. In this instance, the limit of Bazin's conception, it can thus be surmised, is that of the real as the final horizon – Bazin does not go 'beyond the real', as Henderson puts it (in 'Two Types of Film Theory'; *Film Quarterly*, 1971; Henderson 1976b: 390), despite relatively sustained (when compared to Eisenstein, by Henderson) attempts to define film's relation to the real (albeit attempts that are prone to slight differences).

Nor does Bazin 'bargain down' his fundamental conception – rather, he dilutes opposing positions through their forcible dissolution within his conception. Thus 'The Life and Death of Superimposition' (first published in *Écran Français*, 1946) begins by refusing the 'opposition that some like to see between a cinema inclined toward the almost documentary representation of reality and a cinema inclined, through reliance on technique, toward escape from reality into fantasy and the world of dreams' as 'essentially forced'. Rather, the 'fantastic in the cinema' (Bazin here refers to Méliès) 'is only possible because of the irresistible realism of the photographic image' so that '[w]hat in fact appeals to the audience about the fantastic in the cinema is its realism – I mean, the contradiction between the irrefutable objectivity of the photographic image and the unbelievable nature of the events it depicts' (reproduced in Bazin 1997: 73). This applies both to Méliès and, later, to Bazin's phenomenological position on the unreality of expressionist-equivalent aesthetic strategies. For both trips to the moon and to the interior mindscape, the real remains the alpha and omega – both the structure of the showing, and the material that is shown; the celluloid is still exposed before a reality, no matter how fabricated or suggestive. Some quarter is given to films that emphasise the manipulation of the image (their narrative meanings as constructed through montage and stylisation/distortion of the reality filmed) through a division between films from 'those directors who put their faith in the image' and 'those who put their faith in reality' in the later essay 'The Evolution of the Language of Cinema' (Bazin 1967: 24).[3] The former sacrifices the organic connection between the real and exposed celluloid; it is not a purist's cinema.

Bazin's fundamental reading of film seeks legitimacy in the way in which it openly courts historicism. His reading posits an historic perception of film, from the moment of inception (the 'moving'/animation of photographic images, then still in living memory), which is one of film as *the* art of 'the real'. Such a legitimation of the basis of his reading of film means that Bazin's conceptualisation comes to be problematic on a number of far-reaching counts:

- Cinema, even decades before, had travelled a long way from the early pioneer days of documentary and cinema audiences fleeing from the oncoming (projected) locomotive train; Bazin seems to offer a wide-eyed and stunted reading of film, wholly lacking in sophistication for the middle of the twentieth century – the persistence of a 'Lumièrist' reading.
- At this time, the act of filming was treated in terms that would be better understood as industrial-utilitarian, technological-scientific, for populist and reportage end, rather than sacramental – it was the practice of the profane, not the art of the sacred.
- Bazin's observations seemed, at that point, in direct contradiction to the general direction of film-making – documentary gave way to the fantastical, didacticism to entertainment (especially in the cinema); why affirm 'the real' when it held little or no sway over developments in the mise en scène?
- Bazin's reading of cinema bucked both Enlightenment thinking, and – to resort to Walter Benjamin's terms – idiosyncratically restored the 'aura' to the art of the age of mechanical mass reproduction.[4] Of all the arts, film was surely historically the least, or indeed not, 'obligated to God, to honor God's universe'

(as Cardullo puts it in relation to Bazin's conception (Bazin 1997: xii)) in the manner of Ruskin's conception of art.

Critical responses to Bazin's conceptualisation, while offering useful extensions of his ideas, seem either to move towards damage limitation or to express an angry disappointment over the paucity of the imagination of such a seminal figure in film history.[5] (This study falls into the latter category, tempered – it is hoped – by casting Bazin's conceptualisation as coming to take the role of the 'good intentions' that pave the proverbial infernal road).

Thus Cardullo de-literalises such a problematic conception by the introduction of a staggered timeline for 'actually *re*-presented':

The picture is a kind of double of the world, a reflection petrified in time, brought back to life by cinematic projection; in other words, everything that is filmed once was in reality. A rapt Bazin thus speaks of the ontological realism of the cinema, and according to him, naturally, the camera is the objective tool with which to achieve it. He granted the camera a purifying power and an impassiveness that restored the virgin object to the attention and love of the viewer. (Bazin 1997: xiii)

Here the mysterious is consigned to the moment of filming, which the moment of projection then harks back to, so that the 'transference of reality' is historicised – not as a process fully realised during projection, but as a quality of the recording medium during the moment of filming. There is an echo of Siegfried Kracauer's conceptualisation of film realism in Cardullo's reaction: an access to the zeitgeist or the spirit of earlier times, enabled through technologies of visual reproduction rather than an atemporal communion with 'the Eternal'. Or it could be said, in keeping with Bazin's analogy of choice, that Cardullo offers a protestant vision to counter Bazin's Catholic one – only the enactment of the moment of transubstantiation, not a living continuum of the act of transubstantiation.

A similar displacement of the 'transference', onto the usefully vague area of viewer perception, is more typical (and Henderson notes Bazin's own half step into this area as he 'hedges his doctrine' (Henderson 1976b: 392)). Such displacement allows for the legacy of Bazin's conceptualisation today, which is often tied to notions of indexicality. So, for example, Bordwell writes, prior to a consideration of Godard's flouting of the rules of film grammar, 'The diegetic world of the film is to be seen as possessing a baseline of objective realism; on some plane, the viewer is asked to apply a criteria of verisimilitude to the action' (Bordwell 1984: 9). Here the willing suspension of disbelief is called in; the implication is that Bazin's literalness works as a semiotic code – the understood way of suggesting the look of things, as with (Kolker 1983: 147). Stam thus talks of 'The Phenomenology of Realism' in order to reappraise Bazin's 'overly veristic formulation', offering an 'ontological bond' born of 'a concrete link between the photographic analogon and its referent', as manifest via 'the charismatic indexicality of photography' (Stam 2000: 74). These de-literalisations of Bazin relocate the 'actually re-presented' onto the unwritten pact between film and viewer over this issue of 'the real'; 'real' becomes adjectival and qualitative rather than quantitative. Morgan readdresses the problem, summarising and dismissing this history of such revisionist (mis-) readings of Bazin as mostly mounted on semiotic grounds (Morgan 2006: 445–46). This is a corrective to a general tendency toward misreadings, which the editors of a book on Bazin provocatively refer to as a betrayal of their subject (Andrew and Joubert-Laurencin 2011: xiv). But Morgan winds up conjuring with Bazin's language, especially as translated in English, in order to demystify that which, here, is taken as to be understood in metaphysical terms; Morgan does not consider Bazin's position as a variant of transubstantiation. And even Rosen's discussion comes to turn on what is understood by the word 'faith', which he terms, in this case, 'fundamental subject investment' (Rosen 2003: 54).

Henderson, in 'Two Types of Film Theory', is less inclined to add a pinch of salt to Bazin's conception. He notes that Bazin 'placed serious limitations on the complexity and ambition of cinematic form', and that (along with Eisenstein) this conceptualisation has 'been a source of serious confusion and even a retardation to theoretical understanding to cinema' (Henderson 1976b: 398, 399). Finally, '[i]t is difficult for me to find any value in this approach whatever: such theories would keep cinema in a state of infancy, dependent upon an order anterior to itself, one to which it can stand in no meaningful relation because of this dependence' (Henderson 1976b: 400). Henderson's dismissal implies a bruising encounter with such limitations and/or a fervent embrace of a new conceptualisation antithetical to Bazin's (Henderson makes no such references): something typical of reactions to film culture during and immediately after 1968, as shall be argued. And yet, in Henderson's vociferous and personalised objections, an indication of the degree of the influence of Bazin is also to be found; this is a case of implicitly praising Bazin with faint damnations.

Irrespective of the orthodoxy of these qualifications added to Bazin's conceptualisation, and the displacements and reimaginations needed to restore Bazin's theorising about film to the contemporary frame, Bazin's initial grappling with the essence of the image – fumbled, naive, obscurantist or otherwise – could not be easily circumnavigated by later theorists. Rosen therefore sees Bazin as 'the theorist of cinema's basic realism' (Rosen 1987: 17) and MacCabe is emboldened to claim that Bazin's reading of film in 'The Ontology of the Photographic Image' may be taken as 'axiomatic' to European film, from neo-realism onwards (MacCabe 2003: 63). Can it be added that such axiomaticism is achieved via the flexibility pressed upon Bazin's initial conceptualisation – which is the tendency that is most apparent in this writing?

'The Ontology of the Photographic Image' was published in 1945 in *Problèmes de la Peinture* (Bazin 1967: 173) – that is, at the moment of the very inception of a post-war film, a position to be occupied (in the eyes of critics, at least) by the most Bazinian of methodologies: Italian neo-realism. Thus Stam maps Bazin's conception onto a line of aesthetic development from Lumière to Flaherty and Murnau, fortified by Welles and Wyler, and 'reach[ing] quasi-teleological fulfilment with Italian neo-realism' (Stam 2000: 76). To question the nature of the photographic imagery of realism, still or moving, was to question the 'meaning' (that is, to formulate the conception) of film itself. Bazin's use of the word 'forced' is telling in this respect; it is the medium itself that demands a conceptual correlation between image and reproduction from the viewer.[6] So although Bazin was working 'after the fact' in relation to the existence of cinema, he was writing from the epicentre of the renewal of that existence in the first few months after the liberation of mainland Europe, and a number of its national cinemas, from fascist occupation.

Post-Bazinian Realism

In order to establish a picture of a post-war European progressive film culture, it is necessary to first look to a series of sociopolitical events, and note their wider reverberations. This is not a matter of looking to each extreme – the most concrete of historical events and the most abstract of artistic thought – and then finding cause and effect – that is, of relating film form directly to history, as if positing a symbiotic relationship between the two. Rather, it is a matter of presenting an argument for the radicalisation of film form as, in the final analysis, a consequence of historical forces. We can begin by acknowledging, from the late 1940s to the mid 1950s:

- the contentious persistence of neo-realism, or a neo-realism, increasingly given over to melodrama, beyond the end of the 'Golden Age' of Italian neo-realism[7]
- the existence of a number of French film critics and writers associated with and including Bazin, all still mostly marginal figures, who championed, and continued to champion, neo-realism
- the need for a post-1945 conception of the role of art: as ever-wary of the durability of fascism, and as charged with exploring the historical experiences of European fascism
- the persistence of Stalinism beyond Stalin's death, despite a period of hope for a 'thaw' in the Soviet Union.

The complex situation from which progressive film culture was born arises from the interrelationships between these four phenomena. Questions over the 'Golden Age' of neo-realism can be understood to be refractions of debates concerning Stalinism, where the sides can roughly be divided thus:

- those who understood neo-realism to be subject to an attempt to co-opt it as an Italian variant of Zhdanovist socialist realism – that is, that neo-realism should be the orthodox Left aesthetic dogma for the Italian quarter of the endangered Soviet hegemony, despite neo-realism being historically located in the period of Italian resistance to fascism and Nazism
- those who saw in neo-realism the blueprint for a post-war European cinema, determined more by a liberal humanism than the expediencies of cultural commentators allied with, or sympathetic to, their communist parties.

The growing resistance to Stalinism engendered a tendency to be critical of all manifestations of Stalinism, however great or small. And when such manifestations appeared in an area of resistance associated with Western intellectual leftists – film-making, theorising and criticism, particularly in France and Italy where the Left was strong – then a scornful and combative response could only be expected. The French film critics and writers associated with and including Bazin were minded to be combative – both in relation to Stalin (see, for example, the 'unforgivable blasphemy' (MacCabe 2003: 71) of Bazin's 1950 essay 'Le Mythe de Staline dans le Cinéma Soviétique', where cinematic renditions of Stalin in 1940s Soviet cinema are compared to those of Tarzan in Hollywood – 'the only difference . . . is that the films devoted to the latter do not claim to be rigorous documentaries' (Bazin 1997: 30)), and in relation to their own national cinema (this tendency, as manifest in a lauding of the 'low culture' of American cinema, partly through the auteur theory, became known as MacMahonism).

The stakes were upped through a series of disasters for the Western Left, originating in the renewed Western imperialism of Suez and the renewed Stalinism in the wake of the Hungarian October. Yet the fallout of these eruptions of militarism only whetted an appetite to seize the means of (artistic) production; dissent from the left was institutionalised in the ascendant film culture of the mid to late 1950s. This artistic-political intent was to fill the political vacuum left by the Hungarian October. And the filling itself would be done by those disillusioned and radicalised by the Hungarian October, and disgusted and heartened by ill-advised Suez adventurism. At this watershed moment, then, a number of factors fell into a synchronicity:

> One immediate consequence of the Hungarian revolution or, more precisely, of its suppression by the Soviet military[,] was the mass exodus of the intelligentsia from practically all communist parties . . . [so that] for the first time in thirty years . . . there came about, in the form of the New Left intelligentsia, a leftist theoretical challenge to communism. Even if many defectors had abandoned Marxism, or whatever kind of leftist ideology for that matter, enough had remained to present a problem for the ossified communist ideology apparatuses. (Fehér and Heller 1983: 46)

Film culture, which had not initially picked a fight with the Stalinist Left but had found itself the object of attack, could be a tool for an articulation of criticism of the Left by the left – just such a leftist theoretical challenge. The beginnings of this had been apparent even prior to the hoped-for 'thaw' period. And the fight was, at times, literal; the above-mentioned sides championed their films at the 1954 Venice Film Festival – an event that can be seen as a microcosm of these tensions, but one central to the battle in the area of film culture – with raucous consequences.

In the United Kingdom, where neo-realism had been enthusiastically received by both film critics and 'middle-class cinemagoers with an interest in "the art of the film"' (Murphy 1992: 59), the idea of a new brief for a film culture was also voiced, and most succinctly by Lindsay Anderson, in his 1957 essay 'Get Out and Push' (Anderson 1959). Anderson and Bazin, and both their groups of associates, were predominantly middle-class left-orientated intellectual aesthetes of the 'new arts' who rallied for change and raged against the intransigence of their respective film cultures. This class characteristic, and non-aligned reformism, would prove to be indicative of the direction in which film would be pushed.

From the mid to late 1950s, such 'pushing' can be seen in a number of areas of film culture:

- the British Free Cinema – in which Anderson was a principal protagonist as critic, film programmer (for the Free Cinema programmes, 1956–1959) and film-maker
- the inter-journal polemics between Bazin and Guido Aristarco, mostly over a number of Italian film-makers who had deviated from 'Golden Age' neo-realism so as to make films of a more 'psychological' concern; while Bazin saw an increased sophistication in film-making of this type, Aristarco saw only regression
- the reception of the burgeoning Polish School in the West,[8] and the example of Ingmar Bergman's films. The tired war film had been revitalised with psychological realism in the work of Munk and Wajda, and psychological realism and intellectual preoccupations had made for a potent and challenging mix in the work of Bergman. Film, in these respects, became a reflective, intellectual investigation into the existential condition of man, diagnosing his alienation
- the infiltration and popularity of Brecht's ideas, as articulated in his writing and through his theatre productions (then touring), on a number of levels: as 'committed' artistic practice; as a method of sophisticated (i.e., non-naturalist) artistic practice; as historically embodying opposition to Left artistic dogma – his 1930s polemics with Lukács, newly Stalinist after the Hungarian October, now charged with a new relevancy.[9]

The shaping of film culture by these influences, and the distaste for the 'bourgeois realism' that typified popular film of that moment, led to the will to a politicisation of film form. (Or, with a 'naturally' juvenile pushing against the norms of film form and expansion of film form as a means to expression, to then find a formal, 'mature', context for that occurrence: a politicisation). The manifesto of the British Free Cinema illustrates the reaching for a process such as politicisation – but here it still remains vague, personalised and non-aligned:

No film can be too personal. The image speaks. Sound amplifies and com-
ments. Size is irrelevant. Perfection is not an aim. An attitude means a style.
A style means an attitude. Implicit in our attitude is a belief in freedom, in the
importance of people and in the significance of the everyday. (Hedling 1998:
41–42)[10]

In these occurrences we see a number of figures, with voices prominent in the film cultures of the time, now 'primed' to move from the page to the screen. Their articulations are to be constant in this shift, in respect of being against all facets of the old order. And, at the point of their arrival on the screen, such reformism and opposition were clearly sufficient to be getting on with; the first phase of progressive 1960s European film (here to be divided into the Late Modernist film and the New Waves respectively) operates primarily within the desire to realign film in the cultural context of the times. If the film culture is to be read in terms of a shared subjectivity, then that subjectivity is one given over to a visceral desire to efface and reject the old order – or, on the screen, to continue that effacement and rejection of earlier polemics and stances (MacMahonism, *Cahiers* criticism of the Cinéma de Papa – the French 'tradition of quality' film – and the polemics over neo-realism, together with general critiques of the state). In Godard's reaction to the successes of the Nouvelle Vague at Cannes 1959 (in a 1959 *Arts* comment; reproduced in de Baecque 1997: 155), as noted above, there is the connection between the harrying of previous traditions of national cinema and (and with) the new film of the 1960s. Such sentiments were also discernible in West German film culture, in 1962, with the publication of the Oberhausen Manifesto.

The petulance in the will to lay claim to the new cinema of the 1960s, however, cannot fully obscure the outlines of the position from which this coming new order stood in relation to the old. The redundancy of previous traditions of popular film-making was identified in the relationships of the films to realism in the widest possible sense. Their lack of a 'here and now' automatically short-circuited any relevancy to young cinéphiles, and the resultant deadness (even, in Godard's eyes, ugliness) of their film language made for the staid and studio-bound film, lacking in spontaneity or vibrancy, and with a dramaturgy born of the *conservatoire*, not drawn freely from the streets. So the path to revitalisation was clear: a fuller, even vulgar (to use Bertolucci's term, (Bertolucci 1967: 29)) realism, as arising from an unmannered embrace of 'the real' outside the studios. And factors that would contribute to the beginnings of such a possibility were already in place:

- a number of documentaries that privileged both personal style and realism – from both the Free Cinema, and film-makers shortly to be involved in the New Waves – had been made and were in circulation
- a taste for (that is, the perception of an economically favourable climate for returns from) 'young' work: in the wake of the U.S. 'beat' writers and the British Angry Young Men (at that point, occasionally related to the 'Beats'), and on the cusp of the 'youth' explosion in other popular arts
- the availability of technology that further enabled filming outside the confines of the studio.

Whether, at this point, traditions of realism in European film as discussed by Bazin were understood to represent the best hope for the plans of the impatient potential film-makers is a moot point. (Although it is difficult to place any other tradition that would have figured prominently, bar the intensely personal 'poetic realism' of various underground avant-gardes.) And yet, as shall be argued, the New Waves contained two visible reactions in regards to traditions of realism, and both speak of a conceptualisation of film as the art form of 'the real'. Firstly, film form as 'primed' for a complete immersion in – and a naked exposure to (that encountered reality) – a practice with roots in documentary realism, coupled with a tendency to avoid all practices in film-making that would detract from such an immersion (the manipulations of the image, as categorised by Bazin as emblematic of 'those directors who put their faith in the image' rather than reality (Bazin 1967: 24)). DiLorio places *Chronique d'un Été* (Rouch and Morin, 1961) at this junction: a film that he is then able to read as entirely Bazinian, albeit as evidencing the limitations of 'cinema's power to show the real' in the 'necessary artificiality of filmic realism' (DiLorio 2007: 42). Secondly, and conversely, film form as exposing the manipulations of the image intrinsic to film-making practices, as if warning against such manipulations, or exhibiting a frustration with their limitations, or qualifying film realism by introducing an awareness of them. Generally, New Wave films combined, or held together, elements of both these approaches – indeed, such a textual coexistence of opposites represents a defining feature of the New Wave film, and distinguishes it from the neo-realist film. This combination also indicates that the two different approaches originate from, and so point to, the same conception. Both these approaches share a sense of reality as freely transmutable onto celluloid, with its essence – if not its materiality – intact. And from this flows, as Jameson puts it, 'the "truth content" of art, its claim to possess some truth or epistemological value' (Jameson 1990: 74). In a parallel grouping of 1960s progressive film, here termed the Late Modernist film, a phenomenological filter is inserted between 'the real' and the reproduction – but with the sense of a truth or epistemological value still unimpeded. This conceptualisation of film as the receptacle for 'the real' was not seriously questioned in the progressive film of the 1960s.

So in these respects, the films that arrived so noticeably from 1959/60 held common ground with the Bazinian position in a number of key areas. In the first instance, in:

- the intellectualisation of film of the 'Late Modernist' phase, which can be understood as an expansion of neo-realist concerns, and an outgrowth of the film culture in which Bazin and associates defended the advances of film-makers such as Fellini and Visconti in progressive terms; the advent, therefore, of an increasing seriousness to the art of film
- the heightened, sophisticated and 'critical' realism of the New Waves.

In the second instance, from the mid-1960s onwards, in:

- the failure, even when problematising film realism, to break out of the orbit of the idea associated with Bazin of 'cinema's basic realism' (Rosen 1987: 17)
- the sense of an empowerment over reality in film (and the attempts at a revolutionary utilisation of that empowerment) as predicated from a position of the 'transference of reality from the thing to its reproduction' (Bazin 1967: 13 14); the 'real connection' as manifest in progressive directions in film form.

Yet this final respect finds no textual justification in Bazin's writing, and the steps towards it (intellectualisation, 'critical' realism, the problematisation of realism), while sharing common ground with Bazin's positions, display a strong will not to be 'grounded' in Bazin's positions. These three directions – intellectualisation and a critical and problematised realism – are visible through the way in which they have broken with the realism Bazin championed; they are not, in the final analysis, variations on the same theme. Indeed, the 'empowerment' turns Bazin on his head – to latch onto the internal, organic fundamentals of film language, as also passively observed by Bazin (such as, as shall be argued, the idea of time in the frame, in Bazin's theorising on the long take, in 'The Evolution of the Language of Cinema' (Bazin 1967: 23–39)), and attempt to then wield such fundamentals directly 'against' the viewer. Bazin, when discussing the length of time Flaherty used for the sequence of Nanook fishing, saw a melding of film form (Flaherty's long take) with content (the actual waiting period of fishing); this made for a purity of film as film, whereby Flaherty's film form, as 'primed' for the immersion in encountered reality, is effectively worked into the best-shaped receptacle for it. Extracting the long take form and forcing reality into it to the extreme degrees apparent in some New Wave films, so as to have the viewer reflect on his or her bourgeois impulses of wanting a narrative event to occur, is far from – and, very probably, not implemented in relation to – Bazin's position. And yet this phenomenon of an aspirant empowerment, as evidencing an ontological position, irrespective of its orthodoxy or grounding in Bazin's writings, can be best analysed as arising from an evolving 'milieu' of traditions of film realism. And such traditions, while certainly not re-instigated, or arguably maintained, through Bazin's writings, do find an authoritative articulation, even a shameless 'confession', in them – the writings as a strong indicator of common perceptions as to the nature of film, and as offering no retrospective resistance to the directions in the continuing evolution of such a milieu. And lesser phenomena in this evolution (the taste for actualité through, for example, the persistence of cinéma-vérité form, or the long take film forms of Miklós Jancsó that sport the appearance of being observational) can be traced directly back to a fundamental belief in film realism as the best receptacle of the transferred reality – a low-level continuum of Bazin-identified film realism, through the 1960s.

Putting to one side the appropriateness or potential of Bazin's conception of film at the moment of the onset of 1960s-era progressive film, the character of 1960s progressive film points to Bazin as an indexical figure, even when increasingly distant – in but not of this phase. Thus, in identifying this phase of a post-Bazinian realism, the organising structure with which to explore the observable directions in 1960s progressive and radical film becomes apparent; the framework in which a series of concerns and purposes finally reveal themselves. Thus post-Bazinian realism breaks with all but the fundamental conception of Bazinian realism, and so readily presents itself as straying from or undermining Bazinian realism – a transgressive end phase that seems to exist in a state of opposition to (but not negation of) previous certainties. Thus the shift from Bazinian to post-Bazinian realism is akin to the shift from modernism to postmodernism.

Therefore each side of the above-mentioned principal divide (the Late Modernist film, the New Waves) can now be reviewed in relation to, and as advancing, post-Bazinian realism, in order to take us to the point of the crises in film form – the moments at which post-Bazinian realism effectively mitigates against a considered revolutionary film project.

The 'Late Modernist' Film

There is a need to identify, positively, a strain of 1960s cinema that comes under sustained examination in this study. This is the strain that would otherwise be termed non-New Wave. Looking at critical writing of the time indicates a fumbling towards an identification; Cowie introduces his *International Film Guide* for 1964 by identifying 'those interested in serious cinema (for want of a better term)' (Cowie 1963: 7). A decade later in the same series, writing on 'Alternative Cinema', André Pâquet identifies his secondary quarry (the primary being Hollywood and entertainment cinema) as 'the alienation of a more modest, so-called "cultural" cinema proposed by film-makers like Antonioni, Bergman, Fellini and Truffaut' (Pâquet 1972: 70). 'Serious' and 'cultural' are vague terms and, more problematically, implicitly slur the popular and entertaining as lacking in culture, and unserious – a position rife with class connotations. It would be better, for the writers of these Tantivy Press guides, to simply identify 'the Hampstead film' as revolving around the Hampstead Everyman cinema of the 1960s, its programming and clientele.

Such an idea can be seen in John Russell Taylor's 1964 study of 'some key film-makers of the sixties', *Cinema Eye, Cinema Ear*, which begins: 'If the cinema is an art, who is the artist? Ever since people began to consider, very tentatively, the possibility that the cinema might be a new art-form, this has been a favourite topic of discussion among intellectual enthusiasts. Perhaps the question sounds absurdly academic' (Taylor 1964: 1). The 'intellectual' qualification of 'enthusiasts' (which also differentiates such intellectuals from the film enthusiasts to be found among the 'people'), and the claim that this debate has caught the attention of the intellectuals too, indicates that progressive film-making is considered to be within their domains of interest, and a point of discussion – to address, as Taylor does here, this 'new art-form'.

Often this film culture involved, in the U.K. context, 'continental cinema' – a parochial term that is accurate in that 'continental' denoted exactly the serious and cultural, but was also slang for pornography (although sexual titillation was not exactly unknown in this strain of cinema, which often avoided censorship on the grounds of artistic aspirations). However the notion of the new as originating from mainland Europe points to the key characteristic: the new as not only an address of society in the 1960s (with, therefore, objectivity as the principal choice of framing: these films as surveying rather than, as with the New Wave, entering into, or purveying, the experiences of the new) but the arrival and development of an artistic discourse of and for the new. This strain of progressive cinema had finally been freed (through the sophistication or seriousness lent by an embrace of modernist devices) to address the new – a battle that had seemingly determined questions of contemporary art in the years immediately prior. Writing of the identification of The Movement (of English poetry and prose of the 1950s), for example, Morrison quotes from an anonymous 1954 leader in *The Spectator* in praise of a detectable new direction: 'part of that tide which is pulling us through the Fifties and towards the Sixties' (Morrison 1980: 2). The new in this respect represents a fruition of progressive currents 'in the air': to be progressive, and to break away from older modes of artistic expression, is to find a bond to the here and now, to achieve relevancy, to look forward. And, furthermore, the impulse to address the here and now is typically critical: anti-establishment and dissenting, with questioning as a function of an unhappiness with the status quo. Such critical impulses are also an aspiration to look forward, and so aligns this kind of cinema with that strata of society afforded the chance to look forward, and to anticipate better things (if not for society, then certainly for themselves): the intellectual enthusiasts – that is, the bourgeoisie.

Such films occur after the phase or dominance of an aesthetic realism – particularly films made in the light of the favourable critical reception of Italian neo-realism outside Italy. Such films cannot be said to be truly New Wave in that they avoid reflexivity, and the seeming carelessness (that is, often carefully constructed carelessness) of film form typical of New Wave films. For this reason, 'art cinema', a term applied to both this strain of cinema and the New Waves, does not provide precision in terms of an identification. Often (as in the case of Tony Richardson, as will be argued) these films aspired to a modish New Wave status via New Wave-esque aesthetic flourishes mixed into their non-New Wave form. At other times, in defiance of their naturalism, expressionist strategies, often presented as stylisation in the name of 'psychological realism', are utilised.

So it can be said that their naturalism works as a leavening agent, and that their naturalism ultimately retains a totality to the world presented (to use Lukács's term) and a tendency to a dispassionate – an even coldly dispassionate – objectivity. These aesthetic aberrations of New Wave flourishes and expressionist strategies, in respect of this naturalist schema, merely update and refresh the naturalism: new skins for old wine.

For this reason, this cinema has often been referred to as 'modernist' in critical writing; an ahistorical identification, and one that presumably latched onto such exceptional aesthetic moments so as to declare the films as in a full, albeit belated, bloom of a modernist reinvention of form. Yet if modernism is understood as, in the manner of Cubism, an array of differing views or vantage points on the event, then the modernist cinema can be said to have all but run its course by the early 1940s – even, in terms of populist cinema, via a number of noir detective films (*The Third Man* (Carol Reed, 1949) and *Citizen Kane* (Orson Welles, 1941) are the most apparent examples). Could it be argued that this problematic term, 'modernist cinema', originates from the discussions to which Taylor alludes? The intellectuals now simply recognising the psychological representation of their peers as worthy of reflection on the screen, and hence feeling that cinema (before, presumably, dismissed as a populist and so unsophisticated pastime for the working classes) has finally hit its modernist phase? Such familiarity also accounts for the warm receptions of East European films in the United Kingdom, Wajda's in particular, with their existential and humanist concerns, intellectual anti-heroes, and measured, reformist criticism of actually existing socialism. While commentators of the time failed to satisfactorily name this strain, the commercial sector was more forthcoming. Cowie's 1968 volume carries advertisements on its second page for Contemporary Films (their 1960s prints were still being shown in the Hampstead Everyman into the mid 1990s), the journal *Cinéma d'Aujourd'Hui* on its fourth page, and Connoisseur Films Limited on its sixth page. These three terms exactly describe the intended impact and experience, and concerns, of this strain of cinema.

The term 'Late Modernist' would therefore be more appropriate for these films of the 1960s.[11] What degenerates between the modernist phase and this Late Modernist phase is therefore apparent in the latter's constituency – that is, the new film culture of the 1960s. This is a film culture for a select group of connoisseurs who are for the intellectualised, contemporary-orientated and -situated, 'artistic' cinema. In this identification, the intrinsic problem with the

Late Modernist film or phase is also apparent: such tactical criticism, by 1968, was insufficient. The leavening naturalism was effectively leavening all dissenting sentiments too by locking such sentiments into a bourgeois film form (rerunning debates about the limits of naturalism familiar from an earlier phase: that of the dawning of modernism), and so keeping cinema itself from radical or revolutionary aspirations.

With the transition from later phases of neo-realism to a number of films that marked the beginning of progressive 1960s film[12] comes a new and timely concern: alienation. In the films of Michelangelo Antonioni, and particularly his tetralogy,[13] alienation was perceived to be a condition of contemporary existence – formally apolitical, giving rise to illnesses that the less observant would dismiss as psychosomatic.[14] Alienation, in this sense and during the 1960s, was of variable meaning; it could be utilised in a classically Marxist fashion (to criticise the nature of the state, and Brechtian alienation, discussed below, is a subset of this tendency) in a psychological manner (as associated with the work of R.D. Laing at this time), as intertwined with existentialism (the legacy of Sartre and Camus), or in an apolitical fashion (a condition of 'inner space', of Outsiderism associated with Colin Wilson). Althusser, writing in 1967 and eschewing such imprecision, placed the renewed interest in alienation within the context of the 'profound ideological reaction' of de-Stalinisation; (Althusser 1971: 10).

Alienation, in the 1960s and 'existential' sense, as forming the basis for a critique of contemporary society, was perceived at the time, as it still is today, as representing a late 'modernist' period of film-making, utilising an appropriately sophisticated methodology of psychological realism. The chief point of connection was the stream of consciousness, now given a visual equivalent on the screen. The assailing of the mind of modern man or woman, as rendered in a phenomenological stylisation that marks the subjective disintegration of modern man or woman, represents a thematic step away from Bazinian neo-realist realism. Placing biological-survival problems to one side so as to concentrate on problems of psychology – or walking away from a consideration of biological-survival problems altogether, as if implying such concerns are now no longer valid – severs the direct 'transference' relationship between the object and its reproduction. A foray into a working class area – in *The Servant* or *Blow-Up*, for example – now denotes the way in which the protagonist experiences areas and modes of existence outside his usual sphere, in pursuit of his elusive sense of beauty (homosexual encounters and dealings, creating arresting photojournalism, respectively), and is not an exposure to the conditions and environs of the working classes. This shift speaks of the way in which a straight neo-realism had become entirely insufficient in rendering the consideration of modern man and alienation. Pasolini, with his reluctance to move in this direction,[15] retaining a formally political consideration of the South (the 'Southern Question', so-called after Gramsci's essay of the same name) over the North (the zone of industrial growth and modernisation; something particularly pronounced in Italy at this time) represents the exception that proves the rule.

This shift, and Pasolini's example, also speaks of the way in which the progressive film-maker no longer adhered to a preferential option for the poor in relation to his or her subjects. Indeed, in the British case, the suddenness of the abandoning of the concerns of northern realism for swinging London was so pronounced as to call into question any commitment to the lot of the poorer stratas of the working class in the first place. This realignment of the role of the artist as essentially free to engage with whatever he or she saw fit can be understood to possess an anti-Stalinist subtext, particular to the next generation of Western intellectual leftists: the New Left. Hewison notes '[i]n admitting the aesthetic autonomy of the artist, the New Left avoided the trap of trying to impose an ideological conformity' and comments that this gave rise to 'a new kind of romanticism' that he associates with Colin Wilson, Parisian Left-Bank bohemianism, the writers associated with (and categorised as) 'the Movement' and the American 'beats' (Hewison 1981: 183). This, then, building on a foundation of the intellectualisation of film, was the dividend that defined the Late Modernist film once in its stride.

Despite this new set of influences on film culture, and a new audience for such films, the notional fidelity to reality is not banished from film form altogether. After all, the alienation investigated in these films cannot be disassociated from the experience of modern life if it is to remain the key factor in the exploration of modern life. So any stream-of-consciousness stylisation represents a palimpsest mise en scène, with the 'psychological' written on top of, and obscuring, the 'realism'. And beneath the strong surface evidence of the intellectual-auteur's hand there still remains a Bazinian 'transference' at the point of interaction with everyday reality, or the possibility or echo of such a transference in relation to any direct interaction. So that, for example, despite the extremities of Bergman's *Vargtimmen* (*Hour of the Wolf*, 1967) – fantasy and nightmare sequences, paranoia running rampant through both – everything can be narratively 'explained' once the use of psychological realism is acknowledged. The level of stylisation (the realm of paranoia) is built upon a mostly unseen level of normality (the everyday existence of the protagonist). The former level offers a 'reading' of the latter level, with this reading speaking of *La crisi spirituali dell'uomo moderno* (to paraphrase the title of Maisetti's 1964 study of Bergman), the phenomenological truth of the matter at hand. But the latter level is necessary to support that reading; the paranoia, to be of any consequence, must be grounded in a reaction to material reality – otherwise, we remain adrift in the mind of the madman. Intellectualised film was anything but the domain of 'degenerate' art.

Pasolini, in discussing the stylisation of psychological realism, which he termed 'free indirect subjectivity' ('*soggettiva indiretta libera*') in 'Il Cinema di Poesia' in 1965 (a paper was first delivered at the New Cinema Festival in Pesaro in June 1965; reproduced in Pasolini 2005:167–86), establishes these two levels, and then observes their interaction (which, as it drifts into ambiguity, becomes a 'contamination' of each level by the other). At this point, however, a proviso remains: there is no serious doubting of the material existence of the objects reproduced. Or, as both Nichols and Heath note, free indirect subjectivity remains within the limits of the Bazinian conception of film realism (Nichols 1976: 543; Heath 1973: 102). The extremity of subjectivity on display, at this point, does not break free of the constrictions of the traditions of film realism also evident in neo-realism; a baseline of 'the real' still remains intact. Indeed, free indirect subjectivity effectively works to liberate style – offering a greater degree of artistic freedom – without calling into question the 'givenness' of the real. So 'hard' items in *Repulsion*, for example, are rendered grotesque through stylisation (rotting food, the surface of a kettle), even to the point of non-recognition, but there is no doubting that, in the flat of the film's setting, the rotting food and the kettle exist. And the beset mind of the protagonist 'borrows' their appearance in creating the world of her mental disintegration – rendered for the viewer via psychological realism stylisation. Where non-objects slip in, most notably the threatening man glimpsed in a mirror, objects the viewer knows cannot exist, since they have no narrative justification or explanation (how did he enter the flat? at any rate, he has vanished a second later), are then recoded by the viewer as hallucinatory figments of the imagination – the weightless spectres conjured up by the distressed mind. To use Jameson's term, the fantastical can be cognitively remapped[16] until a sober, everyday version of events occurs in the mind of the viewer and the fantastical is fully accounted for. And this dynamic holds even when the distressed mind 'takes over' the film in its entirety, as with Fellini's 1963 *Otto e Mezzo*, in which, with the ambiguous blending of the real with fantasy, the distinction between 'what you show' and 'how you show' collapses, rendering a free association structure, drawn from the mind of the protagonist – nightmares, fantasies, visions of the dead, flashbacks, alternative takes of the same event and so forth.

So there is a kind of negative pleasure to a film like *Repulsion*: the more it stylises, the more it holds back, and the greater the sense of a truth beneath the processes of mental sublimation and displacement becomes. This notional truth becomes the kernel around which everything is structured, demanding recognition from the viewer in order to make sense of the film and to 'justify' the excursion into the expressive possibilities of film-making at this point. If *Repulsion*'s 'truth' is finally rather mundane (the suggestion of the protagonist's history of abuse, possibly sexual, as a child), the pleasure of the text comes from the intellectual project of translating the imagery 'back into' real life.

In Buñuel's work across this period, however, we see not only the achievement of this 'greater' realism, but the erosion of the baseline of the real, and the beginning of the end of psychological realism as a total system for progressive film. At this point, Buñuel's films were typified by a subversion of the difference between narrative 'reality' and fantasy (or non-reality; Rees refers to this as 'the clash between consciousness and dreams (or daydream)' (Rees 1983: 89)). The fantasies are expressions that 'break' the given sense of realism (that is, scenes that are clearly fantasy retain realism for their expression). Thus the reality, from which the realism is drawn, is thrown into question: not only in terms of its palpability, but in terms of the very factors that govern the behaviour of the protagonists in that reality. This indicates nothing other than the repressions (political, religious and social) that hold sway, even in contemporary society. The subversions point towards psychological damage on the part of Buñuel's protagonists, originating in the same institutions Fellini damns (Catholicism and fascism): the delusions of servitude in *El Angel Exterminador* (1962), delusions of a religious origin in *Simón del Desierto* (1965), of a sexual origin in *Belle de Jour* (1967) and the delusion of civilisation (the assumption of the remoteness of the past in the context of modern and 'civilised' society) in *La Voie Lactée* (1969). The net result, through the broken realism, is a notion of one 'presentness', a phenomenological continuation of the same 'time frame' from primitive times to the sophisticated 1960s present – the present as still coloured by the intrusions of the past (that is, the still active repressions that originate in the past). Thus even in the 'modern' world, fascism and Catholicism determine psychology. This accounts for the religious and sexual nature of the fantasies in *Simón del Desierto* and *Belle de Jour* respectively, and the historical anachronisms of *La Voie Lactée*. The viewer, in surveying the madness, is forced to consider the damage wrought by such systems in order to make a sense of the madness. So a rational reading, a sense, still remains possible, and the reaching for it decodes the fantasy/reality blur.

This, in itself, is far from unique to Buñuel; psychological realism is a mainstay of Losey's and Clayton's films at this time, for example, in addition to Bergman, Fellini and Polanski. However, Buñuel frustrates expectations springing from psychological realism. The palpability of these delusions and fantasies is not eroded, excused or 'accounted for' by the utilisation of psychological realism in the manner of Fellini of this period (where the fantasy is codified as fantasy, and given over to, or able to then move into, caricature and exaggeration; the harem sequence in *Otto e Mezzo*, for example). *Belle de Jour* does not utilise a sense of formal subjectivity (on the part of its protagonist), but presents a structure of seemingly classical narrative linearity, objectively, that only later reveals itself as part fantasy, or entire fantasy, or fantasy drawing on reality, repeatedly and compulsively.[17] After one or two occurrences, the viewer is left with the 'real sense' of the film as constantly, perhaps indefinitely, deferred – the anticipation of the cut to the next scene that accounts for this one. Such a technique, in its execution, is well suited to capitalising on the ambiguities of film form per se.

The opening sequence of *Belle de Jour* uses three lengthy establishing shots to denote the, seemingly, narrative importance of the setting of the film. Yet this soon becomes almost entirely irrelevant to any sense of an 'actual' (i.e., materialist) narrative, since the opening is, it turns out, a rape fantasy on the part of the protagonist. This inducts the viewer into the ways in which, for the majority of the film, the real is not distinguished from fantasy. Indeed, this was Buñuel's direct intention (see Aranda 1975: 228). Although the film lacks a subjective aesthetic, the neurosis of the protagonist 'contaminates' the film as surely as in *Otto e Mezzo*, guiding it away from the reality in which the aesthetic seems grounded. Thus the subjective fantasies, which assume the veneer of realism, become a symptom of neurosis: as if this aesthetic is a form of self-delusion, in common with the madman who believes himself to be quite sane. And, in this way, even the look of the film (garish and overbearing, an expression of the perfect or idealised 'reality' of advertisements that depict the desirable or idealised life in advanced capitalist societies: stylishness, sexual tolerance, ease of living) comes to suggest delusion and unspecified trauma. However, prior to such a critique, the film has methodologically 'lied' in Bazinian terms: the language of objective realism is used to cast seemingly subjective impressions or hallucinations as the absolute real – as if possessed of transferred reality, exemplifying a Bazinian ontology of 'the real'. At this point, the form and the content are in direct opposition: a form of an 'ontological-real', so as to articulate 'hard', palpable images that speak of their objective existence, which nevertheless repeatedly delivers the unreal. Rendering a film form of 'the real' as knowingly misleading offers the potential for a radical problematisation of realism – a radical problematisation that, at this time, was enacted in the New Waves. But here, in *Belle de Jour*, this lie is neutralised by the critique of the aesthetic; yes, the reality on display is structured by fantasy, but this resultant false reality is the condition of this (our) time – the aesthetic of advertising, beautiful people, wealth; the deception, vanity and elitism of these emblematic and trivial characters. The viewer can leave the film with a clear consciousness, and a lesson learnt. The same might be said for the moralist; in the central role, Deneuve exudes an idealised and 'modern' sexuality (that is, she conforms to images of physical beauty and sexuality of these times) and yet here, and also in *Repulsion*, is actually frigid. Automatically, then, she embodies in both instances a disjuncture between outer appearance and an inner self. Durgnat refers to her 'vague sullenness' (Durgnat 1968: 143) and Farber to her 'curiously intriguing detachment' (Farber 1998: 274). Such a contradiction is also to be seen in Bailey's portraits of Deneuve from this time – a dead-eyed chic (see for example Bailey and Evans 1970: 12), and in the models of Antonioni's *Blow-Up*. In *Belle de Jour* her impeccable Yves Saint-Laurent outfits added to this sense of the 'ideal' woman as being closer to a tailor's dummy. This bolsters the sense of conformity as masking neurosis – the wider concern of these films – and sexuality as the area in which these tensions are played out, reaching a 'critical mass', despite the dawn of sexual liberation, and a freer sexual promiscuity available to such a class of people at this time.

But what if there was no such neutralisation? That is, what if the limits to stylisation and objective contamination were lifted – removing from the film any possibility of a complete or satisfactory cognitive mapping? The spectres of *Repulsion* point the way to just such a problematic of a mise en scène that has unshackled itself from the baseline of 'the real' altogether, despite a retention of the seeming fidelity to 'the real'. After all, in terms of the experiences, for the viewer, of *Repulsion* and *Belle de Jour* – which parallel the experience and fantasies of the protagonist – the horror or pleasure of rape and sexual assault is given more 'reality', is loaned a greater dramatic and narrative 'weight' than the 'actual' experiences that 'explain' them (fear of workmen, a bad dream in *Repulsion*; a humdrum suburban life in *Belle de Jour*). If one step further is taken – the deletion of the proviso, the removal of the possibility of narrative explanation – then realism has been left bereft of 'the real'. The viewer is still confronted with the abundant alienation – but of what condition does this alienation now speak? Is it a literal 'losing grip on reality' on the part of the protagonist, who has drifted off to a point of complete madness, unable to distinguish fantasy from reality? Or is it that reality itself has finally outmanoeuvred our comprehension – it is the rapidly changing world around that no longer makes sense; that renders itself nonsensical? And in each of these possibilities comes a further question: if 'the real' has, in the final analysis, been eradicated from the film, why does the film still speak the language of the real, in its surface, aesthetic adherence to realism? While the trajectory of psychological realism in the 1960s offers a number of progressive directions, this theoretical cul-de-sac – which inevitably arises with the freeing of realism from 'the real' (that is, the denial of an absolute sense of veracity in the reality 'transferred' to the image) – awaits. It is not a matter of sectioning off this area and identifying the films within it as nonsensical (indeed, as a value judgement this was often done by critics at the time) or the intellectual/progressive variant of deviant or degenerate art. Rather, it is a matter of examining the non-sense in order to note the nature of this one final direction of post-Bazinian realism, its 'radical' phase – the direction 'out' of post-Bazinian realism, as the Bazinian conception is abandoned – and the resultant crisis of film form. This direction will be considered in relation to *Blow-Up*, below. First, however, it is necessary to examine a parallel development to the phase of Late Modernist film, in terms of a shared negotiation with the ontological-real: the post-Bazinian realism of the New Waves.

The New Waves

From the outset, the majority of French New Wave films, as with the Late Modernist films, also established a qualified, or an ambivalent, relationship with 'the real'. The films resisted a sense of completeness, as if not balancing their elements into a pleasing whole; they adopted 'open' structures (as if presented unfinished, at a rough cut stage), mixing a number of different approaches that evolved 'out' from the films (encounters with places and people, scenes and concerns that only fitfully found their place in any sense of a narrative, aesthetic experimentalism). This initiated the need for a greater authorship of the film on the part of the viewer – that is, the seeming unfinished status created the space in which the viewer would react to the film, or parts of the film, as they saw fit.[18] Such an autonomy of interpretation was formally denied in the films of the Late Modernist phase (beyond a measure of occasional narrative obscurantism); these films had established structures that spiralled inwards to the final point of the readings and critiques yielded – the moment of the completion of cognitive mapping, teleologically sealing the film's narrative, and all its components, to that end. So the critique, and the dramatic and narrative 'weight' of the film, for the Late Modernist film, was to be found – even, in the case of the critique, directly dramatised – in the closing scenes, with those scenes as the final and key pieces of the jigsaw. Whereas for the Nouvelle Vague the end was often perfunctory – or even throwaway (as in the thinness of the dramaturgy, and the nonchalance of the deaths that end *A Bout de Souffle* or *Pierrot le Fou* (1965)) – with the weight of the film coming to reside in earlier moments. In short, there was no guiding narrative thread, no one story, onto which all the elements of the film were to be grafted. In *Le Signe du Lion* (Eric Rohmer, 1959, released 1962) and *Cléo de 5 à 7* (Agnès Varda, 1962), for example, it is a wait, as incidental to the impending fate of the protagonists, that becomes the central concern of the film. The events – or even the non-events, the incidentals and the boredom – that fill the wait come to represent the 'real' stories of these films.

And such a condition of aperture, to use Wollen's term, was continually present. The films self-reflexively switched between a number of different vernaculars (documentary realism, genre pastiche and intertextuality, the art film and low or exploitational comedy, and a flux of Brechtian-equivalent reflexivity devices) that, in their often violent juxtapositions, could not congeal into one single naturalism, or be accommodated within a straight realism. Which vernacular was to be believed? To be confronted with Godard's *Bande à Part* (1964) was to have to navigate a series of responses to the type of film experienced; where was the weight of this film to be found? In the scenes of high drama between modern Parisians in the 'citational' genre pastiche? In the 'artier' moments? In the musical moments? The viewer needs to switch positions – modes of appreciation – constantly, and the freedom to do as much only comes with an abandonment of the willing suspension of their disbelief. In this respect, the Nouvelle Vague finds parallels with the 'waking' experience of the Brechtian artistic discourse, rooted in an anti-illusionism, and as achieved through film equivalents of the Verfremdungseffekt.[19]

With these tendencies, while it would have been unlikely that a question of the ontological-real within the frame could not but be problematised, and from the outset,[20] a number of factors initially mitigated against a radical calling into question of the fundamental realism of the mise en scène. Despite protests against the norm (the Verfremdungseffekt equivalents, and the gamut of attributes noted by Wollen), the films remained within the limits of a post-Bazinian realism. Any substantial problematisation of the Bazinian idea of transference could be initially temporarily deferred, or neutralised, via pastiche or intertextuality. The Nouvelle Vague worked to cordon off discrete areas as self-reflexively unreal or stylised in the midst of the very real (as with *Une Femme est une Femme*, 1961; the intricacies of modern love against the garish mise en scène of a musical), or as a facet of the very real (aspects of the thriller genre that effectively permeate the paranoid ambience of *Paris nous Appartient*, Jacques Rivette, 1960).

At the same time as this knowing appropriation and subversion of these very fundamental escapist falsities of the popular bourgeois film (a cinema, as *Cahiers* would have had it, as predicated from a position of a near-complete unreality), the Nouvelle Vague was daring in its dogged pursuit of 'the real'. Indeed a Bazinian realism lives on, in the first half of the 1960s, in the spirit of the Nouvelle Vague auteurs, filming on the streets, and their renewed deference to the reality to be found there. And it was this pursuit that led to a more thorough rethinking of the position of the real within the frame. The organisation of the real – pictorially, and in relation to narrative – that had existed in the neo-realist film in a controlled and regenerative fashion (to the artificialities of popular film-making, in their image manipulations) was now abandoned. Found reality begins to 'destabilise' the Nouvelle Vague film, disorganising pictorialism, as shall be argued.

At first glance these two approaches, of a heightened image manipulation and a heightened realism, seem to be mutually incompatible. The former, in its intertextuality and the evacuation of the actualité from the frame, in the manner of Roy Lichtenstein's retention of the 'purely' artificial, is readily likened to pop art (by Roud in 1966, for example; see Godard 1966: 9). The latter, in its privileging of actualité and the resultant candour of content, parallels the emergent New Brutalism in British photojournalism from the 1950s onwards – both a 'deliberate flouting of the traditional concepts of photographic beauty' (Harrison 1998: 58) in the name of reportage. But when considered as directions within a post-Bazinian realism, a shared blind spot becomes apparent: these directions both accommodate a conception of film realism that does not fully question its transference relationship between the object and its reproduction. In fact, the contradictions thrown up between these two approaches, for Narboni writing in 1963, actually make for a complete Bazinian approach: 'the *seamless gown of reality*, of which he so often spoke and which evoked for him the Shroud of Turin just as often as Veronica's Veil, only fascinated him to the extent that tearing always threatened it. Beneath the *continuous and homogenous reality*, he sensed the spasm, the grimace of a menacing *real*' (reproduced in Narboni 1987: 59, author's italics). Clearly the Nouvelle Vague disruptions to a homogenous realism were then still conceivable within the limits of a Bazinian conceptualisation of realism. Or, to approach this idea from the opposite direction and to recall the trajectory of psychological realism – the disruptions may test, but they fail to break with, a Bazinian conceptualisation of realism.

A methodical 'testing' of the limits of a Bazinian film realism can be tracked across Godard's work during the 1960s – something enabled, in part, by his productivity during these years. And such testing was apparent from the beginning of Godard's feature film work too. Here, in *A Bout de Souffle*, the clichés of North American B-feature gangster films, as 'knowingly' re-enacted by a seemingly semi-rehearsed cast, are delivered via a documentary-realism style, and one pushed substantially beyond the norm (the longest of long takes, underlit location filming, etc.), and with a film grammar that constantly drew attention to itself (the suddenness of the jump cuts, the inclusion of fluffed lines, straight-to-camera addresses, etc.). The film was initially received as a radical departure – the very embodiment of the 'new' of the Nouvelle Vague through the, as Cowie puts it, 'need to shock – technically, aesthetically and socially' (Cowie 2004: 248).

Yet any radicalism arising from this rests on the film's formal, and showy, experimentation. Beyond this, there is merely a will to achieve something of that state of ontological ambiguity found in the Late Modernist film. In terms of the sociopolitical critiques mounted in (let alone the gravitas and scope of) *La Dolce Vita* and *L'Avventura*, or even the British New Wave, in films such as *The Loneliness of the Long Distance Runner* (Tony Richardson, 1962) or *Saturday Night and Sunday Morning* (Karel Reisz, 1960), *A Bout de Souffle* would have seemed entirely frivolous. Wajda reportedly dismissed the New Wave in 1962 as a 'kind of light-hearted, egocentric cinema . . . We don't forget history, we are a part of history, and we fight against history – but we are not individualists, like those

French are' (Cowie 2004: 107). The ends of the radicalisation of film form, for which Wajda here expresses distaste, were evidently as nothing compared to the import of the psychological/modernist reinterpretation of the Polish School of film-making. While the Polish School articulated and readdressed contemporary existence, and was even under potential censure in this regard, Godard seemed content to dabble with film form alone, while ignoring any sense of an engaged narrative altogether.

Even on this dilettante level, *A Bout de Souffle* fails to make its arresting form overtly or formally political; it is merely vaguely oppositional (to hegemonic, bourgeois or classical norms of film language). Bordwell's consideration of Godard's jump cuts reaches for just such an oppositional context to explain why these disruptions of continuity were perceived as startling, unlike examples found some thirty years earlier. It was only in a Late Modernist phase (as 'the rise of the international "art cinema" in the 1950s') that *A Bout de Souffle* could be 'read as if it were a novel . . . as the statement of an author with an identifiable style . . . [so that] now, like other techniques, jump cuts could be made to be seen' (Bordwell 1984: 9). Thus such innovations were gestures that startled only within the limits of the established norms, rather than a complete transformation of the 'meaning' of film and the perception of the mise en scène. And it was on such grounds that the initial attacks on Godard were mounted, including, implicitly, in Louis Malle's *Zazie dans le Métro* (1960) and, explicitly, Jacques Baratier's *Dragées au Poivre* (1963), which parodied Nouvelle Vague aesthetic traits. However, these innovations do represent the beginnings of the ousting of the language of hegemonic, bourgeois or classical norms, and with that ousting the ideological assumptions that underwrote such norms. And while minimal damage to the old order can be said to be inflicted with Godard cutting to a moving shot (a breaking of the 'good' grammar of film language), for example, a notable intervention against the old order can be seen to be in the ascendant in the nature of Nouvelle Vague imagery – the developments in the mise en scène rather than the montage.

The inflation of the status of 'the real', for the various reasons of opposition to an earlier French film culture as noted above, results in a 'hysterical' relationship between film realism and reality once the floodgates had been opened. Whereas film form had once deftly mastered reality – at very close quarters (neo-realist film-makers had marshalled the images they gleaned from the world around them, representing them as unfolding under the aegis of tight narratives and particular aesthetic concerns) and even at a distance (in the strategies of psychological realism) – now film form was continually outflanked by reality. It was as if the camera, which had traditionally adopted an elevation sufficient to capture the images needed, had now lost the ability to attain such an elevation, and was unsure which way to turn – what to film, from what distance, and how. Reality was perceived as too changeable and fast moving, as if now dragging the New Wave film-maker's camera along in its choppy wake. Thus the Nouvelle Vague cinematographer was typically more noted for mobility and speed than his or her 'eye' and professionalism.[21]

The majority of writing on the Nouvelle Vague notes the use of the innovative techniques with which the auteurs invited reality into their films, and how the films were revitalised – lent an excitement, contemporaneity and spontaneity – with such a capitalisation on the ontological-real. It is clear how this fountain of 'the real' also refreshed the clichés of genre. Gangsters and guns, as an outgrowth or extension of *Cahiers* MacMahonist *cinéphilia*, are seen to have proliferated in the outlandish environs of modern France in the Nouvelle Vague, particularly in Truffaut's films (or, in relation to the musical, in Demy's films), even to the point of characterising much of the oeuvre of Jean-Pierre Melville. But in critical/academic writing this is rarely seen as a destabilising effect, more as an aesthetic achievement, often understood to be a smooth logical progression of neo-realist praxis,[22] to the point of a super-materialism, and not as a fundamental revision of the tradition of realism up to that point. A brief review of the aesthetic characteristics of the Nouvelle Vague points to such a revision, which can be understood to be an attempt to reconfigure a Bazinian conception of film for a less naive time of film making – as Narboni's reading from these years indicates (Narboni 1987: 59).

The essential difference between the tradition of documentary-based realism (incorporating neo-realism, later neo-realism and the documentary movements of the 1950s) and the documentary-based realism of the Nouvelle Vague was, crucially, a refusal to impose a compositional visual order on the part of the Nouvelle Vague – the eradication of a pictorialism.[23] 'Overly' tight framing is emblematic of this tendency. There is a sense, here, that the camera is failing to 'master' the world around it, lagging behind the action or occurrences, unable to 'pull' these events into a visual 'wholeness'. The frequent tight and close-up framing (sometimes a distance inappropriate for the object filmed is used) at the expense of now missing establishing and re-establishing shots, communicates the impression that the camera cannot 'establish' the world of the film. This world is no longer 'given'. The mise en scène now interacts with the surrounding reality rather than offering compositions drawn from reality. Malle's documentary *Vive le Tour* (1962) repeatedly illustrates this; little sense of the overall event, in its entirety, is achieved. The camera literally chases after the Tour de France cyclists, at times cutting from one vibrating tight close-up to the next, snatching what observations are possible in this succession of non-matching shots (or, conversely, semi-frames stationary figures as the camera hurtles by). Such a mise en scène radically revises Bazin's reading of Welles's use of sequence shots, depth of field and deep focus (Bazin 1967: 33, 36; 1971: 28) as exemplifying a filmic praxis of a mastery of the reality in front of the camera, of which Henderson notes 'composition-in-depth projects a bourgeois world infinitely deep, rich, complex, ambiguous, mysterious' (Henderson 1976a: 424), a world of unlimited experiences 'with the screen as its cross-section' (Bazin 1971: 27). The Nouvelle Vague auteurs confess subservience in the face of reality, which is only partially rendered as it speeds by – negating any pictorialism that can arise from framing, and any controlled composition. At its most radical, even a cubist impulse (as the antithesis of Bazin's reading of Welles; a flux of partial glimpses – no one set perspective or angle) is left behind – there is no overall organisation, no final mosaic, no apparent intelligence informing the dis- and reassembly of images; at these points, the awareness of the camera apparatus often blocks as much.

In *Jules et Jim* (1961), for example, the disorientating swish pan becomes a recurring aesthetic motif, and one that has no fixed meaning. It is used in both subjective and objective ways; to emulate POV (point of view) shots on the part of the protagonists and to move between protagonists as they talk – to work as a reverse angle shot (for example, as the characters play the 'village idiot game' while sat around a table). The latter instance is particularly pronounced in this respect, since Truffaut swish pans while the camera is mobile (blurring or distorting the jerky background detail), and then pans 'correctively', so as to keep the figures, roughly, in centre frame as the camera continues to move. In this way – and through the freeze-frames, handheld camera work, the iris-outs and shots that are difficult to understand in terms of camera motivation – Truffaut creates a dynamic, 'open' relationship between the environment and the aesthetic, a relationship in which the environment is continually blurred, moving, shaking, as if interrogated by the camera.

Godard goes one step further than Malle; here it is not a case of a lack of mastery or inability to pictorialise, but of a wilful anti-pictorialism. In *Bande à Part* (1964), for example, heads are never quite centrally placed in the frame, and two characters are rarely shot with a 'balance' between them; the camera crops characters as it pans, the establishing shots are not 'smoothly' executed, the mobile camera unit employed (over handheld work) sometimes wobbles when moved, and images are frequently tilted (without achieving a 'Dutch tilt' effect). The cutting accentuates such 'errors'; scenes are often cut half a second or so after the blocking is broken, as characters begin to move off-screen. This environment is not interrogated, in the manner of Truffaut's realism, but fumbled.

The notion of film as a receptacle for the real remains here – indeed, is strengthened (the auteur does not throw up his hands and down tools; the camera remains defiantly turning in the teeth of this high speed reality) – but the imagery illustrates a new pact between the real and film realism. Rohdie qualifies his description of documentary footage as 'absorbed by the fiction' of neo-realism when he claims, in relation to *Stromboli* (Rossellini, 1949), that the documentary footage in turn 'tears the texture of the fiction. Its reality is too much for the fiction to absorb completely . . . it disrupts that context [of fiction] by moving away from the fiction towards the reality whence it came' (Rohdie 1995: 1). Yet he still finds, in the net result, a palpable sense of the world as presented – its certainties and inevitabilities: of Rossellini's sequence shots, 'time and space were rendered whole. Reality was not disrupted'; and that the 'strangeness and power' of Stromboli, as also rendered in the film, originates from 'the wholeness of reality' (Rohdie 1995: 1). When compared to the operation of a dialectical rather than sympathetic relationship (fictional mise en scène and factual imagery), the Nouvelle Vague refusal to impose visual order is seen to prevent the entire process of absorption – no matter how ambiguous it may be – and so illustrates the notion that the old 'wholeness of reality' was now not necessarily attainable in film. The mise en scène was not something with which to frame the world at leisure – but a device with which one doggedly chases after the world, thankful for whatever partial glimpses are snatched. So there can be no mastery of the image, only a deference to it. In this respect, MacCabe's speculation that 'it would be possible to make an argument that the Nouvelle Vague's aesthetic is little more than a development of Rossellini's practice' (MacCabe 2003: 161) (a frame of reference also used by Neupert (2002: 147)) can be refuted on the grounds that such an argument overlooks this essential conceptual break with Rossellini's practice. Likewise, the 1950s documentaries that represent the prehistory of the New Waves evidence no issues with visual order and its implications. And, as objectivity was so visibly abandoned in favour of the impression-driven aestheticism of psychological realism in the Late Modernist films, the desire for a visual order is understandable. Here framing indicates a control over the free-form subject matter, and a frisson of objectivity in this respect, as if to confirm the veracity of the film's vernacular.

Once again, an aperture is in operation, forming the basis of this new pact. Since an aesthetic control of 'the real' occurs more often than not in terms of the framing, in the Nouvelle Vague any given sense of the use of a straight realism is now itself made visible through the 'poorly' framed mise en scène, which is effectively an attack on the conventional tendency to frame the images in a 'correct' fashion. And this exists continually as an aesthetic condition; a constant violation of aesthetic order through an anti-pictorialism. And this Nouvelle Vague framing, with every blurred and over- or underexposed image, demands an awareness of the presence of the camera in front of this found reality. At its most extreme – in Godard's wobbling dollies, for example – the mise en scène denotes that the frames of film themselves denote such a presence. At its most conservative – in Truffaut's meticulous period films (*Jules et Jim* and *L'Enfant Sauvage* (1969)), films far from alienating or experimental, and which suggest by their very nature the reassembly of a 'wholeness of reality' in the recreation of a bygone era – any burgeoning visual order was still besieged. Thus even Benayoun's above-mentioned *Positif* attack on the Nouvelle Vague – 'a regime of blatant amateurism, of wilful paradoxicality' (Benayoun 1968: 162–63) indicates an awareness of the presence of the camera as the defining characteristic of the films.

Such a violation does not occur in the Late Modernist film, which maintains a revised aesthetic order throughout, as noted. And this difference represents the differentiation between the two traditions – the skeleton underneath the flesh of Wollen's cited list (Wollen 1982: 79), in this study. Eco's observations on Antonioni in *The Open Work* in 1962 provide a post-structuralist foundation for this differentiation. In attempting to locate a precedent to Antonioni's avant-gardism, Eco cites Joyce and the Aeolus chapter of *Ulysses*, which mimics the spectrum of journalistic styles while reporting a conversation between journalists. Eco concludes that this gives rise to a sequence in which: '[Joyce] alienated himself in the situation by assuming its expressions, its methods. But by giving these expressions and methods a formal structure, he can also elude the situation and control it. In other words, he avoids alienation by turning the situation in which he has alienated himself into a narrative structure' (Eco 1989: 148). Eco's implied demarcation between 'control' of alienation and letting alienation run riot touches on the essential difference that gave rise to what was effectively a divergence of films associated with the Western leftist intellectual at this time: adhering to this Joycean technique, consciously or otherwise, ultimately differentiates the avant-garde of naturalism and a Lukácsian totality from the New Waves of 1960. The divergence occurs over the question of what to 'do' with the alienation with which the films reverberate. Ultimately, those films that sublimated a sense of alienation failed to achieve anything more than an awareness of the problems they inherently brought about.

It is in relation to the junking of visual order that the intertextual vernacular of the Nouvelle Vague becomes path-breaking – something certainly beyond just the role of an outgrowth or extension of *Cahiers* MacMahonist *cinéphilia*. The colliding of the language of the ontological-real with clearly fictional subject matter (the reenactments of elements of genre films) without a visual order to mediate the results of this collision into a wholeness (in the sense of narrative and – to use Lukács's term – a totality, of the world of the film) invariably raises questions about the nature and status of the fictional. There is a blurring of the visible boundaries: at what point does the ontological-real inform the fictional, or overtake the fictional, or render the fictional as fictional? Herein is the aesthetic framework for a progressive and questioning realism, as seen in Godard's trajectory; the unresolved – unlike Buñuel – tensions that arise between form and content, and his coming exploration of these tensions.

In such respects, Nouvelle Vague realism was made 'critical'; not only self-aware, but the locus of its own questioning of itself – to return to Wollen's terms, a 'foregrounding' over a 'transparency'. And so, in common with the Late Modernist films, the Nouvelle Vague films wound up effectively peeling the language of the real off the actual 'real', and holding this language – film realism, now bereft of its ontological backing – up to the light for examination. The Late Modernist film played with the ontological-real, teasing it with elements of ambiguity and drowning it with subjectivity. The Nouvelle Vague continually questioned the ontological-real – pushed it as far as possible– only to then have it harried from the mise en scène altogether. But in each case, it was not scuppered or dismissed. If in the Late Modernist film it had been found wanting in terms of its expressive capacities, in the Nouvelle Vague it had remained as a workable proposition – a blueprint for an expanded realism, still the motor for the furthering of a film realism. Consequently the Nouvelle Vague did not wind up in the post-Bazinian realism cul-de-sac of the Late Modernist film, unable to move beyond a hopeless shattering of the very codes of realism, as shall be argued, but could attempt to move one step further ahead. The self-questioning of nouvelle-vague expanded realism required just such a forward movement; such questions needed to be answered in further films, in a further pushing of the shock of the new, an ever more 'critical' realism – and here was the potential for the (revolutionary) future, as seen from 1966 onwards. So the real potential of the 'merely vaguely oppositional' (as diagnosed, above, in *A Bout de Souffle*) would be apparent by the mid 1960s, with Godard's evolved critical realism making *The Loneliness of the Long Distance Runner* seem old-fashioned in comparison. And, ironically, the seed of the worth of this real potential is in the above-mentioned frivolousness itself: Godard's form is not exclusively locked into serving the content (specifically the time and place, as with Richardson). In this way, a 'retroactive canonization-reification' (to use Jameson's term in relation to *A Bout de Souffle*'s critical/academic status (Jameson 1990: 188)) does not render Godard's films as dated period pieces, while this can be said to be true of Richardson's, and the fate of films that are diagnosed here as falling into a Neue Sachlichkeit category. The Nouvelle Vague had posed questions of more progressive use than the pre-mptive answers provided in the Late Modernist film.

Or, less prosaically, in its anti-illusionist strategies, Nouvelle Vague film form represented a more considered response to the apparatus of cinema and questions of realism – and this was something that the 'intellectualisation' phase had effectively displaced (onto concerns with the condition of alienation, the lot of modern man and so forth). The New Wave film form, in that it had made realism critical – the locus for its own self-questioning – thus remained as a possibility, once film was reimagined as a facet of revolutionary practice.[24]

As a structuring element, such a radicalisation of form can be viewed as not particular to film realism, or even particular to the evolution of film in the first half of the 1960s, but as typical of a combative attitude towards the assumptions that underwrite the norms of the art form at hand. From this perspective, the project of the New Wave beyond its early years, channelling a Brechtian praxis into post-Bazinian realism, can be accounted for. Eco, in 'Form as Social Commitment' observes that:

The artist who protests through form acts on two levels. On one, he rejects a formal system but does not obliterate it; rather, he transforms it from within by alienating himself in it and by exploiting its self-destructive tendencies. On the other, he shows his acceptance of the world as it is, in full crisis, by formulating a new grammar that rests not on a system of organisation but on an assumption of disorder. And this is one way in which he implicates himself in the world in which he lives, for the new language he thinks he has invented has instead been suggested to him by his very existential situation. He has no choice, since his only alternative would be to ignore the existence of a crisis, to deny it by continuing to rely on the very systems of order that have caused it. Were he to follow this direction, he would be a mystifier, since he would deliberately lead his audience to believe that beyond their disordered reality there is another, ideal situation that allows him to judge the actual state of affairs. In other words, he would lead them to trust in the orderly world expressed by their orderly language. (Eco 1989: 141–42)[25]

Eco's 'new grammar', resting on an assumption of disorder, had been seemingly – and only temporarily – 'tamed' with psychological realism. This stylisation had articulated elements of disorder, but only from an ineffective quarter and not one that, in the final analysis, would trouble the willing suspension of disbelief. The exploitation of the self-destructive tendencies of the formal system would inexorably come with the problematisation of psychological realism – the breaking free of the formerly tamed 'new grammar', in the films of Antonioni. The 'new grammar' found accommodation in the aperture of New Wave film form, and with this alliance would give rise to a number of arresting interventions against the 'formal system'. In Godard's films in the 1960s, this arises from the interaction of an ontological-real as applied to 'the real', and an ontological-real as used to articulate its opposite – the un-real, or 'the false'. While this certainly problematises a Bazinian ontology, it does not obliterate the Bazinian conception of film – Narboni's 'the grimace of a menacing real' (Narboni 1987: 59) continues to underwrite this experimentation. And this kernel of 'the real', inexorcisable from the mise en scène, finally becomes empowering for Godard, and revolutionary film, at the end of this particular trajectory. These two directions in the work of Antonioni and Godard, as arising from the innovations within a post-Bazinian realism as discussed above, can now be examined in detail.

Notes

1. Such traditions of realism fall on the Lumière (rather than Méliès) side of early film history: an unimpeded visual documentation of found reality, as achieved through the advent of technological advances. The divergence of opinion in relation to an appropriate film language comes after such a 'big bang' moment – a continuing adherence to this technologically enabled 'high' realism (which Henderson associates with Bazin, below), or a consolidation of such realism within codes and conventions associated with the novel, with theatre, or other 'grammars' of meaning associated with visual reproduction (which Henderson associates with Eisenstein, below).

2. Bazin left no sustained or developed, formal or programmatic articulation of his position in written form (see Cardullo in Bazin 1997: xi).

3. This essay is a composite of three articles originally published in the early to mid 1950s (see Bazin 1967: 174).

4. On the connections between Bazin and Benjamin, which begins from the speculative position that Bazin may have read Benjamin, see Dall'Asta (2011: 57–65).

5. Rosen provides a directory of responses and notes that the preoccupation with critiques of Bazin had mostly occurred by 1975 – that is, as part of the first stage of post-1968 film theory (Rosen 2003: 73 footnote 1).

6. Such a conceptual correlation is not always an actual correlation, despite Bazin's taste for high realism. This opens up the space in which a major area of concern in Bazin's work exists – a phenomenological reading of film and film realism, with the auteur theory grounded in this area too. Hence Rosen notes that '[q]uite consistently, Bazin associates the need for realism with "psychology" rather than "aesthetics"; hence "reality" itself is not the primary term of his ontology of the image, except insofar as it is an object of the obsession' (Rosen 1987: 12). Rosen's use of the term 'obsession' echoes Bazin's arresting contextualisation for his reading of film – film as an obsessive desire to achieve immortality, a tendency that is to be discerned in artistic endeavours as far back as the Egyptians; film, therefore, as a contemporary version of mummification. A discussion of these areas – Bazin's phenomenology and his history of art – is outside the scope of this study.

7. The 'Golden Age' is equated with Rossellini's 'War Trilogy'; *Roma, Città Aperta* (*Rome, Open City*, 1945), *Paisà* (*Paisan*, 1946) and *Germania Anno Zero* (*Germany, Year Zero*, 1947). The perception that the introduction of 'psychological', romantic or even titillating elements into nominally neo-realist films – as with Rossellini's *Europa '51* (1951), *Viaggio in Italia* (*Voyage to Italy*, 1953) or *La Ciociara* (*Two Women*, De Sica, 1960), respectively – led to a degeneration. This debate, the 'Crisis of Neo-Realism' occurred in various dialogues but especially between Bazin and Guido Aristarco, with particular reference to Fellini's *La Strada* (1954) and *Le Notti di Cabiria* (*Nights of Cabiria*, 1957).

8. For a fuller discussion, see Goddard and Mazierska (2014).
9. In this study, the nature of their positions over form is used to differentiate between avant-gardism and a Lukácsian 'totality'. It is via a 'totality', Lukács's use of Lenin's term (Adorno, Benjamin et al., 1992: 33), that an ideological critique is presented in a sustained and complete way – that is, in a way recognisable, aesthetically acceptable and useful to potentially revolutionary elements. Although this does not denote formal objectivity, totality achieves a kind of conceptual objectivity – the ability to examine the concerns dramatised from a variety of critical viewpoints. For Lukács, realism is not so much a methodological practice (the striving for ever greater verisimilitude) but an aesthetic rendering of 'the real' that cannot but re-present it 'whole' via totality. Totality, also termed 'wholeness', is described by Walsh as: '[t]he cornerstone of Lukács' thought . . . he perceives contemporary society (specifically capitalist society) as alienated, fragmented, discordant; like Brecht, he sees the function of art as being to raise (proletarian) consciousness to a point where it may actively intervene in the process of social determination, and thereby attack at the roots of that social alienation. But Lukács believes that the chaos and fragmentation of "reality" has to be overcome, transcended, in the work of art, which should present a vision of "wholeness" and "unity"' (Walsh 1981: 18).
10. Lovell and Hillier take 'Size is irrelevant' to mean CinemaScope – an expensive process then in fashion (Lovell and Hillier 1972: 143).
11. For reasons of clarity, this study will capitalise the term 'Late Modernist'.
12. This transition can be seen in *Il Posto* (Ermanno Olmi, 1961) and *Salvatore Giuliano* (Francesco Rosi, 1961), with their by-then unfashionable fidelity to 'Southern' concerns, and Pasolini's early, neo-realist films. Other notable films in this category include *La Dolce Vita* (Fellini, 1960), *Rocco e i Suoi Fratelli* (Luchino Visconti, 1960) and *L'Avventura* (Antonioni, 1959). A strain of social issue films, such as *The Servant* (Joseph Losey, 1963) and *Victim* (Basil Dearden, 1961), together with the reception of the films from the Czech New Wave in the West can be considered in this context too.
13. The tetralogy consists of *L'Avventura*, *La Notte* (1960), *L'Eclisse* (*The Eclipse*, 1962) and *Il Deserto Rosso* (*The Red Desert*, 1964). Some critics, such as Rohdie and Brunette (in their studies of Antonioni), consider the first three to be a loose, thematic trilogy, with which *Il Deserto Rosso* has only tentative connections.
14. Illness in the films of the 1960s invariably means neurosis and psychological disorder, the expressions of which are fairly clearly informed by psychoanalytical theory. Films that forefront neurosis or mental illness in this way include *Il Deserto Rosso* and *Blow-Up* (Antonioni, 1966), *Repulsion* (Roman Polanski, 1965), *Morgan: A Suitable Case for Treatment* (Reisz, 1966), *Jules et Jim*, elements of *Prima della Rivoluzione* (Bernardo Bertolucci, 1964) and of *This Sporting Life* (Anderson, 1963),

Le Feu Follet (Louis Malle, 1963) and *I Pugni in Tasca* (Marco Bellocchio, 1965). This is also true, to a lesser extent, of some of the New Wave films of Makavejev, Chytilová and Godard.

15. Pasolini anachronistically remained with the poor for his 1960s neo-realist films: *Accattone* (1961), *Mamma Roma* (1962) and *Il Vangelo Secondo Matteo* (*The Gospel According to Saint Matthew*, 1964), and some documentaries, his earlier novels and parts of his *Uccellacci e Uccellini* (*Hawks and Sparrows*, 1966).

16. 'Cognitive mapping' may here be defined as the reliance on the viewer to piece together the whole narrative from disparate and unconnected moments of information that surface in the film narrative.

17. The question as to what is and what is not real in *Belle de Jour* is examined by Durgnat, who provides a variety of readings of the film, and likens it to Robbe-Grillet's *L'Immortelle* (1962) in this respect (see Durgnat 1968: 139–43).

18. Such an approach is often read as Brechtian; for example, '[since Brecht] sees the "closure" of the work of art as itself potentially alienating, in that it perpetuates the distinction between author and audience, producer and consumer . . . [in developing] open-ended forms, and attacking the illusionist tradition, Brecht actively worked towards creative participation by the audience: they ceased to be spectators "consuming" art (as they still are in Lukács' aesthetic), and became an integral and necessary part of the production of the work' (Walsh 1981: 18). The 'creative participation by the audience' is required if it is accepted that, in remaining in the cinema when confronted with New Wave films and their difference from conventional films, the natural inclination of the audience is to make sense of what is seen on the screen. And such a provocation works to 'invite' the audience into the film – as co-creators of the film's purpose (so that this, then, is the ticket that will be issued at the cinema door of films of a directly revolutionary purpose, as will be discussed). Such a strategy characterised the experience of structuralist film. Malcolm Le Grise's *Castle 1* (1966), for example, defies narrative continuity or sense or progression in terms of what is seen on screen, and the sporadic flashing of a light bulb momentarily overwhelms the film projector's light while illuminating the auditorium, so creating and maintaining an awareness in the audience of itself throughout. Walsh's contextualisation points the way to a discernible and characteristic difference of mise en scène between the films identified here as Late Modernist (Lukácsian 'totality'/naturalism) and, with some exceptions, New Wave films (Brechtian 'openness'/realism). Wollen attempts to tabulate, in 'Godard and Counter Cinema: *Vent d'Est*' (in the Autumn 1972 edition of *Afterimage*), the way in which the wider New Wave tendencies (the 'counterparts and contraries' to standard 'Hollywood-Mosfilm' fare; Wollen is ambiguous here, but seems to suggest such counter tendencies as evident across the New Wave as well as Godard's own oeuvre), as developed by Godard, had achieved a diametrical opposition to these antecedents, on several levels. Wollen lists the conventional phenomena on the

left (which can, then, be related to the Late Modernist film) and the New Wave outcomes on the right:

Narrative transitivity	Narrative intransitivity
Identification	Estrangement
Transparency	Foregrounding
Single diegesis	Multiple diegesis
Closure	Aperture
Pleasure	Un-pleasure
Fiction	Reality

(reproduced in Wollen 1982: 79)

19. The Verfremdungseffekt is also known as 'Alienation', the 'V-effect', the 'A-effect', 'defamiliarisation' (as in Sinker 2004: 44), 'distanciation' (Sussex 1969: 86; Hames 1979: 170) and '"estrangement devices"' (Lunn 1974: 25) in the context of film criticism. Jameson translates Verfremdungseffekt as 'estrangement' (Jameson 1998: 85 footnote 13) and defines it in several ways. He finds in it only a technique for the bringing together of Brecht's wider ideas (see Jameson 1998: 39). The main target of the filmic Verfremdungseffekt was continuity – an aspect so necessary to conventional (or 'bourgeois' as the radical or avant-garde auteurs would have termed it) film-making that it permeates all points of the production process (from the on-set role of 'continuity girl' to post-production 'continuity editing'). At the Belfast Film Festival in 2014, 'continuity girl' Renée Glynne recalled being handed a sheaf of blank pieces of paper by the production manager of Godard's *One Plus One* (1968) when she asked for a script. Sadoul indicated the result in the first sentence of a 1960 *Les Lettres Françaises* review of *A Bout de Souffle*: 'No experienced editor could watch *Breathless* without trepidation: every other continuity shot is wrong' (reproduced in Douchet 1999: 157); decades later, Reader posits 'asynchrony' as the characteristic of the work of Godard (Reader 2004: 72 and ff). Typically, critics of the New Wave will point to the use of jump cuts for this enterprise, freeze-frames, the insertion of intertitles commenting upon the action and reflexive gestures on the part of the actors, blocking the willing suspension of disbelief required to accept the actor 'becoming' the character – all of these as a refusal to 'hide the brush strokes' of the processes of the making of the film. The continuity of the soundtrack is also broken; MacCabe equates this to Brechtian 'epic theatre': 'for its whole progress is a constant separation of its constitutive elements' (MacCabe 1975/76: 46). But between such 'punctuations marks' the 'quality' of the image itself was made 'critical' (as shall be argued). Indeed, a later phase of the New Wave that mostly sought to utilise the expressive possibilities established for an articulation of 'straight' criticism of the Left, beyond the project of sabotaging the film form of 'bourgeois' film, is marked by the return of associative montage. Thus the Nouvelle Vague was mostly an innovation in the mise en scène rather than montage. The shared and ironic

'knowingness' that arises from pastiche, as noted above, might also be considered to be the film equivalent of the Verfremdungseffekt; Jameson notes Brecht's tendency to utilise 'the element of humour and buffoonery as the very space and realm of the experimental as such' (Jameson 1998: 11).

20. Thus Chabrol's place among the Nouvelle Vague was questioned, during the early years, because of his failure to problematise the ontological-real in favour of more conventional narratives.

21. This question of speed becomes central to Nouvelle Vague. To achieve speed, Godard dispensed with live sound (it was dubbed on later) and tracks (he placed his cameraman Raoul Coutard, a former reporter and cameraman with the army in Indo-China, in a wheelchair for mobility) and used a 35mm Arriflex camera with Ilford HPS film stock (usually used for photographic journalism) (see Dixon 1997: 15; Marie 2000: 159). Thus *Vivre sa Vie* (Godard, 1962) was shot in eighteen days (Shafto 2000: 19 note 63). Chabrol placed his camera operators in car boots and on motorcycles rather than lay tracks, and Truffaut was known to do away with a camera tripod, using balconies or rooftops for support (Neupert 2002: 40). Shooting in low-light environments, even without artificial lighting (see MacCabe 2003: 119) allowed Coutard to add to the immediacy of the Nouvelle Vague methodology: 'Daylight captures the real living texture of the face or the look of a man. And the man who looks is used to daylight' (Coutard 1965/66: 10). Similarly, Henri Decaë, who shot the first films for Truffaut, Chabrol and Malle, used Tri-X Kodak film, which enabled him to shoot with very little light, or without artificial lighting altogether, so allowing for the freedoms that came with a smaller crew and budget. (MacCabe notes such freedoms in the context of both advances in camera technology and an easing of union restrictions, and Neupert elaborates on the effective channelling of state money and subsidies by the Nouvelle Vague auteurs as a major influence (MacCabe 2003: 115–16; Neupert 2002: 36ff).) Such freedoms were less easy to obtain in the case of direct sound; Marie describes the way in which Jacques Rozier had to transcribe improvised dialogue and have the actors dub it back onto the film (the audio recording had been unacceptable) for *Adieu Philippine* (1963) (Marie 2003: 96).

22. This is not to say that there is not a neo-realist subset of the Nouvelle Vague; one of the seminal texts for the Nouvelle Vague – *Chronique d'un Été* (Jean Rouch, Edgar Morin, 1961) – falls into this category. Sections of the portmanteau film *Paris vu par . . .* (various directors, 1964) are true of this approach too; a heightened realist aesthetic at the border of fiction and documentary, with elements of each seemingly commenting on elements of the other.

23. The British New Wave, however, almost always imposed visual order. For that reason, the British films can be considered in relation to Benjamin's reworking of the notion of a New Objectivity ('Neue Sachlichkeit') in 'The Author as Producer':

. . . the bourgeois apparatus of production and publication is capable of
assimilating, indeed of propagating, an astonishing amount of revolutionary
themes without ever seriously putting into question its own continued existence
or that of the class which owns it. In any case this remains true so long as it
is supplied by hacks, albeit revolutionary hacks . . . I further maintain that an
appreciable part of so-called left-wing literature had no other social function
than that of continually extracting new effects or sensations from this situation
for the public's entertainment. (Benjamin 1998: 94)

The British New Wave's modish aesthetic techniques, borrowed from films across
the Channel, represent just such an assimilation; the 'decoration' of an essentially
conservative approach to film-making with, to use Jameson's term, '"experimental"
novelties' (Jameson 1992: 64) – an uncritical realism. The radicalism of the British
New Wave was therefore limited to concerns of its content – the attempts to
present Northern and working-class environs and struggles in a sympathetic manner
on the popular screen.

24. Here, in these general terms, it can be noted that such a film form was not unique to
the French cinema; it was apparent in work from Polish (Jerzy Skolimowski), North
American (Richard Lester), Italian (Bernardo Bertolucci) and Romanian (Lucian
Pintilie) auteurs too, and in the Yugoslav *Novi Film* tendency (of Dušan Makavejev,
Lazar Stojanovic, Želimir Žilnik and Aleksandar Petrović, among others), and in the
more 'experimental' films from auteurs of the Czech New Wave (Věra Chytilová and
Evald Schorm).

25. Despite this applicability, Eco initially failed to identify the radicalisation of form
in *A Bout de Souffle*, reading the aesthetic innovations as another example of
an Antonioni-like avant-gardism founded on subjectivity (see Eco 1989: 267,
footnote 13).

CHAPTER THREE

Crises of Post-Bazinian Realism

'I Confine Myself to Pointing out Existing Problems'

In terms of pushing against the limitations of post-Bazinian realism in which the project of the Late Modernist film is here considered, Antonioni could be said to have gone the furthest. And Antonioni's take on modern Europe across the 1960s, a 'Northern' (rather than the Gramsci-derived 'Southern') question, was perceived even at the time to be of both unavoidable and yet baffling critical importance. The tetralogy – in its particular concerns with and uses of existentialism and alienation – had defined the look and concerns of the Late Modernist film. Taylor's precision about the moment of the emergence of the 'Antonioniesque' ('bare compositions with solitary figures lost in great vistas of modern architecture and scenes between two characters who talk mainly with their backs to each other, to "express aliena-tion", were a fad of 1961–2' (Taylor 1964: 81)), even though derisive, underscores the impact of Antonioni's work on the progressive film culture of the time – hence the use of the term 'Antoniennui' (coined by Andrew Sarris (Sarris 1971)). Towards the end of the 1960s it was with stylistic flourishes highly reminiscent of Antonioni's techniques that film-makers in more commercial areas wanted to address the by then somewhat clichéd themes of man's inability to communicate, the apoliticised society, and the way in which modern, technocratic society isolates man. At the same time, the self-styled avant-garde – particularly the film work of Andy Warhol and Paul Morrissey (*The Chelsea Girls* of 1966, for example), and then in aspects of early Fassbinder – would dabble in a kind of designer boredom; an emulation of modern life with listless characters whose narrative 'point' remains elusive.

The persistence of Antonioni's vision, as indicative of a complete, self-contained articulation of the contemporary condition, was to prompt Deleuze's formulation of his time-image reading of modern film. Antonioni is a major presence in Deleuze's *Cinema 2: The Time-Image*. For Deleuze, Antonioni's mise en scène exemplifies modern (that is, post-war) film's engagement with time over movement: 'Tiredness and waiting, even despair are the attitudes of the body. No one has gone further than Antonioni in this direction' (Deleuze 1989: 189). This element of the use of literal time, or a sense of time, in the mise en scène is here denoted as 'experientialism' – which is how Antonioni's longueurs, in the context of his countercultural films, had been taken at the time. Experientialism, in the 1960s, tallies with the hyper-individualism of many of the films – a sensual, picaresque odyssey, usually hedonistic, on the part of the protagonist as he or she encounters the rapidly changing world around. And this experience, through a number of devices, is presented to the viewer in a subjective fashion – to be experienced along with the protagonist. In the experiential, such a tendency overtakes the 'straight' narrative. This occurs spectacularly in the 'Star Gate' sequence of *2001: A Space Odyssey* (Kubrick, 1968), which was marketed as 'The Ultimate Trip' at the time; other examples include *Apa* (*Father*, Szabó, 1966), *The Committee* (Peter Sykes, 1968), *Barbarella* (Vadim, 1968), *Deep End* (Skolimowski, 1970), and *The Sorcerers* (Reeves, 1967) (see Halligan 2003: 72–73). Even documentaries from the time seemingly 'gave in' to such subjectivity, most notable *Tonite Let's All Make Love in London* (Peter Whitehead, 1967).

Where Antonioni's work was met with appropriately complex responses from many quarters, this can itself be read as another facet of Antonioni's influence: the maturation of aspects of the film culture of the 1960s. Yet Antonioni's films were confrontational to such an extent that the snob value of intellectualisation was lost – these were barely films to be seen at; the films court bafflement and displeasure (to return to Taylor's 'intellectual enthusiasts' – the Antonioni films showing at the Hampstead Everyman would dampen their otherwise 'favourite topic of discussion' (Taylor 1964: 1)). Unlike Bergman and Wajda of this period, the avant-gardism of Antonioni more often than not broke with preconceived sets of expectations, to the detriment of Wollen's diagnosed 'pleasure' in a way far more substantial than the 'un-pleasure' yielded by many New Wave films at this time (Wollen 1982: 79). This provides a point of progressive focus that can be clarified once an examination of Antonioni's rebarbativeness has occurred: the project of the Late Modernist film – running from Fellini's and Visconti's films of the early 1960s (two whom, like Antonioni, had begun in and moved on from Italian neo-realism), and through Bergman and Wajda, was clearly not enough. In

Antonioni's relationship with the Late Modernist film, the growing crisis of post-Bazinian realism is related to this focus – the problematisation of the givens of the 'northern' cinema.

The point of entry to Antonioni's development in the 1960s is in the consideration of the central role of the missing, and the idea of the missing, in the tetralogy. This can be seen in three tendencies. Firstly, the literal loss of protagonists – the unexplained, unresolved occurrence that sets the narrative of *L'Avventura* in motion. Secondly, the effective loss of protagonists; *L'Eclisse* ends with a medium long shot of an empty street in the EUR district of Rome – the protagonists have agreed to meet on this street and, although neither shows up, Antonioni's camera 'arrives' (that is, cuts to that location) and waits (for a discernible period of time) all the same. The protagonists of the film have vanished rather than reached any sort of conclusion in their affairs, prematurely arresting the expected narrative trajectory. Considered in the light of *L'Avventura* – where the camera follows the friends of a missing woman – this represents a development of sorts: it is now as if the camera has arbitrarily chosen to go with the 'missing' rather than the present characters. These two tendencies are well documented in relation to studies of Antonioni. Thirdly, missing characterisation: the protagonists move with ease and nonchalance in the suddenly, and disconcertingly, futuristic society of Italy of the economic boom of the early 1960s. They behave with a 'modern' amorality that comes across as a base hedonism rather than a calculated taking advantage of the new era of permissiveness; since there is no sense of history, the idea of a pre-permissive time seems not to be present. Consequently, the picturesque ruins of ancient Sicily in much of *L'Avventura*, for example, are utilised as incidental background, with the protagonists, passive spectators, as entirely indifferent to these surroundings. (And herein is another resonation of the missing: the eradication of senses of history and place.) The audience of the Yardbirds sequence of *Blow-Up*, to turn to more contemporary settings, are still 'immovable and near-expressionless zombies' (Cameron and Wood 1968: 140). Such absence of characterisation removes a sense of the sociopolitical status of Antonioni's protagonists; they are classless and good-looking, their smooth features and dead eyes taking the place of the peasants and partisan soldiers of neo-realism only ten years before. These negations undermine psychological realism; the narrative cannot recode locations so as to say something of the characters' states of mind – indeed, they seem lacking in states of mind, merely passively adrift in the modern chaos of life. And yet this drifting becomes the vector through which the world is encountered – incidentals, accidents, nonsensical or inconsequential moments; the experience is reproduced for long experiential stretches, in the longueurs of the Antonioni film, and yet appears not to have been assembled for any clear narrative reason. So the Antonioni film of this period, as built on such absences, therefore tends not to justify its existence; where, and what, is the dramaturgical impulse behind the scenes? Thus Eco compares typical Antonioni moments (such as the close of L'Eclisse) to 'long, blank spells of live TV' (Eco 1989: 116). Yet, Eco notes, even live television broadcasts are governed by Aristotelian rules of narrative organisation. Antonioni's avant-gardism is in his breaking away from this tendency; he achieves a 'radical indeterminateness' (Eco 1989: 117) – a pervasive state of being rather than, as with Le Signe du Lion and Cléo de 5 à 7, an unhappy interlude, 'killing time', between meaningful events.

Through these negations and de-dramatisations, Antonioni revises the two principal systems that had operated within and as the tradition of film realism. Firstly, the predominantly 'psychological' way in which the wider world (the sociopolitical situation, societal mores and so forth) resonates in the film is, for Antonioni, now only an aspect of the behaviour of his protagonists. No such substantial information is to be gleaned from the settings alone, or the presence of the poor, or a concentration on or reverberation of historic events – the stratagems of the neo-realist narrative. The Antonioni characters journey from location to location – often bringing about violent juxtapositions in the process[1] – and so it is their intelligence, or assumed character motivation, that shifts the effective narrative onwards. This suggests that the psychology of the Antonioni protagonist becomes the new and primary structuring influence on the film (rather than the primary aesthetic influence – as is the case with 'free indirect subjectivity'). However – secondly – the films remain entirely grounded in a materialist sense of the world around, via Antonioni's method (and herein is the legacy of neo-realism): radical indeterminateness requires long durations. Such a use of a sense of time passing in the mise en scène can be termed 'experientialism'. This tendency only brings us to the point of Bazin's consideration of time as fundamental within the frame, and the long take as, organically therefore, cinema par excellence.[2] Antonioni's break with such a conception – even while retaining the film language of such a conception – comes in a diegetic alteration of reality. Unlike Fellini, whose penchant for the artificial had lent to the reconstruction of swathes of Rome for La Dolce Vita for phenomenological reasons, Antonioni alters reality as 'in process' and 'before our eyes'. The earlier phenomenological tendency, here considered in terms of subjective impressionism, is then revised as a radical problematisation of transferred reality in Antonioni. This becomes a path out of post-Bazinian realism.

Il Deserto Rosso can be identified as an advance on 'straight' psychological realism – indeed, Pasolini discussed the film in respect of 'free indirect subjectivity'. Antonioni alters the colours of the walls of a room (i.e., repaints them between shots that make up the same scene) so that his protagonist, Giuliana (Vitti), awakens to find different colours, without seemingly being aware of the change – unlike the observant viewer. At another point, Giuliana is seen looking at fruit and vegetables that are (painted) grey. In this way, the altered perception, as made corporeal in these 'impossibilities', reflects the protagonist's state of mind. It is a state of mind in which neurosis is ordered, in which colours become coded: yellow, for example, denotes the poisonous industrial wastes, death, the mysterious disease contained in a quarantined tanker, which flies a yellow flag of warning. This is a radical innovation in film form, utilising the solid imagery itself to denote 'abstraction' rather than realism. This tendency, as film style, is termed 'subjactivity' by Viano (Viano 1993: 54) and described by Pasolini thus: By means of this stylistic device, Antonioni has freed his most deeply felt moment: he has finally been able to represent the world seen through his eyes: *because he has substituted in toto for the world-view of a neurotic his own delirious view of aesthetics . . .* (Pasolini 2005: 179; Pasolini's italics).

A more subtle variant of this, in *Blow-Up*, is found in the scenes in Maryon Park; Antonioni has painted the tree trunk that Thomas hides behind, and reputedly painted the grass lawns a different shade of green (Cardullo 2008: 148). No formal 'alibi' for stylisation is given in the film; this scene is not coded as subjective impressionism.[3] And the 'lie' of this altered environment is contradicted by Antonioni's style – the camera records the environment with a distance and coldness (dispassionate or unsympathetic framing, distanced high angle shots, little tracking, little or no highlighting of objects as important in the framing of the mise en scène). In the case of *Blow-Up*, the use of deep focus and the clarity and 'correctness' of – for example – the sound of the wind in the trees (see Sinclair 1997: 347) all work to suggest that the filmic narrative remains at the direct behest of the reportage of the environs of the film. The protagonists themselves do not register the change. This film language lends itself to a tradition encapsulated in Bazin's interpretation of Flaherty. And the technique – the false presented with the language of the ontological-real, has already been noted, in relation to

Polanski and Buñuel. However, the field in which the technique is implemented is different; it is no longer just a matter of cognitive reality 'giving way' to psychology as the primary influence on the mise en scène, as in *Otto e Mezzo*, which is free to eclipse cognitive reality altogether while declaring as much.[4] Rather, it is a matter of the psychology, even in the extreme, only manifesting itself with cognitive reality in an objective frame. And at the extreme – neurosis to the point of a misperception of (i.e., wrongly coloured) material reality – the films touch on a 'critical mass' of psychology disrupting the frame's very materialism. Neurosis here begins to usurp the place of reality within the frame – replacing it with an unreality. To return to the differentiation made via Eco's comments on alienation and form, where the 'control' of alienation is seen in operation in the Late Modernist film and psychological realism, and letting alienation run riot finds accommodation in the structures of the New Waves, we now encounter a rupturing of the control of the former category. Alienation, in Antonioni's *Il Deserto Rosso* and *Blow-Up* 'Late Modernist' phase, begins to run riot – and in forms which, in their 'closure' rather than 'aperture', cannot readily accommodate such alienation.

Indeed, tremors of something serious amiss are apparent throughout *Blow-Up*. The narrative seems to render only fragments of wider events. These fragments seem to allude to other narratives, which – when briefly visible in the film (if at all) – only make partial sense. And the same is true of the film grammar and the construction of narrative meaning. After a halting conversation with two models at his studio, Thomas repeatedly and languidly runs a coin over the back of his hand. The detail would remain insignificant were it not for Antonioni cutting to a close-up of this action. It poses a question as to the nature of the significance of the image – one that cannot diegetically be answered with any certainty. Thomas's conversations also function in this way, often hinting at a more profound comment without actually delivering one:

> Thomas: *Are the models still waiting? With their eyes shut?*
> Secretary: *Yes they're waiting, but their eyes are open.*
> Thomas: *Good. Tell 'em to shut 'em again.*

And this is also true of countless other formally baffling moments in the film (other notable examples are Thomas's impulsive buying of a ship's sizeable propeller and his sudden leap across the floor to answer a ringing phone when in mid conversation with Jane (Vanessa Redgrave)). In that such occurrences suggest that further narrative information would clarify what is seen (which remains challenging to the point of rendering the film nonsensical), cognitive mapping is frustrated. The viewer finally remains unable to see the whole, or a whole – indeed any whole into which such pieces might fit.

Prior to *Blow-Up*, these loose ends, diagnosed as obscurantism or modishness by critics such as Ivor Montagu (see Montagu 1967: 290), may have been read phenomenologically, in relation to interpersonal tensions. By the close of *L'Avventura*, for example, the missing protagonist becomes the shadow over the 'unfaithful' sexual relationship of her partner and her friend. Or in *Il Deserto Rosso*, as noted, the frustrated cognitive mapping, in conjunction with the 'free indirect subjectivity', adds a further dimension to the neurosis of the protagonist, as rendered subjectively or 'subjactively'; the world does not make sense to her – so why should it to the viewer? *Blow-Up* represents a progression in part because of the way in which these elements of confusion are no longer utilised in relation to characters but in relation to its setting: the countercultural, even underground, London of 1966/67. London itself, for the outsider looking in, was a nexus of potential confusion: pop art, happenings, sexual liberation, riotous classlessness, recreational drug use and the dissolving of the barrier between work and play (phenomena almost unique to London at that time and, in part, a forerunner to the idea of immaterial labour). And such an idea of a tourist-like 'experience' of this place at this time – which was a sensual/'head' as much as a physical/'body' experience – is also translated into the film. Thus the former device for translating such experiences – 'free indirect subjectivity' – can be replaced with a more objective aesthetic and experiential formal structure without a loss of the 'experience' aspect of the film. This realigns the relationships of the components of Antonioni's method with each other.

Prior to *Blow-Up*, the radical indeterminateness found a thematic alibi in the disintegrating relationships and neurosis. It was as if the alienation of the radical indeterminateness was sublimated into such devices; the films were not 'boring' as such, merely truthful renditions of the experience of – in *La Notte* – strained relationships. The experiential aspect worked to 'bring out' the radical indeterminateness, in the manner of Bazin on Von Stroheim's long takes ('reality lays itself bare' (Bazin 1967: 27)) – to present stretches of the films in such a way that their function in relation to the plot gives way to their function in relation to the panorama of the world of the North. So whereas *La Notte* nominally follows a couple's relationship troubles, the weight of the film comes to concern the nature of the party that is thrown, and the interpersonal relationships apparent there as indicative of human relations at that point. With the psychedelic films, the reverse process is in operation: the device/alibi is first located, and its nature is sublimated into radical indeterminateness. The modern condition that Antonioni clearly felt to be true in the tetralogy is actually manifest in the counterculture; it possesses radical indeterminateness and experientialism already. Thomas is able to attain that 'heightened' experience on a day-to-day basis – there is no need for a transcending of the everyday, utilising moments of extreme psychological strain or mental disintegration, in order to access as much. The Antonioni character now need not be a case study or an exception.

The next step is to accommodate such experientialism as the norm of such countercultural existence; what was once the phenomenological is now simply waking reality. For this reason, the key moments or happenings in *Zabriskie Point* (1970) (the shooting of a protesting student, the Death Valley orgy, the blowing up of the desert house) need not be codified as 'real' or 'hallucinatory': Antonioni's concern with such things is in their experientialism not in their actualité. Indeed, a sense of hallucination or actualité would lessen the experientialism (raising the questions: 'Why is the protagonist hallucinating such a thing?' and 'Why is such an event occurring?' respectively). Antonioni finds himself, with the psychedelic films, in a situation in which reality itself becomes unreliable, 'unstable', as if the materialism that once underwrote the Bazinian and post-Bazinian realism is now revealed as nothing more than a veneer.

The full irony of Thomas's profession here becomes apparent: he is a photographer, and so interacts with found reality – the physical 'realness' of his surroundings – in a very palpable fashion. Indeed, Thomas needs a physical 'realness' in his surroundings, since their photographic reproduction represents his living; abstraction is for others such as his friend, an abstract expressionist painter. Thomas is first seen after a night undercover in a dosshouse – his desire to get the right photos necessitates such an inconvenience, a physical entry into parts of reality he would otherwise rather not visit. However, even if the palpable fashion with which Thomas interacts with the physical 'realness' of his surroundings remains, the nature of 'the real', in the frame, does not. The film erodes a sense of the reliability of what is seen – indeed, it dramatises this very idea of erosion. The direct alteration of material reality of *Il Deserto Rosso*, prescribed within the limits of psychological realism as Pasolini noted, has now spilt out into the 'actual' world, unqualified by frames of aesthetic abstraction.

At first, Swinging London seems to accommodate this state of affairs. The concerns of the counterculture of 1967 were anything but an engagement with the hard reality 'outside' – the flight into the mind, and the giving of greater store to subjective perception, was the order of the day. In addition, the fashionable Swinging London of Thomas's social haunts had the instability of the self-created phenomenon: it signified only itself. And it was partly the photography and the dissemination of images that brought the idea of Swinging London into being in the first place – something true of David Bailey's work at that point. His 1964 portfolio *Box of Pin-ups* may be identified as a key text in the creation of the idea of Swinging London, precisely in this manner. The similarities between the actual photographer Bailey and Thomas have frequently been noted (e.g., Sinclair 1997: 352); Bailey photographed the Swinging Sixties through studies of gangsters, aristocrats, wide boys, models and celebrities, and this seems to be the nature of Thomas's occupation too, and both are working class and from East London. In this way the uncouth, working-class photographer became an integral part of that glamorous world he presented (and, as Harrison notes, by 1960 the distinction between fashion photography and photojournalism was becoming blurred (Harrison 1998: 97)). Thus his character traits become integral to attaining the angle from which he seems best able to capture the zeitgeist: he is obnoxious (his physical and verbal abuse of models), intuitive rather than intellectual (he instinctively realises that something unseen is occurring in his photographs of Maryon Park) and superficial rather than seeking a deeper connection with the 'scene' that he photographs ('I'm fed up with those bloody bitches. I wish I had tonnes of money, then I'd be free'). This latter trait accounts for Thomas's 'blank-ness' and seeming indifference to, or unthinking acceptance or being 'at one with', such radically different environments. The photographer was engaged in creating that which he seemed to be recording. In this is a parallel between the truthful-ness of the language of the captured moving image (on the part of Thomas and Antonioni), the language of the ontological-real and the questionable nature of the object captured – false, unreliable, misleading, changeable; the 'false' that is presented as, and proclaimed to be, truthful by the language of the ontologi-cal-real. (So that Antonioni seems to be suggesting that Swinging London itself springs from such a contradiction – it lives its own myth.)

This dynamic is dramatised in the film as Thomas photographs models, in a sequence that stands out by virtue of its positioning (fairly near the beginning) and length, and lack of radical indeterminateness (Thomas seems, for once, fired by basic bodily impulses – the shoot becomes an erotic encounter). He arranges the models against props, hangs clothes on them, and at one point abruptly tugs a model's leg forward – out of frustration, but as if she is incapable of movement herself. Eventually he tells the models to shut their eyes and then leaves the studio indefinitely, leaving them as if they were shop dummies. Antonioni thus ultimately indicates the nature of Thomas's interaction with the environment through the very act of Thomas's photography. Thomas antagonistically manipulates the reality of the shoot in order to capture a perception – in this case his idea of the image of the Swinging London girl, again indifferent, but garish, and sexually available.

A second such parallel occupies the film beyond this, and one whose implications are not circumscribed within the praxis of a photographer in his studio. Thomas accidentally photographs an assassination – something he only realises once developing his photographs. The repeated blowing up of the images yields a narrative of the murder, and the possibility of understanding what has happened (which prompts a series of ethical questions for Thomas, briefly voiced at a party). But a sense of any such narrative as grounded in the ontological-real, the veracity of photographic imagery, is lost after an unexplained break-in and theft of the reels of film and the developed photographs, bar one. Whereupon Thomas blows-up that one remaining blow-up in search of the image of the murderer, and so on – until the resultant image, as an image of an image (i.e., now removed from a direct encounter with reality) approaches abstraction. Thomas returns to the park and finds the body, but the next day it has vanished – just as its photographic reproduction has also vanished (to thieves) and 'vanished' (to abstraction). The sorry moral of these parallels is that the truth is not to be found, or cannot be found, in reality, and that taken for the truth is only, at best, a manipulation or arrangement of fragments of 'the real' as allied with a perception of what reality should or could look like. The hope of breaking out of this arrangement – founded on the physical evidence of a hidden truth, in the dead body – is soon dashed.

The murder seems to have overtones of a political assassination, but this goes no further than a gesture; the repeated examination and blowing-up of the image recalls the fetishised treatment of the footage of John F. Kennedy's assassination. In this respect, Antonioni's approach is lent a real force – this is not an avant-garde novelty, but an attempt to articulate something of the unresolved and ambiguous nature of contemporary sociopolitical reality.[5] What seems to be called into question in this moral is the act of seeing. To what extent can reality

Figure 3.1 Existential dissolution as the fate for those who would face down existential crisis: a lap dissolve banishes the protagonist from Maryon Park in *Blow-Up* (Antonioni, 1966)

itself remain palpable, 'found' and comprehensible when the modes of its repro-duction disentangle themselves from their traditional roles of reportage? And such a disentanglement, which seems voguish and modern, in fact allows for the existence of acts that alarm even unperturbed Thomas.

The unresolved nature of the murder and missing body lends itself to a recon-sideration in the light of the final scene of the film: the game of tennis mimed by the ragging students. The camera follows a ball that does not exist – tracking along the grass (when, mimed, it is hit out of the court) until the fictional ball would have rolled to a standstill. After watching, Thomas joins in with the make-believe: he picks up and throws the fictional ball back to the onlooking students. At this point the distinctive sound of a tennis ball being hit, as synchronised with the hitting actions, is introduced into the soundtrack, as – therefore – diegetic sound. Thomas watches the match, his eyes and head following the movement of the ball between the two players. He then looks away, appears introverted, collects his camera and walks away. The camera pulls back, situating Thomas in the middle of the grass and then, with a quick lap dissolve, makes Thomas vanish, leaving only the grass.

The jarring nature of such an ending, as balanced across a chasm of narrative questions that remain defiantly unanswered, prompted Rohdie to refer to it as a 'trick ending' (Rohdie 1990: 112) and, for Arrowsmith, it is a 'coda' (Arrowsmith and Perry 1995: 126). For Rohdie, and Arrowsmith and Perry, it is as if this ending is somehow not quite a part of the rest of the film. Cameron and Wood, likewise, refer to the notion that the murder is a fantasy on Thomas's part (Cameron and Wood 1968: 131), and Orr goes so far as to suggest that the greater part of the film represents such fantasy on the part of Thomas (in fact a vagrant, as we first encounter him 'undercover' emerging from the dosshouse), which serves only to anticipate, and provide leeway for, the absolute retreat from material reality by the film's close (Orr 1997: 133). Mellor offers a metaphorical reading too: Thomas, like his apostle namesake, doubts what he sees (preferring touch for purposes of verification), with the missing body as akin to the missing (that is, resurrected) Christ, and this general preference for a phenomenological reading, as shared with British mid 1960s visual culture, here anticipates an encroaching postmodernity (Garner and Mellor 2010: 124–39).

It is difficult to read the sequence as anything but metaphor: as demonstrating Thomas's complicity in the murder – his willingness to conform to a type of 'reality' that he knows not to be 'correct' through his miming. In this, he finally acquiesces to his colleague's, and the general, indifference to the news of a murder. In this respect the sequence would provide a counterbalance to the blow-ups. The process of blowing-up the photographs revealed something not initially seen, and so this discovery altered Thomas's perception of what he saw. With the tennis match, his involvement in something that cannot be seen – that is, a mimed act of something that does not exist, a lie – seems to indicate that he is content to live without that truer perception. And Thomas's profession, the documenting of the real, seems now to enable this collapse of the perception of the real; Thomas himself has become locked in this eradication of the real. The night before, he insists to a distracted colleague, Ron, at the party that he sees the corpse himself:

> Thomas: I want you to see the corpse. We've got to get a shot of it.
> Ron: I'm not a photographer.
> Thomas [with determination]: I am.

Yet seconds later, realising what has been said, Ron asks:

> Ron: What is the matter with you? What did you see in that park?
> Thomas: Nothing.

It is in this banal exchange that the implications of Thomas's relationship to the act of photography becomes clear in the context of the film. Thomas's reason for returning to the park for a second time that night is entirely uncertain. He had previously dismissed the idea of alerting the police to the murder, so Ron's witnessing of the corpse would have no bearing on the occurrence other than to confirm to Thomas the reality of what he had seen in his photographs, and the park, earlier that night. (This echoes and inverts their working relationship: Ron provides written captions for Thomas's photographs in the projected book – he writes verbal abstractions based on Thomas's photographic reproduction.) To counter this uncertainty, Thomas falls back on the act of photography to justify the return: it would provide a reason to be in the park – it would even retrospectively turn his fumbling examination of the corpse previously into a reason, a 'recce' for future photography. This crystallises, in the Bailey context, the ambivalence of the figure of the Swinging London photographer to his surroundings. Booker's discussion of *Box of Pin-ups*, 'a Debrett guide to the New Aristocracy', concludes by edging towards such a reading of Swinging London, but repeatedly declines to offer any explanation: 'Was the whole phenomenon in fact some sort of hallucination, a collective dream to which for some particular reason at that particular time it suited a large part of English society in some way or another to subscribe?' (Booker 1992: 24, 25). The 'I am' indicates that photography not only provides a reason, but defines Thomas, and perhaps traps him with this ambivalence. To continue to photograph the corpse would be to continue to find out more information about the murder. And Thomas, like Ron, is unwilling to consider photography as anything other than the creation of a photographic image in the final analysis, and so is unwilling to intervene in the reality from which it is drawn. This is anticipated in the switch from the dosshouse to fashion photography: the radical difference between these environments has little effect on Thomas. This unwillingness accounts for Thomas's denial of the corpse; both verbally ('Nothing') and implicitly, in the joining-in with the unreality of the mimed tennis match.

Such actions on Thomas's part indicate a form of neurosis or self-delusion, brought on by the unexpected encounter with a kernel of hard truth (the corpse) in the midst of the untruth of Swinging London. The neurosis springs from Thomas's resistance to a paradigm shift in relation to 'the real' – he cannot accept the found reality, nor can he reject the welcome of an untroubled unreality. Like Giuliana in *Il Deserto Rosso* Thomas now sees what is not there – his eyes moving left and right as he follows the non-existent tennis ball. Unlike Giuliana, however, this observed non-existence is the common and shared experience, for Thomas and the others, and not a figment of a troubled individual imagination.

Chatman sees this as a 'flight from his humanity . . . into a world created by his [Thomas's] camera, a world insulated from the terrible anxieties of being human' (Chatman 1985: 257), a reading shared by Slover (1968). And this flight, the kind of de-alienation the counterculture at that point promised (in the freeing of those enslaved to the material concerns of late capitalism), in fact terminates, for Antonioni, in the realms of the modern ill. The corpse temporarily threatens to derail this progress, in that it looks to that element of a greater truth as denied by the countercultural scene. The role of the corpse is thus that of the sublime (in the Kantian sense, as read by Žižek in (Žižek 2002: 202–3)): it denotes what it has failed to, or cannot, communicate. Thus the corpse is the indication of the inability of this realm to engage with any sense of a wider – found or cognitive, political, ethical, conspiratorial – truth. And, in terms of this resonation in filmic terms, the corpse denotes the inability of Late Modernist film form to now deliver 'the real' of which the, and this, film form of a Bazinian ontological-real speaks. Such a dead end could equally be said to be an engulfing in the postmodern condition (the inability of this realm to register the existence of the real per se); the making peace with the way in which – literally, here, with the vanishing corpse – all that is solid melts into air.[6]

Such neurosis ultimately allows for Thomas's complicity in the face of murder. Antonioni's final act, to disdainfully 'wipe him out' (with the dissolve), seems a judgement; Thomas's links to reality become so tenuous that eventually he is 'removed' altogether. Or, if not a judgement, is this a threat, or a prophecy – Thomas as the next victim, Thomas as the dry run?

At the same time, the wipe reduces Thomas to the ambiguous status of the tennis ball and the missing corpse, raising the question: does the neurosis extend to the viewer? Is this question not also posed by the inclusion of the sounds of the hitting of the tennis ball on the diegetic soundtrack, an otherwise outlandish moment of seemingly pseudo-subjective cinematic language?[7] And, in the camera movements that follow that which is not there, is this question not also extended to the film itself, which, like Thomas, thus embraces the illusions necessary to protect itself from the intrusion of hard reality? The 'crisis' is therefore articulated to the final degree: there is no guiding 'reality' at the heart of the film, for the protagonist or the viewer; the routing of post-Bazinian realism is complete.

Such a reading calls into doubt the whole modernist system of sense-making, as exemplified by psychological realism. Freed of the 'free indirect subjectivity' so much more apparent in *Il Deserto Rosso*, *Blow-Up* delivers an opaque drifter, momentarily gripped by the possibility of murder, who then shrugs off any sense of moral or ethical duty in relation to it. The viewer is now confronted with the notion that psychological realism was a rationalisation of the alienation and apathy of modern man rather than a rendition of his true nature. Is this not the crisis of reality that the Polish New Wave sought to avoid with the aggressive intellectualised use of psychological realism? Baratier's *Piège* (1970) would entirely capitalise on this crisis. The seemingly unreal hallucinations of the protagonist (who is first introduced trying to deal with this problem: he buys animal traps for the seemingly phantom women who assail him back home) are not codified as point of view or hallucinations, and so are rendered as materially real on the screen as they seem to be for the protagonist, as fantastical as these flights of eroticised horror would otherwise seem to be.

In this context, *I Pugni in Tasca*, which refuses alignment with both camps of progressive 1960s film (it is not New Wave, despite its New Wave flourishes, nor is it 'free indirect subjectivity', despite the dissonant emphatic soundtrack), can be seen to go straight to the point in terms of this elusive 'true nature'. In order to free the only son not afflicted by illness from financial burden, the epileptic protagonist embarks on a eugenic programme of killing all the other members of his large family, himself included – a process in which his sister finally becomes complicit. While this initially seems like an extreme expression of the amorality and bourgeois malaise that typified other Late Modernist films, it soon becomes apparent that Bellocchio intimates that the notion of illness is a further rationalisation. The hard 'fact' is that the characters all aspire to the condition of the unhappy child protagonist of *Germania Anno Zero*, the innocent boy turned into a killer within his family – a kind of new barbarism associated with the desperate social conditions in the immediate aftermath of the Second World War, in direct contrast to the wealth and comfortable lifestyles of 1960s industrial Italy.

How is this rather dire situation to be interpreted? Antonioni does not deconstruct to a point of absolute negation. His illustration of the deceptiveness of the foundations of his cinematic language – that of the ontological-real – necessarily has to include that element that is attacked: the cinematic language itself. The limits of Antonioni's radicalism are apparent: a dialectic within his work, a self-contained provocation, the making of a 'subtlety of meaning', which Barthes declared to be 'crucial' and apparent in Antonioni's films (quoted in Nowell-Smith 1997: 65–67). This raises a series of questions that, to paraphrase Lukács, relate to the meaning – in the sense of purpose – of contemporary realism.[8] In the context of this analysis, such questions were amplified by the failure of 1968 and the resultant reconsideration of the tenets of film language.

Discussing the seeming inconclusiveness of his film *Teorema* (*Theorem*, 1968, which ends with a protagonist's screaming, to the camera and at the surroundings, in close-up), and with very similar terminology to Barthes in 1962, Pasolini said:

> ... this condemnation of the bourgeoisie which used before (which means for me up until 1967) to be absolute and inescapable has to be suspended before a final assessment is made, since the bourgeoisie is at present undergoing a change ... it is assimilating everybody to the petit[e] bourgeoisie ... So there are new problems, and these will have to be solved by the members of the bourgeoisie themselves, not the workers or the opposition. We dissident bourgeois cannot solve these problems, and neither can the "natural" bourgeois. That is why [Teorema] remains "suspended"; it ends up with a cry, and the very irrationality of this cry conveys the absence of an answer. (Stack 1969: 157–58)

> Teorema ... and Porcile [1969] are free, experimental films. They propose no outcome nor solutions. They are "poems in the form of a desperate cry". (Betti and Thovazzi undated: 129)

The boundaries of what was perceived to be possible for film, for Pasolini, were to be imposed by the bourgeoisie – and film here, as the art form of the 'dissident bourgeois[ie]' (echoing Antonioni's sentiments of 'I confine myself to pointing out existing problems', (quoted in Cardullo 2008: 38)) is not appropriate as a directly revolutionary tool. In this way, Anderson (of *If. . ..* of 1968), Pasolini, Fellini (for *Fellini-Satyricon* of 1969) and also Antonioni, to differing degrees, problematised film form to the point where they identified the impasse common to both crises: that of progressive traditions of film realism, and that arising from the spread of bourgeois political stagnation. This insight represents the achievement of *Blow-Up* in terms of its pointing to the necessity of a new ideological discourse, born of but rejecting the Late Modernist film. In Hegelian terms, this impasse represents the incompleteness of the process of the 'negation of the negation'. The first negation has occurred, yielding an anti-bourgeois film form (of the impasse), but a failure to move beyond the realm of the oppositional and into a new form of discourse – a non-bourgeois film form – has yet to occur.

Arguably, in the medium of film, as Pasolini indicates above (Stack 1969: 157–158), this moving beyond the realm of the oppositional and into a new form of discourse could not occur. Pasolini remained at this juncture of incompletion across the period when attempts at evolving a new discourse occurred; the controversy to follow sprang from Pasolini's continuing criticism of those attempts to formulate a new discourse (as will be examined in the subsequent sections of this study). It is notable that these attempts occurred after Antonioni's 1966 impasse: the utopian, revolutionary and countercultural period of 1966–1968. These attempts may now be seen as a final push within post-Bazinian realism so as to deliver a film not curtailed, in its radicalism, by its insufficiently radical film form. First, however, it is necessary to examine the parallel developments in the New Waves, which also grappled with the limitations of film form prior to 1966.

The Evolution of a Critical Post-Bazinian Realism

The adherence to post-Bazinian realism shared by the Late Modernist film and the New Waves makes it possible to now read the evolution of the New Waves in relation to the end point of the Late Modernist film. The 1966 impasse identified in the Late Modernist film suggests the legitimacy of the hope that a non-bourgeois film form – a form that is not grounded in a state of oppositionism, but that articulates a revolutionary perspective beyond such a grounding – can be achieved. The pursuit of this goal requires the non-sublimation of alienation (alienation in the sense that Eco finds in Joyce (Eco 1989: 148), as outlined above); to reject, as a point of praxis, the Late Modernist film adherence to a mostly unquestioned realism. Or, put simply, to adopt a position that rejects the limitations Antonioni worked within is to attempt to enter into a territory of a vastly expanded critique.[9] The New Waves of the most non-sublimated kind attempted to storm into that territory. In the first instance, as seen, the New Wave films problematised their form in a more direct manner than even *Blow-Up*. Rather than imply the limitations of film as critiquing contemporary society by alluding to, or even dramatising or illustrating, these problems à la Antonioni, the New Waves demonstrated the limitations via a flux of reflexive gestures. Such logic is similar to the way in which an un-bandaged and distressed patient represents a 'truer' indication of the seriousness of the injuries than an anesthetised and bandaged patient failing to respond to external stimuli as expected. The logical next step for the New

Waves was then to offer an enhanced realism. Such a realism was one in which meaning is no longer dependent on (and so neutralised by) mutual make-believe, but arises from a critical awareness of, and subversion of, the mechanisms of the generation of meaning – now identified as ideological, ethical and representational agents in visual discourse. From their inception, therefore, the New Waves were equipped to deal with the problems raised at the end of Antonioni's Late Modernist film trajectory.

So two praxes are apparent: firstly, working within compromised film form, as with the anti-bourgeois film of Antonioni et al; secondly, the outright rejection of compromised film form, as with the non-bourgeois film (or the aspirant non-bourgeois film) of the non-sublimated New Waves. The anti-bourgeois film rejects the norms, and remains stuck in a process of defining its radicalism in relation to that which it is not; the non-bourgeois film exists in a state of the 'zero point' from which to begin afresh, all norms having already been rejected. The difference between the adherents to either praxis was effectively political, and centred on the question of attaining radicalism: was the radical film one that, realising its fatal limitations, removed itself from the fray, or was the radical film one that, overcoming its limitations, entered the fray? To aspire to a non-bourgeois film form over an anti-bourgeois film form was to set out on a road that would ultimately arrive at a (indeed, *the*) key question of the late 1960s, at the height of this fray: which class possesses actual revolutionary potential as the pre-revolutionary situation seemingly dawns? Thus these tendencies exist on either side of the divide between the self-styled revolutionary and the petit bourgeois radical.[10] The corollary of the more radical responses to the question of film form was that the compromised film form of the anti-bourgeois film, or even a degree of it, was insufficiently consciousness-raising in the face of a possibly revolutionary situation.

This is not to say that such a key question was definitively answered in the more radical films of the New Waves, but a glimpse at differing anecdotal answers within the framework of the aspirant non-bourgeois film, at the end of this road, indicates the centrality of this seemingly abstract or academic question. Such a glimpse is afforded in reports on events at the London National Film Theatre (NFT) in 1968. Godard introduced a screening of his film *One Plus One* by taking a vote on the viability of the screening. Since 'going to the cinema, Godard said, was a political act' (Jussawalla and Bellville 1968: 791), Godard's motion was that the ticket money would be better used by the Eldridge Cleaver Defence Fund (the preceding short, by Varda, concerned Cleaver). Godard would refund the NFT for the hire of their screen for the night and, together with 'Open Films' (who were running an anti-film festival to rival the London Film Festival (LFF), the context for the original screening) had provided a makeshift projection facility outside the NFT, on the South Bank, for a free public screening. (In the event, Richard Roud, the LFF director, refused the refund and the NFT audience indicated its general displeasure with the idea of trooping out of the cinema, and more so when Godard punched his producer, who had prepared a commercial edit of the film, retitled *Sympathy for the Devil*; the police guarded the cinema exits throughout.) Yet Bertolucci, introducing *Partner* the previous night, had told the NFT audience that they represented 'precisely the cultural elite for whom his films were made' (Jussawalla and Bellville 1968: 792); (other accounts of this fracas can be found in Hogenkamp (2000: 142) and Finler (1968: 24)). Both *Partner* and *One Plus One* could be said to be aspirant non-bourgeois film-making. Clearly the conceptual difference between the two, for their directors, was in terms of their complete, or mostly complete, lack of anti-bourgeois elements. The *Sympathy for the Devil* cut of *One Plus One*, with its audience-pleasing inclusion of the finished track by the Rolling Stones (much of the film consists of their rehearsing of the track), was rendered anti-bourgeois to an unacceptable degree for Godard: the seriousness of the critique mounted by the film is undermined by the concession that the film finally gives (the pleasure of the completed song in performance). The importance attached to these seemingly minor gradients of oppositionism are not only auteur prejudices, but speak of the wider political factionism and infighting among cliques typical of the left at this point – decades of debate concerning compromise and hegemony (the Stalin and post-Stalin parameters of the debate), now newly invigorated by debate about the progressive or counter-revolutionary roles of the orthodox Left, and radical elements of the bourgeoisie, during 1968. Film as a social practice of and for the *enragés* in general reverberates in such precise approaches to film.

The difference between these two praxes can also be couched in less contentious, dialectical terms. Here, the Brechtian aspect of the New Wave film form indicates a tactical political position in relation to the proletariat. This is not one of binary oppositionism but, in Walsh's terms, the former of 'two responses – what one might term the "avant-garde" and "conservative" variants of leftist criticism' (Walsh 1981: 19). So familiar is such a tension in leftist debates on the revolutionary capacities of culture that Walsh felt sufficiently emboldened to sketch a framework for this tension across film history: 'This split may be codified by these oppositions: Meyerhold v. Stanislavsky; Eisenstein v. Pudovkin; Brecht v. Lukács; Godard v. Truffaut; Makavejev v. Widerberg' (Walsh 1981: 18).[11] Such tactical differences offer the possibility of many fronts – even co-opting general dissent (as in, say, the 'revolutionary' westerns of the late 1960s) into an inclusive fight against the bourgeois state.

The differing degrees of radicalism that evolve across the two variants that Walsh identifies start from the same point – as seen in both the Late Modernist film and the New Waves (and, in a wider respect, as a common problematic for Western progressive and radical art). Their implicitly dissenting and combative attitudes towards film as it had been known speak of a will to break free of an 'original sin'. That is, the way in which prior films had been totemic of the wider malaise in society, through their ignorance of their, as Adorno would put it, 'tainted origins in social inequality' (quoted in Jay 1984: 113), was no longer tenable. The 1966 impasse could be said to be the manifestation, or fallout, of an ultimate failure of the reformism and modernism of the Late Modernist film, since such innovations, which sought to renew film as a sophisticated medium of expression along intellectualised lines, were finally unable to overcome or rout such 'tainted origins', and so turned to self-condemnation. The resultant extreme anti-bourgeois tendencies of *Blow-Up* and *Fellini-Satyricon* do not formally suggest the hope for a new type of film-making; the wreckage of bourgeois film form in such films signals few possibilities beyond itself. Indeed, the narcissism of the hyper-individualism of these films, in which the odyssey of the protagonists is exclusively hedonistic, conforms to the classic criticism of the decadence of navel-gazing as typifying bourgeois artistic expressions. Marco Ferreri's *Dillinger è Morto* (1969) could also be put into this category: intimacy with a privileged protagonist and his surroundings as he seems to take leave of his senses, suffers in a way that suggests a deeper connection to the ills of his time, and an obscure ending that resolutely refuses to offer a narrative resolution or coherent end point.

However, the non-bourgeois film form does indeed indicate the birth of a new type of film-making. The dissenting and combative attitude towards film as it had been known makes for an outright rejection of, rather than a reform of, previous film-making – thus achieving a carte blanche for the contemporary film-maker on the cusp of the 1960s. The New Wave was the art of the possible (to remake film altogether) rather than the illustration of the impossible (the anti-bourgeois film from and within the bourgeois context). It suggests a coming negation of the negation – a completion of the process brought to a standstill with Antonioni's 1966 impasse. And such a praxis – construction from destruction – informed 1960s culture in general; Gilbert Lascault saw that in radical fine art, installations and sculpture of the 1960s '[t]he primary task of the artist is to destroy, to suppress; the rest is, at the most, addenda. In any event, "[quoting Rosa Luxemburg] what is negative – destruction – can be decreed; what is positive – construction – cannot"' (Lascault 1970: 63). The unbreakable foundation – in this case, that which survived the decreed destruction and remained into the revolutionary period – was the Bazinian element of post-Bazinian realism.

Early negations, comparable to the innovations of the Late Modernist film, can be seen in the first years of the Nouvelle Vague, and the rejection of, or processes of ongoing rejections of and modifications to, the language of the bourgeois film. However, a battle speed is achieved at the moment at which such rejections move from a knee-jerk MacMahonist equivalency to a system of considered critique – that the rejection itself is perceived as twofold: both the particulars of bourgeois film-making (attractive leading men, happy endings and so on) and, in and through this, the ideological system from which these particulars arise (in this case, unthinking aestheticism and a passive optimism). At this point, the movement beyond (i.e., the negation of) the early negations – and into the 'zero point' from which a truly radical perspective can be mounted – beckons.

Film form now becomes indexical; radical film form as the vector through which film must pass to achieve a revolutionary potential. This movement generates an actual realisation of the 'impossibility' of the anti-bourgeois bourgeois film as fatally hobbled by its own language. *Blow-Up*, totality-adhering Nouvelle Vague auteurs (such as, on occasion, Truffaut and Chabrol) and the British New Wave's Neue Sachlichkeit-equivalent tendencies all vanish down this hole. Whereas Pasolini, of the 'suspended' *Teorema* (Stack 1969: 158), evidently felt that such a liberation of form from the bourgeoisie could not be achieved in the medium of film during this period, the New Wave films that aspired to non-bourgeois form begged to differ.

The prerequisite condition was the liberation of film form from totality – the willing suspension of disbelief as the principal mode of bourgeois containment of art. In this respect, in terms of the beginnings of an aspirant non-bourgeois film form, totality had been the first 'structure' deserving of sabotage, as noted above – alienation, unsublimated, was cast as that element that prevents totality, that fractures any evolving 'world view' in the films with a flux of reflexive gestures. In much of the work of Godard of this period (and Robbe-Grillet, Makavejev and Chytilová), to demonstrate becomes to sabotage structurally: a revealing of the image manipulation of the construction of film itself achieves both aspects simultaneously. This is why reflexivity is characteristic of the New Wave film, and anything that would be understood to cause the viewer to reflect on the nature of the medium itself while experiencing the medium is therefore allied to this form of radicalism. And this is why the intertextuality is not just a minor and distinctive facet of the New Wave or, as many critics perceived it to be, a strain of ironic and inclusive cinéphilic jokiness. Rather, it is the very method by which the mise en scène mediates its own ontological worth through a more advanced sense of the limitations of realism (of the neo-realist model). A 'holding together' (rather than a synthesis) of these two seemingly opposing methodologies of the ontological-real and the intertextual creates the framework for Godard's evolving 'critical realism'. Is this not the very opposite of the notion of experientialism and the experiential aesthetic of psychological realism, as given over to hyper-individualism – the process whereby the viewer is 'sucked into' the ontological realism of the film, initiating the willing suspension of disbelief? The only such 'experience' offered by the New Wave films was an intellectual rather than an emotional one, of no protagonist POV, a waking rather than passive sense of the mise en scène. The evolution of the New Waves in these respects, particularly in relation to Godard's films, occurs as the balance tips from straight sabotage of passive senses of the mise en scène (circa 1959–1963) to an attempt to reconfigure film form to be capable of generating meanings uncontained by a bourgeois-totality norm (circa 1963 onwards). This, in turn, is further swept along by a need to generate a meaning of revolutionary import in a revolutionary film form (1966–1968). In this respect the ambitions of the New Wave, as an art of the possible, were stretched some considerable distance – to breaking point and, as Godard himself did not hesitate to note, beyond. Eco, in retrospect, denigrated the limited radicalism of the Gruppo 63's project (of which he was a part) at base – 'this literary club's self-masturbatory hermaphrodite machinery' (Eco 1989: 239). And Godard's project becomes unstuck along such lines; film form as indexical results in a tunnel vision. However, this turbulent process fails to dislodge the Bazinian ontology that remains in post-Bazinian realism – if anything, once all partial radicalisations have been cast aside as insufficient, the Bazinian element, now rarefied, returns for one last stand. This consistency means that the evolution of Godard's critical realism can be reviewed in relation to directions within post-Bazinian realism, aped by, but never supplanted by, the radicalisation of film form.

The balance can be seen to tip at the point of the exhaustion of the first phase of the Nouvelle Vague; aesthetic innovation cannot last beyond the point at which it, itself, becomes the norm – sabotage of passive senses of the mise en scène could be taken as read, no longer as a provocative intervention. Returning to the earlier phase of Walsh's application of the dialectical model of leftist criticism – in its 'Brecht v. Lukács' variant – is instructive in this respect. Lukács's attack on Brecht and the avant-garde anticipates Godard's tendency to sideline content in the name of innovations in form. Here Lukács could have been describing Godard's films up until 1963, and his sentiments are distantly echoed in Wajda's dismissal of the New Wave (Cowie 2004: 107):

> One inescapable consequence of an attitude alien or hostile to reality makes itself increasingly evident in the art of the "avant-garde": a growing paucity of content, extended to a point where absence of content or hostility towards it is upheld on principle. (Adorno and Benjamin et al., 1992: 41)

And Benayoun gladly rendered this service in his 1962 *Positif* attack on the New Wave, riding the wave of a critical backlash against the Nouvelle Vague that had been evident from 1960 onwards (see de Baecque 1997: 156):

> If the cinema looks in upon itself too much, it will be in danger of ending up as a kind of subculture, consisting of approximations, pale reflections, quotations and hazy reminiscences, it will be as though it were shut up in a furnished flat whose walls were covered with photographs of furniture, whose books were only about furnishing. (Benayoun 1968: 157)

In the light of, as Benayoun goes on to point out, '[w]hat is happening every day in Poland and Italy, what is still happening in the prodigious melting-pots of America [the fact of which] pours ridicule on the dilatory experiments of our playboys' (Benayoun 1968: 178), he ultimately diagnoses an excessive intertextuality in the Nouvelle Vague, and with this 'growing paucity of content', the loss of an ideological commitment to reality. In 'Nouvelle Vague or Jeune Cinema', Jacob examined the poor reception that Truffaut's 1964 film *La Peau Douce* had received. As with Tony Richardson, the film had utilised the freedoms of Nouvelle Vague film-making to inject vigour into an Antonioniesque story of existential despair and a fatal extramarital affair. Rather than locate its intertextuality in a dialectical context, the film's final sequence – a gunning down in a restaurant – simply was intertextual, as if a Hitchcock film; that is, it was bereft of critical realism. The way in which the psychological portraits of the film were overwhelmed by such genre-derived spectacle rendered the film sub-Melville (whose MacMahonism had always worked in an opposite direction; the genre-derived spectacle is taken as read, and gives way, in the course of the film, to psychological portraits of his compelling existential heroes). In this respect, the film exemplified the critical perception of the Nouvelle Vague in general: was the Wave, after all, not so 'new' but just more of the 'old', now repackaged? For Jacob, a Nouvelle Vague status was no longer sufficient to justify the existence of a film in itself: 'Something, it became apparent in the reception which awaited *Le Peau Douce* at the last Cannes Festival, is happening in the French cinema . . . the films will now have to make their own way: they will have to be judged on their merits' (Jacob 1964/65: 4). Alain Jessua's reaction suggests not that a 'first wave' is over, but that it has splintered, so that he is able to disassociate *Le Peau Douce* from the Nouvelle Vague altogether: 'I can see no common ground between [Godard's] *La Femme Mariée* and *La Peau Douce*, none whatsoever' (quoted in Jacob 1964/65: 6).

So what, then, of the progressive, Brechtian aspect of New Wave film form? This would seem to have been a false dawn – a praxis that soon became an end in itself. Such a dead end was apparent as early as 1960 with Malle's Nouvelle Vague pastiche, *Zazie dans le Métro*, and in Malle's work in general during (and even just before, with *Ascenseur pour l'Echafaud* in 1957) this period, which was almost entirely orientated to bourgeois concerns, a paradoxical 'fascinated contempt for the hypocrisies of the middle class' (French 1993: xiii). *Zazie dans le Métro* contained everything that is termed a radical problematisation of form, but in relation to a cartoon-like world, relying on caricatures and stereotypes and actors made-up to clownish degrees. So despite the radical pedigree of his aesthetic, there is no provocation, merely an unapologetic 'attitude alien or hostile to reality', as Lukács put it (Adorno and Benjamin et al., 1992: 41). Such mannerism is only possible, as *Zazie* demonstrated, if these devices possessed no ideological import in themselves. And *Vie Privée* (*A Very Private Affair*, Malle, 1961), as a more serious conservative outgrowth of the New Wave, could be said to be even more problematic in its glamorous preoccupations (film stars, intercontinental love affairs etc.) – was this the remade cinema of the Nouvelle Vague? (The review in *Cahiers* – which at this point was effectively the journal of the Nouvelle Vague – was entitled 'A Film of Rare Insignificance' (quoted in Douchet 1999: 217).) Jacques Baratier's *Dragées au Poivre*, which uses a number of iconographic New Wave actors, is explicit in its attack on the New Wave (and, to a lesser extent, Antonioni's films): the protagonists, naive and idiotic, all seem involved in New Wave film-making and subscribe to a cult of cinéma-vérité seemingly rather than addressing the real world, while the film itself is crudely sexual.

Likewise *Un Homme et une Femme* (Lelouch, 1966), *A Degree of Murder* (Volker Schlöndorff, 1967) and *Les Choses de la Vie* (Claude Sautet, 1969) are simply commercial romantic/thriller films that sport modish New Wave aesthetics – by the mid 1960s something of another minor subgenre at the point of the degeneration of the formally radical, and a tendency that had been seen to develop fully in the British New Wave, as noted. But even more retrogressive developments are visible close to this nominally radical framework. *The Angry Silence* (Guy Green, 1960), despite reflexivity (straight-to-camera interviews), psychological realism (as the young worker suffers a mental breakdown) and a portrait of the working class and its environs, is very much a film of the right; the plot revolves around expounding a slanderously anti-union message. *Whistle Down the Wind* (Bryan Forbes, 1961) uses its northern, working class setting entirely thematically, erring towards 'simple country folk' stereotypes, and so effectively renders this then rarely seen milieu apolitical. Radical content, let alone radical form, was not delivering radicalism.

In the light of the conservative impulses identified above, it is apparent that the Jessua-identified splintering can be said to have occurred between the tendency that sublimated Brechtian techniques into a totality – 'Late Modernising'-ising it, as with Truffaut in *La Peau Douce* or, Wood argues, Bergman[12] – and the tendency that continued to work within a framework of critical realism. Or, to revisit Wollen's descriptive terms for the New Wave (Wollen 1982: 79), the former rediscovered 'Single diegesis' through a renewed 'Closure' while the latter continued with 'Multiple diegesis' and remained in a state of 'Aperture'. The latter tendency operated with a new sophistication. While Godard's films of the first phase had identified and articulated only the possibility of structural critique through gestures of reflexivity, they now worked towards evolving an actual critique through a critical realist interface with the structures of the 'other' cinema (that is, of the modes of commercial film-making: science fiction, the musical, the gangster film, the romance). This would necessitate a radical problematisation of content, to fully move beyond the simple strategies of an adherence to the ontological-real. And to move from gestures of reflexivity to the actual critique necessitated another presence 'in' the film: the readers of the structures of the 'other' cinema. For this reason, the notion of inviting the audience 'in' became all-important; it was in, and through, their perception that the investigation occurs – a conceptual strategy. Or, more specifically, and as the events of the 1968 London Film Festival illustrated, to invite a specific audience in – the audience that was perceived to represent a potential political front, those most receptive to, and who stood to gain the most from, such investigations.[13] So to have retained a belief in the use of a primarily structuralist critique at this 'critical' time of a pre-revolutionary situation demonstrates Godard's continued faith in the revolutionary potential of this project.

Such a belief is apparent in Godard's section of *Loin du Viêt-nam* (Godard, Varda, Joris Ivens, William Klein, Claude Lelouch, Marker, Resnais, 1967) and *Caméra-Oeil*, in which Godard himself speaks straight to camera, explaining that his presence is the result of frustration at the hands of the North Vietnamese, who will not allow him to film in their country (nor does he blame them). And, at any rate, as a French national, how could he hope to be able to present 'truth' in the kind of film he envisioned?[14] In this way, the 'structure' of this film (point blank monologue, the absence of narrative and drama) is linked directly to the inability to attain any sense of an objective analysis of the political situation. The viewer is to consider *Caméra-Oeil* both a radical piece of film-making in response to the situation in Vietnam and a structuralist reading of the auteur's position in the face of the crisis. Thus Walsh had described Godard's method as one demanding 'creative participation by the audience: they ceased to be spectators "consuming" art ... and became an integral and necessary part of the production of the work' (Walsh 1981: 18). Ultimately, the use of Verfremdungseffekt is that it creates the sense of critical awareness in relation to the mise en scène that could allow for this participation to occur: alienation cannot be only for alienation's sake. Here the Verfremdungseffekt frustrates the desire for a documentary engagement with the Vietnam situation, in all its facets, on the grounds that Godard cannot, organically, achieve the ideological perspective necessary for such an engagement shorn of retrogressive ideological prejudice and misunderstandings – which is the case, the viewer now ideally understands, with bourgeois documentary engagements, its news and reportage, on this subject.

Figure 3.2   Despite Che's instruction, Godard makes zero Vietnams: confronting the audience with the impossibility of the subject at hand. Clapperboard and *Caméra-oeil* in *Loin du Viêt-nam* (1967)

This full-blown structuralist critique evolves from the intertextual gestures of the earlier Nouvelle Vague films. In this respect, the dialogue it continues is with the image manipulation element – the falseness of film language in relation to its 'better half', the Bazin-identified ontological truth of its mise en scène. However, this latter concern was also reconsidered in relation to an integration of the viewer. The fictional framework now supported a 'raw', Rouch-like investigation – the chunks of undigested 'reality' from which the viewers could draw their own opinions. *Masculin-Féminin* (1966), for example, reflects disparate aspects of life in Paris during the 1966 elections, mostly through lengthy interviews. The actual dates of scenes are given in voice-over, didactically highlighting this specificity. The film's documentary aesthetic matches the sense of an 'actual' investigation into political attitudes, which are invariably radical, as Godard diagnoses oppression at all levels of society (through the threat of conscription; workers complaining about the abolition of their breaks; the imprisonment of Brazilian artists mentioned by an activist) and shows a militant response to such radicalism on either side (in one scene, an American ambassador's car is defaced while the protagonist distracts the driver with approving talk about North American action in Vietnam; the film winds up with a further series of interviews – now conducted in a police station). When these directly political concerns are offset by forays into non-political spheres of life (the protagonist chasing women, a pop singer called Madeleine, and the commonplace settings – cafes, roads, a laundromat), the two areas of concern suggest the potential for an overlap, and in this the import of the political into the realm of the personal, and vice versa. So, during one interview Paul (Jean-Pierre Léaud) pushes a girl to talk about artificial contraception and elicits a telling response: she can talk about women's liberation but is too bashful to talk about contraception. Whereas the 'political' front is grasped in terms of the personal, the 'biopolitical' – as Hardt and Negri later term it – has not been.

The multifaceted manifestations of oppression, which link the personal and the political realms, are only partially visible in such a local and particular investigation. Interviews with individuals naturally fail to attain the whole picture, and in the reassessment of such an investigative praxis comes a major shift in Godard's work. As Loshitzky notes, in relation to *Deux ou Trois Choses que Je Sais d'Elle*, 1966 marks Godard's first full 'move to radicalism' (Loshitzky 1995: 144), to 'a series of explicitly political films' (MacCabe, Eaton and Mulvey 1980: 20) (Reader places Godard's '*engagé* period' in 1965, with *Pierrot le Fou* (Reader 2004: 83)). For MacCabe, while *Deux ou Trois Choses* is 'to a large extent [still] the world of the early Godard romance [*Vivre sa Vie*] . . . it's breaking up under the impact of Godard's absorption of Brecht' (MacCabe 1975/76: 58). Here the radicalism arises from a wider application of the conclusions of the local investigation, so becoming 'explicitly political', and renews its Brechtian component in this endeavour in order to implement this wider application. Brechtian method thus carries forward the evidence gathered on the ground; the systems that oppress, as voiced by the Parisian women, can then be tracked into, and considered in the context of, the wider world. And this wider world is one of the policing of meanings, the isolation of experiences, the segmentation of the continuum of life – in short, the stratifications that Brechtian method cuts through. This results in a number of strains of radicalism, which are more often than not intertwined in Godard's films of this period.

Makavejev's New Wave films also presented different 'strands' – in *Ljubavni Slucaj ili Tragedija Sluzbenice PTT* (*Tragedy of the Switchboard Operator*, 1967), for example – but Makavejev retains an intimacy between them (the lecture from the sexologist and the love story of the film; the erotic nudity of the latter and the nudity of the female protagonist during the autopsy, for example) that operates despite the lack of totality binding them together. Makavejev invites the viewer to find the connections between such strands, to create a convergence and discover the lesson. Godard, on the other hand, challenges the viewer, in the light of the seeming lack of connection, to find an ideological critique that unites them. For Makavejev, an associative and emotive relationship between strands is created, while for Godard the relationship remains juxtapositional and dialectical.

As apparent in *Caméra-Oeil*, the application of this expansive method implicates the act of filming. The anti-illusionism of *A Bout de Souffle*-type intertextuality has evolved into a form of ontological anti-illusionism: a consideration not
of other films, but of the *actualité* of the process of filming. Godard places the
very processes of film-making in-frame. This is evident in *Masculin-Féminin*, in a
metaphorical way; Paul is both a character in the story and interviewer of other
characters – a stand-in for the director as documentary-maker. In *Pierrot le Fou*,
however, Godard separates the different discourses that make up the mise en
scène – making for, as Benayoun aptly termed it, 'rough-draft cinema' (Benayoun
1968: 163): a state of (seeming) incompletion, or a work in process, or unfinished
or abandoned. With such a 'failure' to synthesise fiction and fact within the frame,
Godard remains within a state of ever-present aperture – now an actual, rather
than gestural, reflexivity.

The manifestations of such aperture are apparent throughout *Pierrot le Fou*.
An on-screen journal appears periodically, commenting abstractly on the film,
filmed in close-up, often partially obscured by framing or shown too briefly to
be fully read (a very provocative lack of visual order). The distinctive amateur
performances of neo-realism and the flux of 'real people' extras from *A Bout de
Souffle* are no longer background detail, but are placed at the forefront: characters introduce themselves, straight to camera, as currently employed working
as extras on this film. Elsewhere in *Deux ou Trois Choses* the protagonist is first
introduced by her actual name, by Godard in voice-over (VO), and both she and
Godard speak straight to the audience on many occasions. At this point, with
Godard inaccurately describing actress Marina Vlady (Juliette) when she is first
seen, the need for the critical intervention of the viewer into the 'text' of the film
is invoked – the invitation could not be more blatant.

The soundtrack for *Pierrot le Fou* bears every trace of having been mixed in a
couple of hours in post-production; the music lags behind its cues, or seems to
take no cue at all from the events on screen. Such dislocation of diegetic sound
had been previously utilised by Godard to identify the fiction and non-fiction
aspects of his imagery, as in Godard's 'Montparnasse-Levallois' section of *Paris
vu Par . . .* Here stretches of shots of the protagonist walking are accompanied,
seemingly at random, by extracts from a full orchestral score, transforming the
scene into one rich with the promise of the potential of the unfolding narrative
(who is the girl? why is she entering a cafe? why does she post two letters? and
so forth). In response to the gravitas lent by such music, the viewer looks for

elements or actions that suggest the potential for the 'meaningful'. Yet Godard interrupts such a process by abruptly dropping the orchestral score at seemingly indiscriminate moments. This renders the same images as 'standard' cinéma-vérité, in which the meaningful renders itself in quite different ways (the protagonist's appearance, manner, the street in which the protagonist walks, and so forth). Such techniques prompted Pasolini to comment 'Godard . . . destroys the "grammar" of film before we know what it is' (Pasolini 2005: 194), and Sontag, of this sound technique in *Vivre sa Vie*, 'Godard restores the dissociation of word and image characteristic of silent film, but on a new level' (Sontag 1967: 200). The dislocated use of sound in *Pierrot le Fou* moves beyond such a dichotomy of fiction and non-fiction; it casts the entire mise en scène as an unsettled – i.e., totality-resistant – amalgamation of the two.

Thus Godard's point of reference becomes his own film-making, not that of others, moving forward from this initial MacMahonist impulse; he now displays the techniques for the generation of narrative meaning in his own films. As with the 'revealing' of a screening room in *Chronique d'un Été*, the film becomes diegetically aware of itself, by situating itself in relation to that which is filmed:[15] a critical realism of auto-critique and anti-illusionism. A reverberation of this is the way in which the films continually articulate their own methodologies – another Godardian trait (Vlady, for example, in her aforementioned introduction, even quotes 'old father' Brecht on declamatory acting).

These directions initiate the framework in which the formerly 'straight' approach, as orientated to the ontological-real, is now reconsidered – indeed, becomes a focus of consideration in the films themselves. It is at this point that a limited negotiation with a post-Bazinian realism can be claimed for Godard's work of this phase. So, in *Deux ou Trois Choses*, Godard talks of readdressing, in VO, 'what actuality is: it is both what one calls actuality in the cinematographic and journalistic sense'. Indeed, the film is founded on such a notion of investigative journalism (it is based on an article in *Le Nouvel Observateur* that Godard had chanced upon, concerning housewives prostituting themselves in the council flats on the outskirts of Paris) and, at times, aspires to the didactic status of documentary. But the 'cinematographic' side of the investigation shifts these standard concerns – which typified the investigation of *Masculin-Féminin* – away from an ontological-real approach. The 'documentary' tenets of veracity and objectivity are now abandoned in favour of an interrogation of the images found, as they are found, using Godard's voice-over commentary for this purpose – that is, the exposure of the process of filming, a questioning of the images generated; a critical realism born of an auto-critique:

> This is how Juliette, at 15.37, saw the pages of that object that, in journalistic language, one calls a magazine being turned over. And here, some 150 images further on, is how another young woman, similar to her, saw the same object. Where then is the truth? Full face or in profile? And first of all, what is an object?

The voice-over is subservient to the images, a reversal of the documentary standard; it cannot impose meaning on the images, but seeks to find meanings.

Such questioning – or, rather, refusal to settle on any one 'answer' – is even apparent in a prototypical way in the most 'throwaway' of sequences, in *Le Mépris* (1963).[16] After the opening credits, Godard frames Camille (Bardot), lying naked on a rumpled bed, in a highly aestheticised way, to the extent that '[h]er reclining body even seems made to order for the scope format' (Silverman and Farocki 1998: 33). Godard is able to offset the exploitational nature of such an image – albeit via sublimation into narrative structure – by having Camille interrogate her own (that is, Bardot's) image. Camille questions her off-screen husband about her attributes; does the husband prefer her ankles, her behind, her breasts, and so on. In this way, the question of the voyeurism implicit in Godard's film language 'vernacular' (commercial/exploitational) framing of Bardot is sublimated back into the diegesis of the film; the narrative self-consciously 'names' the very crisis it seeks to quell. And just as this dialogue draws attention to the spectrum of differing perceptions of Bardot (can we begin to quantify or qualify a notion of carnal beauty as she, a supposed visual manifestation of these things, invites the unseen husband to do?), Godard intervenes in the aesthetic, switching between colour filters to render the static image red, blue, 'natural' and yellow. This achieves the visual equivalent of the dialogue: different views of the same object, which are all attempts to capture something of the changing perception of the characters and actors in his films, and the inability to settle on a 'correct' mise en scène – that is, the inability to fix a straight meaning to the shot, determining how the object 'should' be shot or 'should' look. Such digressions can be described as cubist – the desire to present all angles simultaneously, and in so doing refrain from privileging any one angle. It suggests that there is no 'correct' way of shooting the scene, no objective vantage point from which the camera can be positioned, and so the only honest possibility left is to articulate this conundrum. Silverman and Farocki's reaction to this scene suggests just such a flux of readings: 'In a way, the film never says "Camille", no matter how the camera lingers on the image of her body. It says: "Eve", "Penelope", "Bardot"' (Silverman and Farocki 1998: 55).

Yet this auto-critique, refined in the narrative of *Deux ou Trois Choses*, rapidly 'degenerates' – it becomes confessional and rhetorical – that is, particular to the 'auteur's cinema' of the mid 1960s. Godard speaks of his own doubts and feelings of isolation, and continually questions the veracity of the images he is presenting (while Vlady continually describes her surroundings and the impressions of her character). It is as if Godard wilfully wrecks this new methodology – a final moment of auto-critique; anything settled must be dispensed with (in keeping with Pasolini's comment on Godard's film grammar; that the antithesis arrives ahead of the thesis). Such self-doubt, as manifest diegetically (and which will be examined below) pushes the film ever onwards, blindly adhering to the Nouvelle Vague's art of the possible, despite such ominous rumblings. Godard abandons one framework after another until he is – literally, with his camera – peering into the inconsequential objects in front of him (coffee cups, the detritus of cafes and clothes shops) in the search for meaning.

And it is on such a level of abstraction – a preoccupation with a tracing of the relationships between objects and the world in which the protagonist moves – that Godard is able to discern the lineaments of the 'wider picture'.[17] Thus prostitution is not an exceptional aspect to the lives of the Parisian housewives (as *Le Nouvel Observateur* undoubtedly had it) – rather, it is the aspect. And it is not only an aspect of Western society, but the very condition of living in the West. In this way, the theme of prostitution is both particular and universal – and the mounting of such a claim represents an evolution of critical realism; it is seen to yield (not just present) this claim. Whereas *Masculin-Féminin* could posit itself as being 'about' (or attempts, in a number of ways, to be 'about'), as well as set against the background of, a particular event (the 1966 elections in France), *Deux ou Trois Choses* is able to present a more sustained approach to the contemporary, and one that suggests a justification for finding the universal in the particular, and vice versa. And as Godard moves 'beyond' the specifics of the sociopolitical and into the area of more abstract themes, this represents both a match and a rebuff of the intellectualised, non-specific universal themes that characterised Late Modernist film. It can also be seen to be the full flowering of Godard's renewal of the Brechtian component of his film-making.

This allows for a capitalising on the actual critique, as rendered. Sontag notes a prior use of universal themes in Godard: 'The twelve episodes of *Vivre sa Vie* are Nana's [Anna Karina] twelve stations of the cross. But in Godard's film the values of sanctity and martyrdom are transposed to a totally secular plane' (Sontag 1967: 206). Now, such notions of sanctity and martyrdom are first to be found in the secular plane (the lot of the prostitute) and transposed to sociopolitical specif- ics (the 'prostitution' of life in an era of late capitalism). Hence the theme of prostitution, first encountered in *Vivre sa Vie*, is re-approached from the opposite direction in *Deux ou Trois Choses*. Whereas prostitution had been a concept for dramatisation in *Vivre sa Vie*, and in a 'straight' Brechtian manner (to 'make con- crete' an abstract idea through the story of the ill-fated protagonist), with *Deux ou Trois Choses*, the concept is a given – a fact of Parisian life – and is now made abstract so as to make for a wider investigation. Even the '*Elle*' of the title (. . . *que Je Sais d'Elle*), as Godard's voice-over explains, refers to both the protagonist – the modern housewife-prostitute – and the setting of the film, the Paris-as-building- site familiar from 'Gare du Nord' (Rouch's section of *Paris vu Par . . .*) of the previ- ous year. Such a strategy could be said to be broadly Althusserian: considerations of the personal and the political meld – ideology becomes ever-present and ever- pressing, all-applicable, even in the most mundane of circumstances.[18] Were this a film of sublimated alienation, the net result would be a form of 'identity politics' whereby, even though the protagonist comes to work as the lens through which wider superstructural concerns are evident, the film predominantly concerns itself with human interaction. But with alienation channelled into a radical prob- lematisation of form and content, the net result seeks to plot the actual intersec- tions of the personal and the political – to articulate the 'real criticism' rather than a flux of gestures and representations. So, at the end of the film, in a literal realisa- tion of Marx's phrase 'commodity fetishism', products themselves are lined up as if they were the protagonists of the film; the human element removed entirely.

If the particulars of the actual investigation are shaky, as noted above, the results of this exploration of a preconceived thesis are progressive. The actual manifestation of the intersection between the personal and the political occurs in relation to the idea of, appropriately enough, the connectedness of images. While prostituting herself, Juliette-Vlady will not allow her client to view her undress- ing – that is, he may not see the actual transition between the states of 'dressed' and 'undressed'. To expose this transition would be to allow for a connection to be made between the images of herself as housewife and herself as prostitute.

To make such a connection would be to cease to deny the way in which modern Western society ensures the sexual servitude of its subjects. To cease to deny this is to attain a revolutionary understanding of the oppression of the proletariat. And so therefore that same society works to create a schizophrenic sensibility that, in the figure of Juliette and her mores, will prevent the connection of the images of housewife and prostitute. Likewise, her client prefers to watch the lovemaking in a reflected mirror image – to deny the reality of the bought lovemaking by considering it at one remove, as an aesthetised, utopian act – that is, to 'return' the image of brisk prostitute to that of loving housewife (significantly in this respect, the mirror is removed from a wall covered in glossy posters of exotic locations – more 'removed' images that seek to 'remove' Juliette from the drab surroundings of her apartment). MacCabe finds such a fragmentation of images-of-self on the part of the protagonist as evident in operation, in embryo, in *La Femme Mariée* (Godard, 1964):

> When we are made privy to her [the protagonist's] inner thoughts they offer no coherent account of her situation but rather a stream of disconnected phrases. This lack of a coherent view enables the film to break down a unified image of a woman's body, held in a man's look, and to provide instead a series of disconnected images which resist attempts at unification. (MacCabe, Eaton and Mulvey 1980: 35)

Or, put another way, at this point of an 'excessive' ontology – the journalistic truth Godard relentlessly pursues, his documentary camera pushing itself into very private areas of existence on this basis – Godard encounters the very opposite of 'the real' that underwrites post-Bazinian realism. Whereas this encounter becomes Antonioni's major theme, it remains a minor consideration in Godard at this point – although both Antonioni and Godard interpret this shaking of post-Bazinian realism in a way understood, above, as postmodern. So, for Godard, the condition of living in French society in the mid to late 1960s is that of moving in an environment of visual pastiche, ironic homage, knowing allusion – a cacophony of competing signifiers (Neupert terms this 'parodic overcoding' (Neupert 2002: 130)). How else could Juliette herself shun the ontological-real via a disassociation of images-of-herself, fragmenting the totality of her own reality?

This was no chronological discovery for Godard, apparent for the first time in 1966. There is a sensibility in *La Femme Mariée*, through *Masculin-Féminin*, to *Deux ou Trois Choses* that suggests that the inverse of the ontological-real is also true. Prior to this conclusion, the MacMahonist gestures and the image-manipulated aesthetic of *Une Femme est une Femme* only gestured towards such a possibility – but the possibility becomes a full-blown, 'legitimate' reading of the world in this later phase of Godard's work. This is apparent in Godard's third 1966 film, *Made in USA* (made after *Masculin-Féminin* and before *Deux ou Trois Choses*). Here the language of the ontological-real is in operation, most notably via its lengthy long takes. Yet the content is utterly bereft of the 'real': garish and glossy colours abound, often 'unreal' primary colours, heavy make-up, flat imagery (often using walls to block depth of field, often walls covered with loud posters), a necessarily fictional 'future' setting (of 1969) and a fictional location ('Atlantic City' – although clearly a Paris suburb). There is a proliferation of objects of fiction or reproduced reality: books, newspapers, the act of typing, films posters, billboard advertisements, advertisement-like painted petrol pumps and even flashes of comic-like still illustrations (an intertitle 'Bing!' is seen as Karina is felled by an underworld heavy, as in the 1960s *Batman* TV series), a game in a bar that reduces words to meaningless sounds, and the same effect is achieved with two characters delivering monologues simultaneously, or a distorted recording of Godard's own voice playing on a reel-to-reel tape recorder. The final 'contradiction' is an intertextual dedication of the film – to Nick Ray and Sam Fuller, *Cahiers*-favoured masters of a cinema of emotion and realism. So when confronted with such widespread image manipulation, MacBean places the film with Demy's 1964 musical *Les Parapluies du Cherbourg* in which all dialogue is sung (MacBean 1975: 30). And very similar, and similarly widespread, image manipulation in *Rote Sonne* (Rudolf Thome, 1969) pushes this film into the realm of science fiction: the high genre of the unreal-as-real.[19] Von Moltke notes Thome's indebtedness to Godard in terms of image manipulation (Von Moltke 2000: 272), but in converting this direction in Godard into the identified praxis of Thome, Von Moltke is able to go one better: Thome copies Godard's copying (Von Moltke 2000: 267) – hence 'the real' as endlessly removed from the mise en scène.

These dialectical frictions between form and content indicate that the inverse of the ontological-real is also possible; an ontological-false, or intertextual-real with which the film language refuses to accept that such excessive intertextuality cannot be considered outside the language of 'the real' – a kind of pathological denial that there is nothing appropriate to an ontological-real sensibility that cannot still be salvaged from such unreal pastiche. This could be accommodated within Bazin's above-mentioned consideration of Méliès and the fantastic/ un-true as 'possible only because of the irresistible realism of the photographic image' (Bazin 1997: 73), (and indeed this could be said to be the case with Peter Watkins's methodology)[20] were it not for the way in which, from Godard's vantage point of excessive ontology, it is the found world that seems 'unreal'. Those structures that Godard criticised via genre pastiche are now – or soon to be, the 1969 of the future, or the city of *Alphaville* – evident in found reality. The world of *Masculin-Féminin* is described by Paul – who graffitis surreal, sexual and political slogans in public places – as the 'age of James Bond and Vietnam' and by Godard, in a final intertitle, as 'This film could be called "The children of Marx and Coca-Cola" – Make of it what you will'. Such 'unrealness' is made subtle with *Deux ou Trois Choses*; it is no longer the 'contradiction' evident in contemporary existence – it is a condition of contemporary existence.[21] Such a reading is only possible when, despite extremes of intertextuality, the post-Bazinian realism remains.

At this point the endeavour of outright intertextuality comes to be seen as one of a very limited scope. Once the content has been problematised in this fashion, and the idea (that, in words from *La Chinoise*, '[a]rt is not the reflection of reality, it is the reality of that reflection') 'proven', there was little more Godard could do or say in relation to this line of investigation. Thus in *Made in USA*, after the first act of violence (highly stylised; bright red paint clearly substituting for blood), Paula (Karina) comments in VO, reminiscent of Paul's graffiti: 'Already fiction triumphs over reality. Already there is blood and mystery. It's like a cross between a Bogart and a Walt Disney film: a political film ["*donc dans une film politique*"]', and later concludes 'Indeed this was a political film. A mixture of Walt Disney and blood'. This represents the limit of the use of intertextuality in problematising the ontological-real aspects of New Wave content. Thus, MacCabe finds the film extremely wanting: 'the complete inability of the form to deal with the reality of a politics which eludes the easy solutions of the thriller genre. In some ways, the simple and sombre message of the film is the inability of the left to cope with the developments of consumer capitalism' (MacCabe 2003: 177). And, from the perspective of over three decades, the major movement of Godard's work in the 1960s was away from such conditions of intertextuality. Arguably, intertextuality had come to re-establish a totality, as in Thome, foreclosing aperture, and continuing to work to sublimate alienation into narrative structure regardless of the provocative results. (And of all the traits of the Nouvelle Vague that have come to offer, in Benjamin's words, 'new effects or sensations . . . for the public's entertainment' (Benjamin 1998: 94), intertextuality is most prominent.) Unlike *Deux ou Trois Choses*, the voice-overs of *Alphaville, Une Étrange Aventure de Lemmy Caution* (1965) and 'Il Nuovo Mondo' (Godard's segment of *RoGoPaG* (1963)), even across the ontological-real of the 'future-in-the-present' (Wollen 1982: 89), still impose a singular meaning on the mise en scène. The liberating force of alienation had been dissipated via exercises in intertextuality along the lines of (in Godard's words, in relation to *Le Mépris*) 'to film an Antonioni subject in the manner of Hawks or Hitchcock' (Armes 1976: 44); something not unlike Eco's 'self-masturbatory hermaphrodite machinery' (Eco 1989: 239).

This failure is, naturally, addressed by Godard, at times literally (in his voice-over commentaries in these films, and as in *Caméra-Oeil*); as much as the films interrogate the images, they must also interrogate their own fumbling of these images. Such disappointments mark the way in which an aspirant non-bourgeois film form has failed to outflank problems associated, earlier, with an excessive intertextuality – an oppositional gesturalism. And just as Godard's films of this phase voice their own methodologies, so too do the films implicitly note a frisson of failure in their excessively melodramatic endings, as illustrative of the above-noted thinness of the dramaturgy. Farber found such a literary realism as characterised by 'mock profound conversation' (Farber 1998: 262), evident throughout in the cumbersome language employed by characters, continually referring to events as they occur (one character cries 'Paula, you've stolen my tomorrow!' after being shot in *Made in USA*; *Bande à Part* repeatedly uses descriptive voice-overs over 'standard' cinéma-vérité shots – '[u]nder crystal skies, Arthur, Odile and Franz crossed bridges suspended over glassy rivers, the moats frozen, the water dead. A taste of blood was in the air', and so forth).

Initially Godard romanticises his own failings; such a failure of nerve within the films is continually articulated to the point of – in the manner of the 1966 impasse – coming to constructively suspend or 'wreck' the narrative. In *Le Mépris*, Fritz Lang, playing himself, quotes Brecht to Bardot (in which Brecht terms Hollywood 'the market where they buy lies'), and after the spoken opening credits comes: 'For what we see, Bazin said, the cinema substitutes a world that conforms to our desires. *Le Mépris* is the story of that world' (over an image of a camera pointed straight at the audience). Thus Godard announces, in the film, a film about a film of uneasy 'lies', made in the knowledge of its opposite: 'what we see' (and with such self-defeating sentiments finding their fullest expression in *Made in USA* for MacCabe and others).

Yet this is only to acknowledge the problem and, in the manner of Antonioni, temporarily work within the boundaries of the problem rather than transcend it. And this problem arises from the failure of praxis and film form, and non-specifically at that; thus Godard's rough draft cinema is one of a series of abandonments and re-beginnings, forever failing to overcome one particular problem – the nature of the praxis and film form as indicative not of insufficient radical-ism in itself, or doggedness in its pursuit of meaning, but of the limits of post-Bazinian realism. Godard's refusal to countenance any one meaning, while all the time refusing to doubt the existence of a meaning born of ontological truth within the images, represents a deferral of the investigation at the point at which it approaches the final norm of bourgeois film: the ontological-real of a reality transferred. It is for this reason that the negotiation with post-Bazinian realism mentioned above is of a limited scope.

In the meanwhile, however, with *Deux ou Trois Choses*, such problems with an 'outright intertextuality' are recast as solutions to the ontological-real. The 'living state' of intertextuality as contemporary existence is evident in the way in which the lives that Juliette represents are infused with romanticism as much as the earlier Godard films – but of a commercial kind, of commodity fetishism, even to the extent of initiating prostitution (since Juliette spends her earnings on consumer goods).[22] So *Deux ou Trois Choses* contains a tension between the expressed desire to shoot a documentary on the Paris region and the living condi-tions of the Juliettes, and the 'invasion' of the frame with pop images of unreality: the posters of faraway countries (or even those taken as 'fantasy' countries – a poster for Israel is frequently seen), consumer products, voguish new fashions, the unreal interiors of shops. In this respect, the Bazinian ontology of the film image is equally given over to the 'unreality' of Juliette's life. Thus Cavell posits Juliette as a portrait of modern woman, alienated by the pervasive and damaging nature of her late capitalist environs, and so can connect *Deux ou Trois Choses* to *Il Deserto Rosso* in respect of voicing this critique (Cavell 2005: 34). Such a connec-tion suggests the possibility of an illuminating point of comparison between such films of differing uses of alienation, not least since Godard's re-looping of an 'out-right intertextuality' back into his postmodern mise en scène comes to make for a methodological end point comparable to that achieved in Antonioni's tetralogy.

From his position, Godard succumbs to the evidence of this critique by allow-ing the frame to be become crowded, and ultimately overrun, by the inanimate, fetishised consumer commodities. And Juliette, enslaved by her conformist consumer impulses, is herself transformed into such a consumer product, a prostitute. The prostitute is then considered in the same 'disassociated' way by the client, who, with the mirror image of lovemaking, turns the tawdry purchase of her time and body into an aesthetised, utopian act. In such ways, Godard is able to declare the critique by allowing it to disrupt the mise en scène, a mise en scène now overtaken with commodities, or given over to commodification-like processes (the selling of the Juliette, and the contamination of 'the real' with the 'unreal' of garish, 'consumer'-style aesthetics). Thus he is able to show the very battle for critical meaning in operation, with the mise en scène as its very 'arena'.

Antonioni, on the other hand, illustrates the problem by presenting it as a determining factor within free indirect subjectivity. This is evident in the 'escape-fantasy' (Cameron and Wood 1968: 112) sequence of *Il Deserto Rosso*. Giuliana tells a story to her son, visualising it in her mind's eye as she does so. The resultant sequence is vastly at odds with the rest of the film; its quietness is pervasive, and the aesthetic is not degraded (that is – the colours are not rendered as false but as clean and rarefied, as fantastical as the story about a girl who lives on a beach). In short, the aesthetic is not 'contaminated' by the industrial world of the film. Yet both aesthetic and story also illustrate something amiss – perhaps the very ontological-real of the Bazinian representation of the world; the image allows no 'weight' to the reality it represents, carries no ontological gravitas. And both aesthetic and story speak of the banal and empty ideals of the glossy imagery of lifestyle advertising; escapism measured in terms of harmonious and 'natural' existence with nature, a world without pollution – indeed, without a sense of time passing.

Despite the way in which this sequence is so removed from the film, it is far from a utopian interlude. With its story of ships and a lonely young girl, it is a distorted reflection of Giuliana's situation. Thus the clean imagery of advertisements renders a 'negative' reflection of Giuliana's harsh world: where the harsh is cleaned and beautified. And, true to the rest of the film too, the sequence contains unaccountable occurrences (the unmanned ship that briefly appears and then leaves, and an audible diegetic singing without a source). Thus the fairytale-like unreality of the sequence illustrates its very opposite: the depth of Giuliana's repulsion of reality, the intensity of her inner reality, the desire for an escape into this man-less world, 'written' with imagery of advertisements, and her failure to hermetically seal this world from the psychic tensions of her actual, lived life. It is another dead-end fantasy, as with Giuliana's earlier talk of opening a ceramics shop. In this way, in Antonioni's critique, the commodity festishism has encroached even into the unconsciousness. Antonioni here illustrates the psychological damage to the subject, while Godard shows the causes of and the conditions that inflict the psychological damage – in the knowledge that the audience is then expected to make sense of this confrontational and alienating experience. In this respect, Godard's critique may be said to be materialist (rather than psychological) in nature.

From this perspective, it could be said that Godard was not only a part of the climate of political dissent, but contributed to that climate, politically, with his own evolving analysis grounded in the reality of that climate. Thus MacCabe notes that 'one of the most remarkable features of [Godard's] work is its closeness to the contemporary moment . . . La Chinoise, apparently aberrant when it appeared, [was] yet confirmed in its actuality less than a year later by the events of May 1968' (MacCabe, Eaton and Mulvey 1980: 84). La Chinoise, made in March 1967 and set in summer 1967, concerned a revolutionary Maoist cell at the Nanterre campus of the University of France. The film anticipated the Nanterre unrest in a manner termed 'terrifyingly prophetic' by Roud (Roud 1970: 133): the March 22nd Movement was founded at the University of Nanterre, similarly revolutionary in its intentions and coming to represent a major component of the civil unrest in France in 1968. Rosenbaum and Reader relate La Chinoise directly to this short era of political upheaval (see Rosenbaum 2000: 32–33; Reader 2004: 76–79); for Reader, this foresight distinguishes Godard's entire oeuvre: 'the cinema, for Godard, has fulfilled the function of visionary scientific instrument, foreseeing patterns of emergent social change before they occur, and then confronting and testifying to the reality and/or atrocity of those events' (Reader 2004: 72). The notion of a 'scientific' (as objective, disinterested, unblinking) examination of found reality, so as to predict social mutations to come, can be said to be close to a post-Bazinian realism, as identified here.

The materialist critique cannot be considered as the outcome of the more fruitful of the two discourses (ontological and intertextual) at this evolved point. The entire dialectic of Godard's work had led to such a materialist critique, in its progressive innovations and dead ends. This dialectic was forged from excesses on either side of post-Bazinian realism: excessive image manipulation (the intertextual concerns, to the point of an encroaching, postmodern realm), and excessive Bazinian ontology (the journalistic/investigative impulses, implemented via a film language of cinéma-vérité). Merging these two streams had allowed for a series of reinvigorated Brechtian analyses, exposing the tyranny of meaning in the system of interpretation of the world that surrounds and oppresses the protagonists. This had shifted Godard's political discourse away from the given terrain of political concerns (French bourgeois politics) and into more abstract and 'pressing' areas (the condition of prostitution and the actual phenomenon of prostitution, respectively, for example) that were appropriate for an increasingly politically radical outlook and, indeed, an 'intervention' predicated from a materialist critique.

The particular nature of the materialist critique, and the potential it offers for such intervention, can be seen with greater clarity when considered in relation to a number of films that, as if an outgrowth of the Late Modernist film or a literal realisation of the inferred calls of the Oberhausen Manifesto, simply dramatised the social-political situation for leftists at the time, as if a direct leftist theoretical challenge to communism. These 'interjections' into the wider debate represented, in Gordon's description of Pasolini's films from this period, a 'discourse of ideology' (Gordon 1996: 235) – that is, a literally critical realism, and often taking the sophisticated form of 'a speculative, essayist cinema' (as Aranda describes Buñuel's La Voie Lactée (Aranda 1975: 230)). Sweet notes this tendency, in relation to Resnais, Costa-Gavras and Makavejev, as one of 'internal socialist criticism raised in one of the most public of media. These films are examples of leftists airing their dirty laundry in public, an activity universally condemned by communist central committees' (Sweet 1981: 92). Although many insightful observations on the collective state of the European left can be gleaned from this area – the defeatism of Prima della Rivoluzione and La Guerre est Finie (Resnais, 1966); the dialecticism of struggle in Uccellacci e Uccellini and 'La Ricotta' (Pasolini's segment of RoGoPaG); the politicised reconsiderations of sexual and religious mores in Makavejev and La Voie Lactée; questions concerning the revolutionary potential and role of art in Die Artisten in der Zirkuskuppel: Ratlos (Artists under the Big Top: Perplexed, Alexander Kluge, 1968); and the general state of the European left imagination via a variety of portmanteau films (Loin du Viêt-nam, La Contestation,[23] RoGoPaG) – such films avoid wading into, or attempting to directly intervene in, such areas. Pasolini's Marxist Crow, in Uccellacci e Uccellini, can identify a variety of salient tensions ('It's the twilight of the great hopes. These wretches [the film's comic protagonists] are the first to be left in the shadows along with Rossellini or Brecht while the workers, in this twilight . . . [sic] Ideologies continue to go forward but this fellow goes on talking . . . nobody knows about what . . . to people who are going they know not where . . .'),[24] but these tensions are not presented proactively – merely critically. In Godard's materialist critique, and with a number of radical films that adopt comparable praxes, comes the attempt to 'activate' such a dormant critical tendency. Only a small leap of the imagination would be required to see disruptive gestures, born of such a dormant critical tendency, as actual political interventions, particularly in the context of the mounting civil unrest of 1967 and 1968. Outside the East Bloc, the leftist theoretical challenge became not so much one of provocation and analysis, anti-illusionism and reflexivity, but one that would attempt to situate the Verfremdungseffekt in relation to revolution – as a revolutionary tool in itself.

For Godard, the resultant possibilities of an even wider consideration, as in *La Chinoise* (the first film of 1967, after the three 1966 films considered here), had unsurprisingly added a Maoist sensibility to the expanded critique. Despite a number of theoretical dead ends (*Made in USA* and excessive intertextuality), born of the failure to fully break with gestural MacMahonism, and irrespective of the stated frustrations with the evolved praxis of *Deux ou Trois Choses* (the disappointment with the attempts to expand the scope of the 'political' on film, and the resultant identification of the postmodern political in contemporary France), Godard was at anything but an impasse. Rather, the element of the expanded and radical discourse (Brechtian method, a film form that delivered actual rather than gestural critique, and a post-Bazinian realism capable of delivering undigested chunks of reality – however qualified that reality was – into the laps of revolutionary-minded viewers, constructively and didactically alienating them, rather than bolstering a subjectivity and totality) provided a critical realism well equipped to accommodate and materially further an increasingly militant sensibility. In shaking himself free of the limitations embraced and subverted by Antonioni, in tandem with the continuing push from an anti- to a non-bourgeois film form, Godard and like-minded auteurs were ready to utilise the potentials of post-Bazinian realism for formally revolutionary ends.

Notes

1. The violent clash of locations in *Blow-Up*, presented just ten years earlier, would have served only to illustrate a notion of social inequality (in any Free Cinema or British New Wave film, and even in a relatively mainstream film such as *Victim* – the

lawyer's excursion to the building site, for example). In relation to the dosshouse that opens Antonioni's film, virtually identical shots can be found in Karel Reisz's *We Are The Lambeth Boys* (1958); buildings dominate the screen and blot out the sky, people are seen as dwarfed by this grimy urban environment. Now, audaciously, such 'classic' juxtapositions of locations are used for atmosphere and the creation of the experientialism of the film – they do not function as they once would have been expected to.

2. Bazin's analysis of the long take is expressed in his essay 'The Evolution of the Language of Cinema'. Here, of Flaherty's long takes, Bazin found: 'the length of the hunt [in *Nanook of the North*, 1922] is the very substance of the image, its true object' (Bazin 1967: 27), and of Stroheim's, 'In his films reality lays itself bare like a suspect confessing under the relentless examination of the commissioner of police' (Bazin 1967: 27). Kolker find in this an inherent 'reliance on the image itself, a faith that the image, uninterrupted and barely tampered with, would reveal the world the filmmaker wanted observed. Neo-realist theory fell directly in line with Bazin's belief in the analogue nature of the film image, "analogue" in the sense that it seems to correspond to the way we ordinarily perceive the world it records' (Kolker 1983: 147). The long take montage, by shedding the element of the manipulation of meaning in film, is a peerless device in terms of channelling 'pure' reality into the mise en scène – of film possessing the ontological-real.

3. Rohdie notes that 'the change from female to male protagonists [a difference between *Blow-Up* and the films of the tetralogy] . . . is accompanied by a change from a subjective camera and narration to a rigorously objective camera and objective narrative position' (Rohdie 1990: 184). Although Brunette points out that 'this claim is not borne out by a close analysis of individual shots' (Brunette 1998: 111), Rohdie is correct in identifying a greater spirit of objectivity in the language of *Blow-Up*. In terms of the text itself, it is not always clear. The mise en scène often suggests itself as the rendering of a subjective perception (the correct framing for this used; the POV shot, from over Thomas's shoulder as he drives, for example, now also an element of the experiential aspect of the film) while the distance of the camera suggest an anti-expressionistic objectivity.

4. For example when Guido dreams of meeting his deceased father: he comments, aloud and to himself, upon the scene as it unfolds, acknowledging its metaphysical – i.e., unreal – elements.

5. A measure of this force is seen in the influence *Blow-Up* visibly exerted on the cycle of New Hollywood paranoia films that dealt directly with the fallout of the Kennedy assassination, extending this into the Nixon and Watergate eras. This is particularly so in the strategies of cognitive mapping, which are alternatively frustrated and bolstered in the films of Alan J. Pakula in the 1970s.

6. In this respect, the film offers a possibility in Stephens' thesis that '[i]t is possible to posit a passage from a modernist to a postmodernist aestheticism in various

expressions of the aesthetic radicalism of the sixties decade'. *Blow-Up* can be categorised as 'the shift from representation to simulation in critiques of mediated reality' (Stephens 1998: 99), and this comes about through a 'deni[al of] the autonomy of the referent, instead emphasizing simulation over and above anything else . . . Without a referent, an objective reality or notion of a genuine source, reality was seen to comprise [of] only images, and all equally illusory ones at that' (Stephens 1998: 115). As applied to this context, post-Bazinian realism readily takes on the mantle of such a referent.

7. Other interpretations exist – (Tyler 1969: 133; Harris 1987: 61 and ff; Ward 1995: 139 and ff and Brunette 1998: 124) – as do readings of the film that pick up on the seeming reflexivity of the act of photography on Thomas's part (Huss 1971: 4–5; Brunette 1998: 121).

8. Antonioni had noted this limitation as circumscribed within his own status and the use of film at this stage, in answer to such questions of purpose, in 1961: 'Lucretius . . . once said, "Nothing appears as it should in a world where nothing is certain. The only thing certain is the existence of a secret violence that makes everything uncertain" . . . What Lucretius said of his time is still a disturbing reality, for it seems to me that this uncertainty is very much part of our own time. But this is unquestionably a philosophical matter. Now you really don't expect me to resolve such problems or to propose any solutions? Inasmuch as I am the product of a middle-class society, and am preoccupied with making middle-class dramas, I am not equipped to do so. The middle class doesn't give me the means with which to resolve any middle-class problems. That's why I confine myself to pointing out existing problems without proposing any solutions. I think it is equally important to point them out as it is to propose solutions' (quoted in Cardullo 2008: 38).

9. If placed on a sliding scale, Antonioni merely articulates, (as quoted in Cardullo 2008: 38), and works from (as evident in *Blow-Up*), one position alone; the slightness of the role of the bourgeois film-maker as hobbled by his adherence to bourgeois concerns via exclusively bourgeois means of articulation (i.e., a revolutionary-level radicalism of film form as an impossibility). In Third Cinema film theory, Antonioni's position – that of the Second Cinema – is, indeed, seen as organically incapable of anything beyond a consideration of such 'local' problems.

10. This was clearly not a universal problem for political discontents. There were those who rejected or dismissed, or remained unaware of, such a divide altogether; Buñuel's *Le Journal d'une Femme de Chambre* (1964) was an exemplary anti-bourgeois film with a 'neutral' form; nothing overtly psychological, subjective, avant-garde or (bar one moment) New Wave-like. Much the same could be said for the anti-clerical *La Religieuse* (Rivette, 1966) yet, despite its conservative form, the film was still banned. Such films do not demonstrate a crisis in their language, as both 'against' and 'of' the very system they critique.

11. Walsh was to have gone on to apply this specifically to Makavejev and Godard (whose 'total oeuvre constitutes a superbly "Brechtian" evolution' (Walsh 1981: 130)). This would have constituted the fourth and fifth chapters of *The Brechtian Aspect of Radical Cinema*, which now only exist in draft form.

12. Wood notes Bergman's Brechtian devices in *Persona* (1966) and *Skammen* (*Shame*, 1968), which he contrasts favourably to Godard's (Wood and Walker 1970: 173) on the grounds that they do not cause the 'spectator's analytical detachment' but rather 'draw the spectator into the film, demanding total emotional involvement' (Wood and Walker 1970: 145).

13. And it is from such an elitist position that Godard was to abandon conventional film-making in all senses during 1968 for the 16mm *Ciné-tracts* newsreels. (*Film-tracts*, each lasting no more than a few minutes, various directors including Resnais and Marker, all anonymous, some shot in Godard's flat. Godard himself shot the Latin Quarter protest; an Italian equivalent was also in operation, the Cinegiornale, and a fledgling British chapter – Red and Black newsreel – was established.) The *Ciné-tracts* were shown to student assemblies, striking factories, 'arts lab' cinemas and so on, often by the Etats Généraux du Cinéma Français – the logical conclusion of Godard's tailoring his work to such specialist and revolutionary-minded audiences. Thus *IT*, in 1969, could quip '[s]tudents in Italy became tired of seeing themselves on film, occupying their own university buildings. Nothing worse than being a worker at Renault in Paris and seeing a film, by Godard or someone, about last week's worker occupation at Renault' (Dickinson and Giannoni 1969: 5). Roszak attacked such cultural-political elitism from a straight class perspective as symptomatic of 'the spoiled middle-class young amus[ing] themselves': 'what can the Beatles' latest surrealist LP mean to an unemployed miner' (Roszak 1971: 70). The connection between such documentaries and radicalising the proletariat is explicit in the *Ciné-tract*-like *Columbia Revolt* (New York Newsreel, 1968) – a 'how to' guide, filmed from within the occupied university buildings; during one conversation the stated aim is given: to encourage other students to rise up, over the need to fight the police. The talk of the 'red bourgeoisie' in the similar *Lipanjska Gibanja* (*Student Demonstrations*, Žilnik, 1968), along with the documentary footage of the founding of the Red University Karl Marx (formerly the University of Belgrade), offers a similar target.

14. Godard voices such a position to students, albeit in general terms rather than in relation to this film, in the documentary *Two American Audiences* (Mark Woodcock, 1968). A similar moment opens *Nicht Löschbares Feuer* (*The Inextinguishable Fire*, Harun Farocki, 1969). A 'statement given at the Vietnam War Crimes Tribunal in Stockholm', by a Vietnamese man, is read out by a narrator sat behind a desk who, after discussing the impossibility of showing the horrors of the effects of napalm (not least as Western viewers would simply be psychologically unable to accept the images), offers a 'hint' by extinguishing a cigarette on his arm. The perception

problem for Western viewers that is identified recalls Arendt's position on Nazi concentration camps 'horror [that] can never be fully embraced by the imagination' (Arendt 1966: 444).

15. Rouch claimed the origin of this technique (showing the rushes to the subjects, and then filming their reactions and the subsequent conversations) was to be found in the organic process of cinéma-vérité production, following Flaherty's lead in this respect (Rouch 2003: 268), rather than aspiring to a moment of reflexivity.

16. The sequence was reputedly only shot to placate a producer's wish for more nudity in the film, although Silverman and Farocki speculate on a possible revision of this well-known story (Silverman and Farocki 1998: 230 footnote 5).

17. Or, more precisely, Godard can claim that at this level such lineaments are discernible; the film's actual investigation is barely more than a footnote in illustrating a preconceived thesis. Such a limitation became the basis for the condemnations of Godard from the Situationist International (see, for example, 'The Role of Godard' in *Internationale Situationniste* (archived at Anon 1966)). As with many of Godard's films of the 1960s, the ideas usually have more import than the actual films – this is the cost of a refusal to sublimate alienation into disrupted narrative structures; a lack of completeness, through the embrace of 'rough-draft cinema', blocks the kind of perspective that would arise from a totality of vision. Thus Godard's films from this period cannot be taken as considered praxes – manifestos of film-making – since they repeatedly implicate themselves as failures. This partly accounts for the volume of Godard's films from this period; a series of new beginnings with the end rarely in sight.

18. MacCabe relates Althusser to Godard's work, in relation to Godard's Maoism (MacCabe 2003: 197), as quoted in *La Chinoise* (1967) (MacCabe 2003: 197), as influential on *Vent d'Est* (1970) (MacCabe 2003: 225) and as the very basis for *Lotte in Italia* (Dziga Vertov Group, 1970) (MacCabe 2003: 229). This Althusserian framework, as a perspective that can be seen to be mirrored in Godard, goes some way in redeeming the problem of non- or only partial implementation of praxis identified above.

19. However, *Rote Sonne* is not a straight continuation of the New Wave tendency of image manipulation. Thome 'cleans' the frame of the detritus and crowding of objects and people typical of the New Wave mise en scène; reality is now only glimpsed – scenes outside the claustrophobic apartment rooms, the occasional extra in the background, or the modishness of the characters (their dancing, poise and clothing).

20. For *Privilege* and *The Gladiators* (1967 and 1969) the science fiction genre allows for a vision of a possible future. As with Godard, Watkins's 'realism' is fantastical from the outset, while his mise en scène indicates the immediacy of an encounter with the ontological-real. However, Watkins's realism merely makes real a future fascist state – his reluctance to take the fantastical seriously, which occurs with his refusal

to force it back into found reality, inhibits any interrogation; here, the future fascist state simply 'is'. In *The Gladiators*, which seems a direct response to 1968, a French revolutionary student finds he is co-opted by the computer system, which runs 'live' war game exercises. However, there is no context for such a tendency; no wider application to historical precedents – the co-opting simply happens. Compared to Watkins, the found reality of and in Godard's mise en scène, no matter how alien, remains intimately connected to the here and now.

21. *Trans-Europ Express* (1966) illustrates the results of such extremes removed from post-Bazinian realism; Robbe-Grillet's reflexivity resultantly concerns itself solely with the film, at hand, as a film. Any problematisation of form occurs within, to use the term found in Robbe-Grillet's script for *L'Année Dernière à Marienbad* (Resnais, 1961), a 'monde clos' (Armes 1968: 151) – that is, the radical problematisation of form is not permitted to have a 'knock on' effect in relation to the ontological-real. The lessening of the assumed import of such reflexivity results not so much in a Brechtianism but, as Gieri terms it, a 'Pirandellism' (Gieri 1995: 9). Unsurprisingly, Robbe-Grillet himself faults Godard on Bazinian grounds; 'Godard found himself drowned by the realistic theories of Bazin' (Fragola and Smith 1995: 133), so that, as Van Wert argues, 'Robbe-Grillet faults Godard for attaching political reasons to his technical experiments' (Van Wert 1977: 15).

22. The resultant encounter with the postmodern represents the point at which a collective alienation (in the Marxist sense), as the condition of Western consumer society, is now perceived to be the motor for the actual alteration of the physical surroundings. Such a sensibility was not an unusual idea in the mid 1960s; Sontag's 1968 essay 'Trip to Hanoi', for example, readily ties this new sensibility to North American imperialism. She describes the military outpost of Vientiane as '"River City USA" . . . We passed the movie theatres showing skin flicks for the GI's, the "American" bars, the strip joints, stores selling paperbacks and picture magazines that could have been transplanted directly from Times Square' (Sontag 1969: 267–68). Such a sensibility, in Godard, can be related directly to the sustained strategies of the ontological-false or intertextual-real, but it is readily identifiable in any number of more local Godardian flourishes. Neupert notes a shot in *La Femme Mariée* in which the protagonist finally seems to momentarily walk 'into' a magazine advert for lingerie, which prompts him to claim that '[t]he world of ads is literally the world that Godard's characters must walk through' (Neupert 1987: 52).

23. This 1967 portmanteau film, intended as a dialogue between Marxists and Christians, was originally entitled *Vangelo 70* (*Evangile 70*), and then retitled *Amore e Rabbia*. It was released as *La Contestation* in France in 1970.

24. 'The age of Brecht and Rossellini is finished' is often quoted in relation to this film, for example (Schwartz 1992: 489), but does not appear in all versions of the film.

CHAPTER FOUR

Film and Revolutionism

A Film Culture of and for 1968

By 1966 Antonioni and Godard had problematised form to the extent that they had isolated the one remaining, material 'truth' of their medium – the nature of the medium itself. For Antonioni, furthering the Late Modernist film to the nth degree, this had shaken the very foundations of a film language predicated from a Bazinian 'greater' truth of transferred reality. In this respect, Antonioni's post-Bazinian realism phase had ultimately revised and then razed the 'Bazinian' element altogether. Those with Antonioni, at the resultant impasse, encountered a paralysis of purpose: if the nature of film itself is unsettled, then how is the role of the progressive film-maker, in relation to wider, societal questions, to be assessed, let alone enacted? A temporary answer was achieved via a paralleling of these two problems, as anticipated in Gruppo 63, and as evident in *Fellini-Satyricon*: the uncertainties of the project of the progressive or the radical film also speaks of, or to, or can be mapped onto, the uncertainties of the 'project' of 1968. In this way, problems of form become problems of politics; both are indicative of the same crisis of purpose. That is, this impasse is able to situate itself in relation to a bigger impasse: the conception of 1968. And yet this useful proximity was not coincidental: the very problems of agency (that is, the role of the film in society, specifically that of the dissenting film within – and indeed 'of' and of a concern with – late capitalist society) rather than straight protest also confronted those who sought a direct confrontation with the state apparatus. More precisely, those who had abandoned a faith in progressive change as a possibility, and a possibility to be wrought from within the progressive wing of the bourgeois-state system itself (and these were the forerunners and architects of 1968), were now grappling with a new constellation of possibilities: the freedom to act outside that system had been attained – but how to act, and to what ends?

For Godard, working within New Wave methodologies, the arrival at the one material 'truth' of the medium had led to an enhanced praxis – if there was an impasse, or a paralysis of film language, it was easily discarded or overlooked. Language had only been a means of interrogating found reality; Godard's focus had been external – to find slogans that encapsulate and critique, therefore, rather than a lexicon of ever-diminishing certainties. And, by 1966, the New Wave methodologies that had evolved would not necessarily 'wind down'; just as the impasse had indicated a hope for a non-bourgeois film form in its very failures, the fledgling methodology of the non-bourgeois film had indicated that even more was possible. The viewer's revolutionary consciousness had been raised via critique, but it could now be galvanised and even prompted into action; the process of watching the film was to be understood as an act that was itself political, that had acquired, or came to be seen as possessed of, agency – and one seemingly without limits. This was a logical destination for Godard – to move beyond the self-effacement of *Blow-Up*, and beyond even the comparable pessimistic end points of other Waves (particularly the Czech New Wave).

Such an aspiration to 'even more' was first evident in a number of timely focuses: the political militancy of *Masculin-Féminin* in Godard's case; the Reich-derived notion of sexuality as possessing the potential for political radicalism, as seen in the films of Makavejev; the nostalgic nature of *Prima della Rivoluzione* and the paralysis identified in the polemics of *Loin du Viêt-nam* as indicative of a disillusioned yet revolutionary-minded cohort – where the unspoken aspiration was to reject such degrees of helplessness.[1] And in the growing restlessness on the streets, just such a non-acceptance was to be glimpsed. The activism apparent in 1966, with smaller incidents of civil disruption, notably in Rome, and a growing militancy in these endeavours, was to reach the point of seeming mass insurrection, particularly in Paris, in May and June 1968. The writers of graffiti slogans – those who had once made radical gestures – had, by now, progressed to hurling paving stones at the police from behind makeshift blockades, incinerating cars and mass occupation; they no longer just engaged in radical gestures. In all, the progress of post-industrial Western capitalism was temporarily waylaid; Hardt and Negri conclude that '[b]y the end of the 1960s the liberation struggles, whose influence had come to be felt in every interstice of world space, assumed a force, a mobility, and a plasticity of form that drove the project of capitalist modernization (in both its liberal and socialist guises) out into an open sea, where it lost its bearings' (Hardt and Negri 2001: 250). And so if the collective imaginations of the protestors ultimately outran their collective abilities, it would have been some comfort to those then vainly erecting the barricades to know that the collective imagination evidenced in May and June of 1968 was seemingly limitless in its revolutionary zeal and intention.

Radical and dissident film and film culture had not only resonated with a growing sensibility of spontaneity and the happening, but had expressed that sensibility and aspired to advance it in several cases. That initial element of the 'debate' of 1968, one that illuminated and questioned the impact of political stagnation in all spheres of life – something apparent during the long lead-up to 1968 – was deftly articulated in the films of the Czech and British New Waves. Meanwhile innovations in film discourse – the expansions, problematisations, positions and provocations that are apparent in general, from intellectualised to radical film –illustrated a similar dissatisfaction with respect to such political stagnation and suggested, as if propelled ever onwards by their own momentum, a step beyond the sense of this debate as a final destination.

And such zeal was to give rise to a literally expanded cinema during this phase – a culture that worked to overturn the industry. The attempted seizing of the actual means of production led to the founding of 'non-capitalist' production and distribution models and networks, identified in a Cahiers August 1968 editorial as 'Revolution in/through the cinema' since 'making the revolution in the cinema [also implies] making it before or at the same time everywhere else' (Harvey 1980: 18).[2] This is analogous to the attempts to reform or overturn the institutions of higher education, which were also perceived to be microcosms of society – from the radical internal reforms to occupations and the establishment of 'anti-universities'. Generating, and generated by, such a hothouse atmosphere was the most utopian and wayward period of film-making of the leftist theoretical challenge, which involved sharing tactics and aspirations with the 'soixante-huitards' actively working against the state. The year 1968 mandated the radical film-maker, and radical film became a front in and of the struggles of 1968. Indeed, as noted at the outset of this study, film became a microcosm of 'the event' of 1968, in which the ideas, subjectivities, militant tendencies and general excesses of 1968 can be – then as now – examined and experienced. This was to prove to be a unique tactical attribute in the radical film culture of the time; the previous rallying for a 'here and now' (as originally flowing from the Angry Young Man sensibility), and

Godard's preference for a materialist critique, now resulted in, at times, a commentary running ahead of events – as with *La Chinoise*.

The specificity of the film culture of and for 1968 was such that a brief review of the shared concerns will follow, so as to note the common themes and flashpoints that are echoed in, anticipated by, and form the concerns of, the '1968 film'. These are: internationalism, counterculturalism, and the analysis of 1968 arising from the awareness of a false revolutionism. Such a review needs to be qualified by an acknowledgement that no single formal agenda united the protestors – indeed, many blocs adopted diametrically opposed causes, even when the protests were understood, even by the protesters, to be united across borders, including the Iron Curtain. The one commonality was an uncontained disillusionment with the inert structures, and opportunist personnel, of state power.

- This disillusionment, in the first instance, was galvanised and found evidence and cause in the escalation of the war in Vietnam. The resultant solidarity with North American anti-war activists and the Vietnamese strengthened the sense of 'internationalism', and the belief in the international dimension of the 1968 struggle (and the internationalising of that struggle) against the bourgeoisie during this seemingly belated phase of imperialism. Internationalism can be defined along such lines: 'the actions and movements which developed regardless of national boundaries, subverting the nation states' framework' (Young 1977: 33). The cause of nuclear disarmament movements – a cause that necessarily required an international contextualisation – bolstered this sensibility.

In terms of facilitating empathy and solidarity with the plight and struggles of those terrorised abroad, film was a medium with few parallels. Film was one of the few export products of a non-utilitarian kind that circulated in ideological spheres other than its own. Through internationalism came communalism: those who had felt anger at political intransigence and social stagnation were now not alone, finding themselves empowered and numerous – and with the space and inclination, and reason, to protest. Film, therefore, as at the service of internationalism, could bring home the wars abroad, and in so doing situate itself on an intersection of that which Ali identifies as the three fronts of 1968: 'Third World in revolution, crisis in capitalist Europe and turmoil in the "socialist camp"' (Ali 1987: 229).

- The expansion of the realm of the 'political': that nascent sensibility (which was to fully flower in Second Wave feminism) that all that was personal was political, and vice versa. A bohemian counterculture that represented a way of life opposed to the norms of capitalist society (that is, that exhorted a degrading of the body's ability to function in such a society) through hedonistic pursuits and, or along with, the refusal of work thus arose.

Such a sensibility was readily relayed into the 'sensibility' of countercultural film, from tropes of modish counterculturalism (already encountered in this study in relation to Antonioni and Fellini) to full blown experientialism. And such a sensibility, in film, in turn, could come to take on a radical agency: the propagation of that counterculture, bohemian or dissident/political, or a mixture of both, for biopolitical ends. Whereas internationalism fed the nature of the protests in its world-political terms, counterculturalism fed the nature of the protests in terms of a radical imagination, and the lived experience, of the protestors, of social and civil inequality and of revolutionism.

• The non-revolution. Since such widespread revolts did not, finally, constitute anything like the 'revolution' that had seemed possible in the midst of the disturbances, the events may be seen in terms of a convulsion or a 'huge ideological spasm' (Hanley and Kerr 1989: 7). The seeming revolution turned out to be an opportune running battle – opportune since those in power in both Eastern and Western Europe seemed no longer to believe in the structures of authority they maintained. And yet the decisive role of the European communist parties and labour unions (mobilised at the dangerous point of the meeting of protesting students and workers) in channelling dissent back into the power structures of the (bourgeois) state illustrated that no quarter finally fully supported the protestors, despite the lip service paid to those engaged in civil disobedience. This was no state secret or whispered conspiracy; as student leader Cohn-Bendit noted shortly after: 'during the months of May and June, the ["bureaucrats running the"] Communist Party and the CGT [union] played the game of the State and the bourgeoisie in theory no less than in practice' (Cohn-Bendit and Cohn-Bendit 1969: 168).

Inevitably this gave rise to a questioning of the 1968 project, at the time – and such questioning (when carried out by, say, Sartre, (Cohn-Bendit and Sartre 1968: 100), or Habermas (Habermas 1968: 58–59) or even the Situationists (Viénet 1992: 19)) invariably identified the lack of a revolutionary programme as critical. The conclusion, therefore, was unavoidable: the convulsion of 1968 had effectively occurred within the bourgeois sphere, for its own purposes, and the state would reorientate itself around the movements, swallowing them, so as to reconsolidate its power. In 1972 Pasolini described 1968 as a 'false revolution – which presented itself as Marxist while it was in reality only a form of self-criticism of the bourgeoisie' (quoted in Schwartz 1992: 532). So, whereas elements of the dissident and militant left believed that the degenerate nature of the then phase of 'late capitalism' particular to 1968 represented a time that was ripe for revolutionary intervention, Pasolini's use of the term 'neo-capitalism' indicates a more pessimistic reading.[3] The year 1968 was a reordering of historical fascism and capitalism (the former a system to sustain the latter, the latter the 'front' for the former) for the beginnings of an expansion of capitalism – so that 'neo-capitalism' would soon be termed 'globalisation'. Such readings are to be found in the films of 1968; the hope of a late capitalism 1968 (implied in Godard) against the pessimism of neo-capitalism 1968 (articulated in Pasolini).

To return to the questioning of the 1968 project: the response garnered from protestors when asked about their programmes fetishised an anarchistic distaste for dogmatic political strategies, and exalted countercultural spontaneity for its own sake (see, for example, Cohn-Bendit and Sartre 1968: 103), sometimes on the grounds of de-alienation. Such a position suggests 1968 as a '"festival of the oppressed" – the figuratively oppressed, that is' (Hall and Critcher et al. 1979: 241) rather than a reprise of Moscow 1917 on the streets of Paris. Such a position is not based on an historical analysis of the prevailing situation; it merely articulates a will to rebel, and this will seems as much psychological as class-based – an exercise of freedoms, rather than a consolidation of them. This 'street-level' understanding of 1968 can be said to account for the lack of theoretical rigour that is so characteristic in the West at this point (on the street, and on the screen); it was possible to be revolutionary irrespective of an understanding or comprehension of the objective requirements or need for such a state of being. And this is why so much revolutionary artistic expression, particularly in relation to sexual liberation, is concerned with utopianism and idealism. Such states are the corollary of such an essential blind spot in the revolutionary methodology, now filled with hopes for a better future in the absence of a sustained analysis of the actual present. And expressing such utopian yearnings through a critique of the stasis of a liberal-bourgeois status quo achieves a circumnavigation around this blind spot. This is the murky area in which a gesture of defiance comes to be confused with an act of defiance. And, conversely and tragically, an actual act of radical defiance (the Prague Spring), from the vantage point of Moscow, was read as a wider gesture of defiance.

The film culture of 1968 certainly represented the will to radicalism, as historically fired by the will to transcend the helplessness or inconsequentiality of the anti-bourgeois bourgeois film, but in a climate in which such things were evidently 'freed' from theoretical rigour and historical analysis. Utopian ideals could simply be used to express condemnation of, or even transgress the norms of, bourgeois society as part of a wider revolutionary milieu; radicalism and revolutionism, on the screen, were 'enough' in themselves. If the blame for this is to be attributed to petty-bourgeois radicals, then this state of affairs could only arise once the orthodox Left had jettisoned any possibility of a progressive foundation for the expression of discontent. And the renegades of ultra-leftism (a 'catch all' category for discontents of the left; a tendency now isolated by the actions of the Left, and increasingly polemical) had their own cinema of 1968: a period of filmmaking every bit as problematic as the events of 1968. The crux of such a period was in the nature of the rejection of helplessness and even of the critique itself – in the attempt to create a cinema of, or an alignment to, material action.

In this respect, radical genre films, despite the militancy of their intentions, as evident in the films themselves, can be consigned to a lesser category of revolutionism, akin to 'entryism'. And such an 'infiltration' of revolutionary concerns into otherwise supposedly apolitical areas (that is, the film of entertainment – of recognisable types, humour, thrills, suspense and violence and a standard filmic construction and language) came, paradoxically, from an embracing and reinvention of genre conventions, a willing capitulation to the rules of genre, rather than a New Wave-style deconstruction of them via a critical realism. Such films ultimately adhered to the rules of genre rather than capitalised on post-Bazinian realism; their consciousness-raising was a by-product of subversion from within the codes of bourgeois cinema, codes that were otherwise accommodated by bourgeois cinema. For this reason, the political lessons imparted were invariably allegorical. Gillo Pontecorvo's *Quemada!* (1969), despite its Hollywood star and period setting, dramatises the underhand dealings of the imperial West – fomenting, and then quelling, revolutions in developing countries all to their own sordid, financial ends. It is difficult not to read the film as a diatribe against revolutionary zeal – a reading that finds an accommodation with 'neo-capitalist' readings of 1968. The allegorical element is particularly strong in radical spaghetti westerns; Sergio Sollima's *Faccia a Faccia* (*Face to Face*, 1967), for example, with its incongruous hippie commune, invites a reading of the film as directly applicable to its year of release; since those in power are 'morons' and academics are marginalised through their teaching posts, a history professor joins an outlaw gang, making the transition from revolutionary theory to practice, in the manner of Timothy Leary. *La Resa dei Conti* (*The Big Gundown*, Sollima, 1966) and Corbucci's *Il Grande Silenzio* (*The Great Silence*, 1968) suggest that notions of law and order in the West are illusory – the agents of capitalism are those that exert real power.

These film-makers tend to present a defence along the legitimate lines already encountered in relation to Antonioni: a maturity of conception of film, as a minor facet of the revolutionary struggle, albeit one with the potential to gently urge radicalism across the masses – as a mass (rather than elitist) form of communication (see, for example, Sergio Leone and Pontecorvo, who evokes Lenin, on this model (Frayling 1981: 231 and 242 respectively)). This occurs via populist revolutionary didacticism, a breaking of taboos and mores, as/or a continuation of anti-bourgeois preoccupations.

This tendency is evident in Truffaut's *L'Enfant Sauvage* (1969) and Chabrol's work – particularly, of this period, *Les Biches* (1968), *La Femme Infidèle* (1969), *Le Boucher* (1970), and *La Rupture* (1970). The worth of injecting dissonance into situations of a bourgeois milieu is arguable; Neupert assembles condemnations of Chabrol along the lines that such an approach is made in bad faith – the films remain bourgeois whatever the nature of their criticisms (so that Fassbinder could condemn a 'complete fascism . . . The question is: is he knocking [bourgeois values] in order to overcome them or to maintain them? I think the latter is more likely' (Neupert 2002: 133)). Even Wood and Walker, on Chabrol at the end of the 1960s, despair that '[t]he savage derider of the bourgeoisie has become its elegiac poet' and note that *Cahiers* had 'abandoned Chabrol' for this reason (Wood and Walker 1970: 19 and 132 respectively).

There is plenty of evidence of the attempt to create a cinema of, or aligned to, material action in *Vent d'Est* (featuring and from a script written by Cohn-Bendit); from the voice-over commentary: 'Today the question 'What shall we do?' presses forcefully at militant film-makers. It's no longer a matter of what road to take. It's a matter of determining – determining what they must do practically'. In attempting to 'begin again', to 'begin from the beginning' the film denounces film-makers who have condemned the bourgeoisie in the language of the bourgeois film, as well as film-makers passing themselves off as Marxists, named as

Eisenstein, Vertov and Pontecorvo (over images of actors applying make-up) – itself a tendency akin to Stalinist betrayals (Franco's Spain and the PCF (French Communist Party) over May 1968). For these film-makers:

> *Your method is false. You think it's enough to quote Mao, to go into the country to film farm workers and then to mix the two together to demonstrate that it's necessary to identify, unite with the rural masses . . . you shout, make predictions, spread opinions, but you don't really investigate . . . you're practising bourgeois sociology . . .*

The question of 'what to do' is answered by the close of the film – an exhortation to urban terrorism, refuting any 'humanist-bourgeois' condemnations of the murder of 'innocents' as a way of avoiding the real question of class struggle. Such sentiment is the filmic equivalent of (or even aspirant annex to) the Red Army Faction in Germany, the Red Brigades in Italy and the Angry Brigade in Britain.[4] The Argentinean documentary *La Hora de los Hornos* (*The Hour of the Furnaces*, Fernando Solanas, 1968) juxtaposes images of the sons and daughters of the Argentinean bourgeoisie at a party (free and contemporary; the males sport Beatles haircuts) with images from a slaughterhouse (the throats ripped out of bulls, blood covering all surfaces), as if to suggest that this is an appropriate fate for the offspring of the Argentinean ruling class. How is one to read the Molotov cocktail section of Bertolucci's *Partner* (1968) – the bomb strapped to the camera tripod as it pans, obscuring the view with this pertinent symbol of civil unrest and the self-empowerment of the protestors? (The film also includes a didactic scene in which a Molotov cocktail is made.)

Such ultra-leftist articulations also denote a 1968 constituency. Despite their provocative nature, these sentiments are expressed from a standpoint of inclusivity. The assumption is clearly in operation that the films and the viewer (or, at least, the ideal viewer, to whom such films are addressed) are at one with this stage, or outgrowth, of the leftist theoretical challenge. And just as the Verfremdungseffekt was utilised for the 'intellectual' aspect of this challenge, arriving at this point, its opposite was also to be called upon for the revolutionary aspect of this challenge: consciousness-raising appeals to revolutionary feelings (rather than thought) via experientialism. This was to be understood within the radical maxim of Che Guevara's 'Make two, three, many Vietnams' (quoted in Eaden and Renton 2002: 144), building on the way in which the counterculture was 'above all, a revolution in consciousness – because it was, in essence, a revolution *of* consciousness' (Hall and Critcher et al. 1979: 254–55). Thus film was reconceptualised as a front line in the militant struggle against the state. This determined a number of directions in this revolutionary period: populist entryism (here noted in relation to genre films), sexual liberation (the radical eroticisation of experientialism) and a form of filmic situationism (a Brechtian method-like politicisation of experientialism).

Three factors propelled the methodology of such a cinéma-militant (as these films were occasionally referred to at the time), beyond 'just' articulating the actual criticism. Firstly, the Brechtian New Wave had radicalised the Bazinian sense of a direct relationship between found reality and film. For Bertolucci, for example, writing in *Cahiers* about Godard, this had yielded an 'extraordinaire discours moral', a 'vulgarité' arising from an ability to remain open and susceptible to the reality all around (Bertolucci 1967: 29). So how could film culture not be 'in tandem with' the increasing civil unrest? Secondly, with the structuralist critique, the legacy of intertextuality, when the point had been reached where (as with Gruppo 63's stance) a 'critique of language was designed not to be a summary of the existential situation but a critique of the political status quo' (Eco 1989: 246), then '[t]he goal was to proceed, by way of a criticism of the miniature system of official culture, to a critique of the grand system of bourgeois society' (Eco 1989: 239). And so the critique, on the screen, in terms of its direct relationship with reality, should then aspire to initiate an actual solution. With *Deux ou Trois Choses* Godard had found a methodology based on the notion of an intrinsic connection between the minutiae of society (ever-present; the longueurs in coffee bars and shops, the close-ups of coffee and consumer products, etc.) and the mise en scène so that the minutiae of French society had, at times, constituted the mise en scène. In this respect, how could Godard's film not engage with, in a proactive way, changes in society? Gruppo 63's stance was articulated in the manifesto *UNEF Proposes*[5] in relation to the growing discontent on French university campuses ('the radical challenge to the university is inseparable from a challenge to the established authorities' (UNEF National Executive 1968: 109)). The notion of extending this struggle to all areas of society, to all institutions, had also been intrinsic to Godard's political analysis of *Deux ou Trois Choses* and the use of the concept of prostitution as a universal critique – from micro- to macrocosm. Godard's work in 1967 and 1968 is close to the manifesto's call for '[t]he extension of the struggle to all those sectors that disseminate the ruling ideology, that is, the media … the whole artistic sector should join in the battle for the creation of a new type of popular culture' (UNEF National Executive 1968: 110–11). So there is a direct line of progression from critique to action, founded on the evolving methodology of Godard (and those who aspired to make comparable films), and determining the role of the radical film-maker of 1968. This progression and determination occurs along the lines articulated by the Dziga Vertov Group and like-minded militant film-makers, in the paraphrasing of Lenin's question 'What is to be done?'

It is at this stage that the idea of the actual solution begins to falter, caught up in the 1968 sufficiency of the idea of questioning the status quo. So Lenin's question, in *Vent d'Est*, becomes, for the radical film-makers of 1968, rhetorical. Was the asking of that question, or engaging in actions that aspired to articulate such a question, also the end in itself? The answer brings us back to the above-mentioned blind spot, now in terms of whether a revolutionary situation is objectively being approached or has even been achieved. That is, the project of questioning can only be justified if it is assumed that it represents a front in the progress towards the pre-revolutionary situation. A variety of different film responses to 'What is to be done?' exist in the 1966–1968 period, as well as a majority of films that shy away from a direct answer while remaining within the realm of dissent. This latter tendency is possible in a situation of a lack of theoretical rigour and historical analysis, since the revolutionary or dissenting gesture, in itself, could be perceived as 'sufficiently' political, the degrees of its bluntness equated with the measure of its radicalism. The cinéma-militant lacked the nuanced and considered nature of the Czech New Wave – or even the Late Modernist film (the entirety of which could be dismissed as bourgeois from the vantage point of revolutionism).

The third factor intrinsic to the methodology of such a cinéma-militant was that the fight had come to French – or, arguably, international – film culture, not vice versa, when the esteemed Henri Langlois, one of the key figures of MacMahonism, was removed from his position at the Cinémathèque Française in early February 1968. His removal was termed by Pierre Mendès-France as 'un épisode du grand conflit ouvert entre la démocratie et la technocratie administrative' (Houston and Roud 1968: 115). Truffaut, Renoir, Godard, Bresson, Chabrol, Carné, Lelouch, Rivette, Malle, Vadim, Resnais and Barthes (formally associated with the Cinémathèque Française) demanded Langlois's reinstatement, which eventually occurred (for a full history, see Roud (1983: 148–60)). Such government interference became a rallying point for dissent and a dry run for the 'evénéments' of May and June, 1968 (for Roud, May '68 was the 'logical conclusion' of the Langlois protests (Roud 1983: 148); a connection also made by Harvey (Harvey 1980: 15–16), Truffaut in 1982 (Roud 1983: viii) and Bertolucci (Cowie 2004: 200). Truffaut, Godard and others would soon help facilitate the abandonment of the 21st Cannes Film Festival that year. They, and other New Wave film-makers, would be active in the civil disturbances of 1968.

Experientialism and the Revolutionary Consciousness

By 1966, the choice of sexuality as a vehicle for political radicalisation was inevitable, with, firstly, experientialism as the evolved methodology for a subjective communication of the ontological-real; with, secondly, the appearance of a politicised counterculture that was perceived to be intrinsically, even potentially radically, anti-bourgeois; and, thirdly, with the now freer ability, and appetite, to reproduce scenes of sexuality on the screen. The choice of sexuality as a vehicle for political radicalisation was inevitable. Sexuality could be considered to be a locus for the oppression and alienation endemic in capitalist society and so, in the task of liberating individuals from such conditions, there was a potential uniting of the masses – and on less esoteric grounds than considerations of neuroses, commodity fetishism and a leftist theoretical challenge to communism. The manifestation of this sensibility in the 1967 'Summer of Love', bolstered by a tinge of criminality through widespread recreational drug use, suggested that a radical undercurrent of the so-called 'permissive age', a politically unformed revolutionary consciousness, was only waiting to be tapped. Ideally, this would occur in the politicisation of the individualist, 'hippie' wing of the counterculture (for whom 'social change began with the individual freeing herself or himself from the social conditioning that made inequality possible' (Grunenberg 2005: 195)): the revolutionary consciousness, fully formed in the head, to be directed out against the counter-revolutionary institutions and apparatuses of society at large. In practice, since a multitude of 1968 'projects' were in existence, some saw reconstructed individualism as the end point in itself, as achievable via sexual liberation – and any political goal that would arise from this process as hopeless, or inappropriate.

Individualist pioneers of sexual liberation, or revolutionaries of such a spiritual kind, move towards a limited liberalisation – one circumscribed within the parameters of a 'one-issueism'. The argument has been made that 'permissive-ness' was merely a Machiavellian strategy, conjured up and used by those forces of authoritarian societies to exert further control over 'misguided "liberals" lead-ing an innocent public into decadence' (Hall and Critcher et al. 1979: 239). Or that 'free love' was a lesser evil for the state in 1968 than, as Home argues, groups such as the Dutch Provos, Kommune 1, the Motherfuckers, Yippies and White Panthers – to the extent of a state reaction 'greatly over-emphasising the "peace and love" aspect of hippie culture in the media' (Home 1991: 68). Indeed, in most Western European countries at this time, the new age of sexual promiscuity had a juridical facilitation (the legalisation or decriminalisation of abortion and homo-sexuality, the reforms of divorce laws – and the fuller availability of artificial con-traception in the form of 'the pill'). Yet in the climate of the times, permissiveness and illegal drug use, despite the way in which such things may equally be claimed for left-libertarian or straight libertarian[6] causes, came to assume a radical import. In this way, national liberation – even in a Third World context – found a reso-nance, or even an equal, in notions of sexual liberation. There was an ascendancy of, to use Reich's term, 'sexual politics' so that, as the slogan of the time had it: 'I take my desires for reality, for I believe in the reality of my desires' (quoted in Katsiaficas 1987: 101). This suggests a component of Reichian theory and practice (or just radical sexual activity)[7] in tandem with other choice theorists of revolu-tionist praxis: Marx and Lenin, Mao, Marcuse,[8] Laing, Guevara, Aron and Fanon. The emancipatory potential of the politicisation of the European countercul-ture of sexual permissiveness and free drug use was understood to be enormous; insurrectionist 'Bommi' Baumann, for example, outlines the first step through the need to 'integrate dope into praxis too, no more separate shit, but a total unifica-tion around this thing, so that a new person is born out of the struggle . . . This is how many of my buddies around Easter of '68 were in part politicized' (Baumann 1979: 49) and thereafter to recover and convert drug addicts through the therapy of urban terrorist training. Julian Beck, writing in 1966 and 1971, claims an estab-lishment war against hallucinogenics since they engender '[t]he dream – the col-lective dream – the vision of earthly paradise [that] inspires the revolutionary uprising. The Structure tries to obliterate this dream, substituting its own "image of the model life". Cannabis and psychedelics smash such images and stir the col-lective dreams' (Beck 1974: section 79). In such imaginings, a 1968 revolutionary consciousness seems to offer the potential for mass activism – the remade man, and the subsequent overturn of the state via love, rather than napalm.

In such a context, almost any breaking of bourgeois mores (or, indeed, laws) via documentations of or representations of permissiveness 'automatically' rendered film anti-bourgeois – a status confirmed by the legions of moralists, who, while also choosing sexuality as the focus of all that was stagnant in society, counter-attacked any manifestation of permissiveness as socially dangerous. So to even court censorship was to question the system of governance of free expression, to enter into a form of filmic 'confrontationism',[9] transforming a radical gesture into a radical act. The correlation between the fields of sexuality and revolution was not lost to denizens of either persuasion; as a May 1968 slogan had it: 'The more I make revolution, the more I enjoy love' (quoted in Katsiaficas 1987: 10). And, more specifically, this connection could be said to be a utopian response to:

> ... the [New Left]'s theoretical and strategic lacuna ... [derived from] the fatal gap in Marcuse's thought [which] was still the lack of a connection between the existentially derived belief in personally authenticating political action, and the non-repressive civilization that was to be achieved by it. (Young 1977: 345)

The uninhibited expression of 'love' suggested itself as both existential and, in this utopian sense, the basis for (or, indeed, in the founding of communes, the

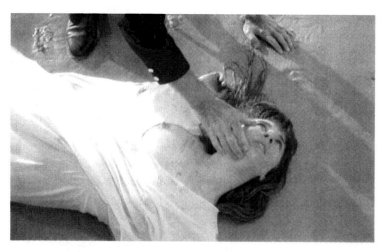

Figure 4.1 Sensual sub(counter)cultures: the free love vampires of a utopian commune in *Le Viol du Vampire* (Rollin, 1967)

making of) a society of the future. Thus many 1968 radicals spent their time and energies forming such societies, as macrocosms of the commune-state to come. This makes for the substantial concern of Varda's *Lions Love* (1968), which documents improvisations around a ménage à trois, which, in the bohemian milieu of California, seems entirely everyday (rather that risqué, in the manner of *Jules et Jim*). Even Jean Rollin, for *Le Viol du Vampire* (1967), seemed more concerned to place his hippie vampires in such a context, rather than as simply genre types. Here, the 'ultimate' stance against bourgeois norms, for better or worse – in the undead, naked and sensuous vampires – finds accommodation within the radical formulation of a free love utopian commune.

Scenes of sexuality rendered experientially made for a mise en scène that was fundamentally anti-bourgeois (rather than just risqué, in terms of content) and for the communication of a countercultural experience to the viewer – the 'tuning in' aspect of countercultural existentialism, the 'surrender' to the wider, collective experience founded on inclusivity. Thus sexuality and experientialism, with its double potential for consciousness-raising, readily came to represent a 'happening' aspect of films of sexual liberation – consciousness-raising via the collective 'giving into strange forces' that, Lachman notes, was intrinsic to the 'mystic sixties' (Lachman 2001: 129).[10] And the notion of such a spectacle of liberation, founded on the repeated violations of the norms of good taste or civilised behaviour on film, finds a precedent in Artaudian theory.[11] Surrealism, which was commonly understood to provoke in the manner of confrontationism, would have offered a lesser revolutionary potential: whereas surrealism threw bourgeois society into sharp relief, Artaudian consciousness-raising seeks to eradicate the traces of bourgeois society from the revolutionary consciousness altogether. (Surrealism, therefore, is well placed within the Late Modernist film – the inexplicable, the overwhelmingly and disturbingly strange, as with Polanski; intimations of all not being what it seems and so forth, as with the end of *La Dolce Vita* or most sequences of *Otto e Mezzo*; and in the way in which Buñuel's work readily found a place in progressive 1960s cinema.)

It is with direct transgressions that radical film makes the transition from critique to intervention, from analysis to act – the refusal to accept the helplessness (that is, ineffectuality or essential and self-defeating uselessness) of the anti-bourgeois critique in the face of bourgeois society. Thus the films could be said to attempt to 'liberate' the viewer through the violation of the norms of bourgeois society in the subjective context of experientialism – 'forcing' the event on the viewer, a situationist strategy.[12] This tendency represented a reading of the use of cinema, rather than just a timely strategy; thus Makavejev could claim:

> From the start I had the idea of using cinema as a zone of liberation, as an ensemble of explosive ideas, images, relations, associations. Then it struck me that we could trigger a chain reaction in the spectator, so that the film could be, not just a film, but a sort of action . . . (quoted in Durgnat 1999: 55, Makavejev's emphasis)

In the East Bloc, in the work of Makavejev, Reich is used as a direct response to Stalinism in *W.R. – Misterije Organizma* (*W.R.: Mysteries of the Organism*, 1971), so as 'to be free of mental Stalinism' in Lebel's words (Lebel 1968: 105). *W. R.* denoted both the subject of the film, Reich, and 'world revolution' (for Durgnat 1999: 51): the suggestion that the anarchic force of the orgasm can be channelled into mass revolutionary uprisings (which was only taken semi-seriously in the film). Here, with the high tide of a Reichian cinema of consciousness-raising, sexuality was posited as offering the potential for mass mental liberation, achieving socialism and communalism as the horizon 'beyond' authoritarianism, as a natural state of being.

However, few films of this era offered such a perspective, let alone actually 'arrived' at such a destination; the above-noted lack of theoretical rigour and historical analysis is nowhere more apparent that in the films of sexual liberation. This seems to be the central tension of Marco Ferreri's *L'Harem* (1967), which may be taken as a critique of the assumed radical import of proponents of free love. The film follows a woman who assembles all her lovers in the same Dubrovnik villa, as if a dramatisation of the 1968 slogan 'It is forbidden to forbid'. But the orgiastic soon gives way to listlessness: the new society suggested here, of free love, as if on the other side of bourgeois morals, does not seem to be enough for anyone concerned, and the characters soon turn on their host. A baby cheetah is seen in the villa, which initially causes alarm to the guests but is revealed to be toothless and so harmless, and so is merely an exotic, and ever-present, ornament. Ferrari seems to suggest, in this visual metaphor, that what was once taken for dangerous (liberated sexuality) is easily tamed and rendered incidental.

In a very general sense, when, for example, a figure as un-radical as Richardson describes *Mademoiselle* (1966) as being about 'sexual awakening and the violence and fantasy erupting from sexual frustration, isolation and loneliness' (Richardson

1993: 168), this could be said to be a Reichian sensibility of revolutionism, or an Artaudian concept of 'cruelty' – and the debate will go little beyond this point. Thus one-issueism begets gesturalism. And bourgeois society needed little time to assimilate the new sexual mores, after a somewhat belated start. So cynicism is not a prerequisite to see a 'cashing in' on this new sensibility, although many films found a middle ground between commercial exploitation and 'revolutionary' gestures concerning sexuality: free love in *Joanna* (Michael Sarne, 1968), *Vampyros Lesbos* (Jesús Franco, 1970), *The Breaking of Bumbo* (Andrew Sinclair, 1970) and *Age of Consent* (Michael Powell, 1969), for example; and hippie ideals of free love and mind-expansion, in *More* and *La Vallée* (Barbet Schroeder, 1969 and 1972 respectively), both positing hallucinogenics as a way of achieving a freer and non-capitalist sensibility.[13] As a commercial tendency, which owed much of its economic viability to the enthusiastic and youthful 1960s audiences of the New Waves, a woolly counterculturalism soon came to colour aspects of the majority of films per se,[14] even those of otherwise staid concerns. In *Women in Love* (Ken Russell, 1969), D.H. Lawrence is reimagined as sympathetic to, or a forerunner of, a 1960s sensibility (free love, nature mysticism, emancipation through revolt, the importance of culture). Richardson's *The Sailor from Gibraltar* (1966) is both literary in a highbrow sense (from a novel by Marguerite Duras; a Graham Greene-esque narrator providing a novelistic VO), and an experiential sexual odyssey, with eroticism forcing the subjective to the fore, as if this is an end in itself. Richardson's Duras adaptation of *Mademoiselle* finds a very limited form of revolutionism in sexual liberation in a more evenly matched way, so as to equate an expression of eroticism with a degree of anti-bourgeois radicalism. As with *Women in Love*, sensuality in *Mademoiselle* is seen to derive from the primal and anarchic forces of nature, which awaken sexual and destructive impulses in the protagonist, a schoolteacher. She spends her time committing anonymous acts of arson in the village and making love in the surrounding countryside. As with *The Sailor from Gibraltar*, the film's heightened sensuality is located in a continual sense of the subjectivity of the mise en scène (denoted with New Wave-type close-up montages of the protagonist's face, lap dissolves from faces to locations and so forth). Thus the very landscapes are 'eroticised', and so while the film is rustic in its setting, that setting turns out to be contemporary in its sensibility (a disjointedness that matches the protagonist's mindset; her contemporary sensibility in a period setting – in fact, the condition Laing often diagnosed). This eroticisation suggests itself as a form of Verfremdungseffekt: the film invites the viewer to both keep it at a distance (the period drama aspects of the film) and to 'give in to' its atmosphere (the eroticised landscapes). Such a film suggests an implicit distrust of the repressive and alienating nature of industrial society (another Lawrencian attribute; it is also present in the adaptation *The Virgin and the Gypsy* (Christopher Miles, 1970)), as does the hippie reimagining of Thomas Hardy in *Far from the Madding Crowd* (Schlesinger, 1967). This connection illustrates the anti-capitalist (in the 1960s literal sense of that term) spin given to Marx's anti-industrialism in relation to alienation, as noted above in relation to the role of Marcuse's writings at this time. These films implicitly rewrite Lawrence's anti-industrial stance as anti-capitalist – the common denominator being free love and free expression as contra the ills of the modern age and contemporary bourgeois society. But these mostly inconsequential manifestations of 'revolutionism' are achieved in the use of the ambience of revolt through expressions of sexual liberation, more often than not in a simple acknowledgement of sexual desires as pushing at the boundaries of bourgeois norms. In this respect, these films represent the intellectualised aspects of that diagnosed by Marcuse as 'repressive tolerance'; and in so doing their unbridled sexuality unbalanced the aesthetic formula of the Late Modernist film so that neurosis is pushed out of the frame in favour of expressions of sexual desire, which, in spite of its Reichian orthodoxy,[15] is an otherwise poor substitute as a lens for examining contemporary society – and with all other aspects essentially remaining the same. The problematic nature of this realignment, skilfully masked by Schlesinger, Richardson and Russell (and with canonical novels to assist in this matter), was apparent in the non-intellectualised film, such as sexploitation genre films of the time, made in earnest (as with Malcolm Leigh's *Legend of the Witches*, 1969), or otherwise (as with Derek Ford's *The Wife Swappers*, 1970), or their mainstream counterparts (such as *Barbarella*), or countercultural films often made in bad faith by industry figures.[16] *La Sua Giornata di Gloria* (Edoardo Bruno, 1969), made on the other side of 1968, is unique in its seemingly ambiguous distrust of free love as a radical agent: the protagonists make love rather than participate in the insurrection they have organised, which is heard (not seen) occurring outside. Such a reading of love and lust as simply a distraction from and sapping of revolutionary energies would come to be articulated in Second Wave feminism; eroticism as merely signifying '*the displacement of other social/affection needs on to genital sex*', as Shulamith Firestone put it in 1970 (Firestone 1988: 140; her italics).

So what of the 'zone of liberation', as predicated from the experiential position accommodated within post-Bazinian realism, once attained? In the literal realisation of 'fucking in the streets' (Caute 1988: 274), as with the love-in sequence of Antonioni's *Zabriskie Point*, the radicalism of this act, outside itself, is less incisive. In the context of the film, perhaps overcome by the existential moment (the feeling of insignificance in the presence of the vast Death Valley scenery in front of them), the protagonists make love. They are then seemingly 'joined' by numerous other couples and triples, all also making love, in the valley. This occurrence remains ambiguous, suggestive of a rendering of subjective impressions on the part of the two protagonists. This moment can be said to be one such filmic happening, and such ambiguity is central to the happening; as Lebel notes 'a deep link between the actual and the hallucinatory, between real and imaginary' (Lebel 1968: 93). The film refuses to disrupt such blurring of the real and the imaginary, while at the same time (unlike the ambiguous orgy scene of *Il Deserto Rosso*) spending considerable time in the sequence.

This love-in is an affirmation of life (in the act of procreation) in the face of the dead landscapes of Death Valley (the ancient rock formations on which the love-in occurs). As a re-reading of the givens of the countercultural scene, and in this respect reminiscent of Antonioni's London of *Blow-Up* (the re-reading of which attracted critical condemnations concerning Antonioni's apparent misunderstanding of the scene he sought to document), it would seem that the couple do not make love because they are free from the constraints of society, liberated of bourgeois mores, as would have been assumed and expected at the time of the film's release. Rather, they make love in the light of a taste of their own mortality – the 'deathscape' of Death Valley, the very anti-eroticism of their surroundings. It is a primitive rather than cerebral act, driven by fear and the desire for comfort, rather than freedom. The camera continually frames bodies against rock, looking on at them, often at distance, even from above, as if observing frantic insect activity; it does not present the close-ups that would communicate the totality of the experience for the people involved, or deliver the frisson of voyeurism typical of the more opportunist films of 1968 permissiveness. This unreal love-in does not illustrate a free-love America but rather indicates the way in which the couple embrace a limited and fleeting sensual world rather than accept their political responsibilities (that is, the un-illusory world, from which they are on the run) and their mortality. Thus the sequence is another retreat into the psychological and fantastical, in the manner of Thomas's acceptance of the vanishing corpse in *Blow-Up* or Giuliana's dream in *Il Deserto Rosso*. In these terms, although it would be fanciful to claim Antonioni is directly interjecting against the given 'sexual solution' to the New Left's 'theoretical and strategic lacuna . . . the lack of a connection between the existentially derived belief in personally authenticating political action, and the non-repressive civilization that was to be achieved by it' (Young 1977: 345), his problematising of radical sexual liberation seems to point to the grounds on which the 'sexual solution' has been made in this regard.

Here, as noted above, Antonioni's experientialism removes from the ontological-real of his key sequences (the Death Valley love-in, the explosive destruction of the desert house at the close of the film) a sense of their actualité. So the question remains, in relation to the narrative of the film: have these events occurred? Even the shooting at a campus protest – the turning-point of the entire narrative (and anticipating a decisive historical moment in the gathering protests among North American students of the time, at Kent State University, just a few months after the film's release) – remains ambiguous. Antonioni thus intensifies his suspension of meaning, now from the outset, so moving towards a cognitive mapping that suggests esoteric readings of the world presented. To be confronted with the film is to experience a flux of questions – how is one to interpret scenes in *Zabriskie Point*? What does the painting/graffiti-ing of the stolen aeroplane 'mean' – assuming this sequence is not pointless – and so forth. The withholding of answers reduces the film to a 'ponderable' artefact, an item for meditation, and one whose parts fluctuate between cliché and profundity. In this way, the experience of *Zabriskie Point* is that of a critical distance from the counterculture: the film seems not so much to 'buy into' the scene but, lacing its profundity with cliché in a disarming manner, to mimic it. The concerns of the film are not those of a sense of 'living history', but the very failures to make history – the unfocused nature of the radical and dissenting will that emerges in the 'dead time' between activism and protests.

So the sights and scenes of the film's setting (North America of 1969) are present and correct – the hippies and their dress sense, the love-in, the psychedelic happening, the campus debates, the civil violence, the police brutality and the generation clash – but now stripped of their standard symbolic meanings. As with *Blow-Up*, Antonioni disconcertingly prevents such voguish imagery and sentiment from determining the structure and narrative of the film itself. The two central spectacles of film (marked by their cathartic nature in the narrative) work in a dialectical relationship that contextualises the revolt of the young in a seemingly demeaning way. These spectacles are the hypnotic montage assembled from Antonioni's seventeen camera set-up of an exploding luxurious desert retreat (extreme slow-motion shots of consumer goods, the detritus of contemporary American civilisation, flying through the air to the accompaniment of Pink Floyd's 'Come in Number 51, Your Time is Up') and the Death Valley love-in, the Zabriskie Point of the film's title (explosive formations of rock, frozen – the slow-motion of millennia rather than minutes). Antonioni's filmic language at this former point also problematises the ontological-real status of the imagery. The house may explode only in Daria's (Daria Halprin) mind's eye; a kind of reversal of 'free indirect subjectivity' where the 'mind' of the character is now the shown object (an expression of explosive or destructive anger or dissent), implying the nature of the unseen material object (the actual desert house).[17] In this context, and with this sequence as the culminating moment of the film (Daria leaves the vision of the exploding house and drives away; Antonioni imposes an end title onto the framed setting sun), the exploding house may be related to the explosive energy of the students during their debate on activism – a sequence that opens the film. The use of Pink Floyd on the soundtrack connects both sequences too. Both indicate an inarticulate anger and destructive inclination towards modern society. These two happenings (Death Valley, codified as the 'love' aspect of youthful revolt; the desert house, codified as the destructive aspect of youthful revolt), suggest that the energy of youth is a natural energy; that what is taken by the authorities (present as well in the film) as violent dissent, anarchic revolt and a shirking of civil responsibilities is, in fact, evolutionary rather than revolutionary, and present in the very landscape of America. Likewise, the high jinks of Jerzy Skolimowski's *Le Départ* (1967), with the carefree protagonists engaging in criminal and hedonistic pastimes, suggests that such abundant energy, and wilful disregard for civil norms, exists already in the metropolitan youth, and needs only to be channelled into political action for the entire city to come to a standstill.

The destruction of the desert house allows Antonioni to have it both ways when it comes to revolutionism; the violent destruction of the symbols of capitalism and, as a hallucination, the will for an overthrow of the capitalist system subsumed into non-violence, inaction and silent protest (in Daria's exit). The latter tendency is a radical refusal to engage in the workings of society, akin to the examples of militant action against conscription taken by U.S. conscientious objectors at the time (such as the public burning of draft cards), and the refusal of work. And experientialism itself allows for the expression of such protest; the passive protagonist who aggressively imagines such acts of destructions. In terms of a cinema of Artaudian spectacle, such spectacle should be able to contain opposing sentiments. And in terms of a 1960s sensibility of revolutionism, Antonioni is able to speak revolutionism and speak of revolutionism. The two meet at the point of the happening, in which the narrative, and its ontological-real, becomes radically ambiguous – a catharsis that is finally attained.

Performance (Donald Cammell and Nicholas Roeg, 1970) embraces such a position of radical ambiguity from the outset (here related to the recreational use of drugs), so that the entire film could be said to be a happening, with the hallucinogenic sensibility giving rise to an experiential narrative. The film utilises a series of 'psychedelic happenings', achieved technically and structurally – cutting across time and space and even into bodies (a tracking shot of a bullet penetrating a brain) and flashbacks that interchange the principal protagonists, whose personas (ruthless gangster on-the-run and burnt-out rock star, the latter initially played by Mick Jagger) then merge. In the first instance, this can be associated with their subjective states of mind, under the influence of drugs,[18] a will to perform (the generic gangster and the generic rock star) and a playful swapping of roles. But, by the close of the film, the exchange of personas seems to be psychically and physically complete (with the gangster's bosses carting off the 'wrong' body when they finally catch up with him). The wider 'happening' aspect of the film locks this ambiguity into its sense of the ontological-real; MacCabe notes that an 'infinity of interpretation is foregrounded' (MacCabe 1998: 78). The beatings inflicted on Chas (James Fox) early on in the film even resemble a happening: stylised, explosive and with liberal streams of red paint (as blood but, in a Brechtian or Godardian manner, implausible blood) splattered across walls. This works to remove *Performance* from the framework of articulating subjective impressions, in the manner of *Repulsion*; the film resists reductive readings founded on hidden, or invisible, subjective vernaculars, and retains a theatricality and presentness that re-enforces the notion of an actual merging of characters.

Working with this contradiction, the film is able to posit connections across the divide in a consciousness-raising manner (and in a manner that suggests a mimicking of the meanderings of a mind under the influence of drugs). The film gestures towards a relatedness between displays of sexual prowess, technological advance and financial acumen (the opening intercutting of sexual activity and an aeroplane and speeding car – that of the gangster's driver), and between a pacifistic 'dropping out' of society with the violent underside of late capitalism (as Chas embraces the psychedelic experience with as much gusto as his job as an underworld thug, and as Turner (Jagger) brings his visionary and artistic sensibility to the workings of the underworld). Thus in terms of the film as a happening, the elliptical editing is not a rearrangement of the 'straight' narrative, in a classic modernist manner; the elliptical editing is the straight narrative.

Despite such a mining of contradictions, and the 'infinity of interpretation' (MacCabe 1998: 78), Wollen notes the key connection in the way in which the film finds the intersection between the counterculture and political action: the very 'blind spot' that is avoided by the vagueness of much revolutionary praxis in this area. This occurs thematically and iconographically, in the way in which the film signals beyond itself by effectively dramatising the notorious police 'bust' of the Rolling Stones.[19] In Wollen's response (Wollen 1995: 22), the film works as a reading of the counterculture, illustrating those elements that will not be tolerated by society, as if an index of confrontationism. Both *Performance* and *Zabriskie Point* seem to require an interdisciplinary sensibility, and a knowledge of key events of 1968, to organise otherwise seemingly inconsequential moments into a narrative of signification (or problematised signification). But the signification reveals – beyond a standard procedure of connecting the personal to the political, of positing liberation in the context of societal repression – little more than previously apparent in otherwise straight dramatisations of such problems, and is certainly no more dramatically richer or more nuanced for the communication via this new vernacular. To acknowledge the way in which the films reconfigure their lessons – experientially, at times wordlessly, and in an attempt to envelope the receptive viewer in an experience of 'total cinema' (so that the cognitive experience itself outweighs any need to adhere to narrative clarity, let alone Aristotelian rules of narrative organisation) – does not detract from the ultimate failure of the films to move into (rather than towards) a zone of liberation. These films of sexual liberation and counterculture, in their very confrontationism and speaking of revolutionism, reproduce the structure of the anti-bourgeois film; the film that defines itself in relation to that which it is not. The very evolution of the structure of the film of sexual liberation, outlined above in relation to Bava and exploitation, suggests a movement within the framework of the changing boundaries of bourgeois expression, allied to the Marcusian 'repressive tolerance'. And, as noted in relation to the conservative impulse of an almost exclusive concentration on the heterosexual libido in this endeavour, these above-mentioned films fail to achieve an absolute radicalism, fail to break certain boundaries. Their radicalism, in the manner of Antonioni of *Blow-Up* and Godard of *Deux ou Trois Choses*, still stems from problematising found reality via form. In this countercultural phase, the process of the problematisation itself – the uncertainty about the whereabouts or veracity of the ontological-real – can be dramatised in a suitably experiential way. And is not the happening simply a way of raising such questions in relation to found reality? As long as form is used for radical expression, the films remain in a position from which they can only comment on found reality for the benefit of the viewer, regardless of the radicalism of their gestures and disruptions of narrative norms in terms of spectacle, happening, ambiguity and so forth; they cannot go further and their potential as action is thus curtailed, circumscribed within a contribution to the bourgeois pastime of debate. Even Wollen's analysis of the emblematic nature of *Performance* boils down to a 'realisation that . . .' (Wollen 1995: 22); the ultimate referent for the films – that element that they need in order to function – remains entirely outside, in the 'real world'. In this way, the radical consciousness, while unavoidably on display, only ever seeks to enhance a critique of – verified by and predicated from – found reality – the very dynamic that has been consistently in place since neo-realism. Post-Bazinian realism has offered no further advance from this staging post. However, a more progressive variant than the examples discussed here is possible within the horizon of post-Bazinian realism. A logical solution to this problem of critique and debate – and the rejection of the lowly position of the film in this respect – and one apt for films of sexual liberation, is a radical redress of content and a realignment of form to content; in the context of Antonioni, and Roeg and Cammell, a de-intellectualisation of form. That is, to bring the 'real world' into the film to the extent that strategies of ontological ambiguity are redundant in the face of a documentation of intrinsically 'actually existing' consciousness-raising happenings. (And, it might be added, no 'expanded cinema' – or the enveloping multimedia environs of the liquid light show – is required to provide a progressive experience for the viewer.)

In the Commune films associated with Otto Muehl,[20] also an exponent of Reich, the question of an ambiguous reality is still raised (the films are performances, performative and ritualised) but is of little consequence: the events are real enough in their cruelty, and performance or ritual only facilitates and organises the situation in which such events can occur. These films of uninhibited sexuality, something almost always associated with 'love' in the wider countercultural context noted above, do not aspire towards utopian gestures but simply reproduce, in an ontological-real fashion, elements of the dystopian. As such they could be termed happenings of a 'collective exorcism', as identified by Lebel

(Lebel 1968: 99), for those involved. The visual motif of the enema is appropriate in this respect – an explosive expulsion of excrement; not Antonioni's explosion as grand visual metaphor for the yearnings of student radicals, but the body as a messy machine of self-purification rather than the perfumed terrain for mutual exploration in the films of and for the permissive society. And the ontological-real, in the recording of the very epitome of un-simulated bodily acts, is mostly reduced – or returned – to a form of straight documentation and not a manipulation of its vernaculars.[21] Thus Vogel describes Muehl's method, in which: 'To Muehl, the only way to exorcise this cruelty is by recreating it in the protected environment of theatrical space, cruelly confronting the spectator not with fraudulent, fictionalized simulations but with the act itself' (Vogel 1974: 251). Here Muehl's method is simply to move towards the showcasing of a decisive moment of reality as it occurs. In this respect, Muehl 'realigns' film form and content into the most direct of relationships; the films represent more than just a utilisation of film as a recording device, since such happenings require a frisson of the real in order to be authentic – to transcend their representational nature and attain a materialism. So real bodily functions and fluids ('the act itself') are encased in a 'real' and un-manipulated mise en scène of post-Bazinian realism. Muehl's mise en scène restores the primacy of content; the camera exists to yield the content, and record the human dynamic in which the event occurs. This realignment undoes Brechtian method, and the 'abstraction' of 'the ideological consciousness' so that (with Brecht, in Althusser's reading) 'the centre [of the world] is always to one side . . . deferred, always in the beyond' (Althusser 1971: 144–45). Here the event itself occurs 'centrally', un-deferred, confronting the viewer with the difficulties arising from the fact of its occurrence. And yet a simple correlation with 'atrocity footage' (more than abundant in the late 1960s, with the freer circulation in the news media of footage of the Vietnam War) is inappropriate; Muehl rejects moral or ethical codifications – no, or no infinitely interchangeable, victims and perpetrators, prisoners and imprisoned. Muehl's radicalism persists as long as the events are deemed 'unacceptable' to bourgeois society and therefore cannot be assimilated as filmic representations, but remain as transgressive acts, as re-perpetrated via their filmic reproduction.[22] And, in their unacceptability, Muehl's films represent sexual liberation of a non-bourgeois kind.

This methodology is found in the Materialaktionen films, such as the *Mama und Papa* cycle of short films (1963–1969) and the *Sodoma* cycle of short films (1968–1970), which can therefore be seen to function as 'cinéma-vérité, or old-fashioned neo-documentary' (Durgnat 1972: 310). Barber notes the film-making, in the case of *Action Stress Test* (1970), as a 'performance-document that follows the sequence of events with the maximum objectivity, closely pursuing and transmitting Brus' action . . . shot anonymously by the cameraman Werner Schulz, in colour with sound recorded directly in the performance space' (Barber 2004: 109). These films shun any sense of recreated reality by playing up their theatrical settings at the outset – bare rooms (with a token amount of furniture), rarely venturing outside such settings, participants openly delivering 'performances' – the audiences of which are sometimes glimpsed at the edges of the screen. But here the theatrical setting is used to showcase the happenings, to witness this instance of 'psychic subversion' (Vogel 1974: 254) of the Commune's activities. Such 'live happenings . . . real and extravagant acts of sexual violence and defilement' (Vogel 1974: 250)[23] automatically deliver an anti-illusionist mise en scène in the aspirations to authenticity. In some instances, such as *Stille Nacht* (H.P. Kochenrath, 1969), *Investment* (Muehl, 1970) and *Manopsychotik: Otto Muehl* (Muehl, Joerg Síegert, 1970), long takes are used to retain the actualité of the act of transgression; the event cannot be assembled through a judicious use of montage. *Manopsychotik: Otto Muehl* shows the audience surrounding the events, with little or no demarcation between an area for audience and performers, and the nominal crew (sound recordists, someone who may be operating lighting, photographers and musicians). Naked cameramen are seen in the midst of the event and at one point a camera itself is used to penetrate, vaginally, one of the performers.

This sense of place and event is even retained in the most frantically cut films, which is the other extreme of Muehl's method. The editing destroys the notion of a sexual 'narrative', creating a flux of non-specific images that function as expressions or snapshots of pansexual and physical occurrences, a digest of innumerable acts that have occurred; the sense of actualité remains – or is even heightened, as the individual moments are ripped out of any narrative or event that might mitigate them. Where, elsewhere, such mitigation begins to suggest the straight tropes of pornography, as in the orgy of *Psychotik-Party* (Muehl, 1970), the use of frantic montage in de-eroticising the events is particularly apparent.

After realigning a methodology of the ontological-real with the unavoidably real, the films attempt to recreate the immediate past in microcosm. The real of Muehl's happenings creates a 'psychic' connection with the real of the histories they signal towards; these cruelties are re-enacted, not enacted for the first time.

Figure 4.2 Bare life: eschewing the conceit of bourgeois psychological realism, the camera now penetrates its subject vaginally. And, shortly after, indigestible happening is allied to the digestive cycle, with defecation marking the film's ending (*Manopsychotik*, Muehl and Siegert, 1970)

So when such happenings raise the inevitable question as to what it is that the participants are being liberated from (that is: what is the nature of the ills that require such graphic exorcisms?), this is prompted by Muehl's materialist rather than gestural engagement with the lineaments of liberation.[24] In rising to this question, Vogel finds a telling similarity between the uninhibited presentation of the unwatchable in Muehl and *Le Sang des Bêtes* (Franju, 1949) (Vogel 1974: 251). Both resonate with a sense of the horrific and immediate past: 'Muehl cannot be understood except as the product of a continent that experienced within half a century two world wars and the crushing trauma of Nazism' (Vogel 1974: 251). Muehl and *Le Sang des Bêtes* also counterpoint their horrors with wildly inappropriate music (a forceful illustration of the uselessness of 'art' in terms of the historical reality of fascism). The Commune films play on notions of victim and oppressor (the nude, defiled bodies recall those documented in *Nuit et Brouillard* (Resnais, 1955)), and they directly utilise the imagery of torture and genocide associated with the Nazi past. *Investment* includes a sinister and non-descript character, dressed in a black overcoat in the manner of a state torturer or chief of police, sporadically wandering past ritualised group sex in a chamber (or is glimpsed through a window, passing by). Whether engaging in the activities or ignoring them he remains nonchalant – these events are nothing out of the ordinary for this envoy of state. And, as with Franju, Muehl's films contain the slaughter of animals, now incorporated into simulations of violence (as in *Stille*

Nacht: a pig's blood and innards cover a writhing, naked woman) or unsimulated sex, with frequent penetrations of the vagina by live or decapitated birds (as in *Manopsychotik: Otto Muehl*).

The ceremonial nature of the happenings even overrides, at times, a sense of their epistemological value. In *Investment*, group sex becomes ritualistic, or as if a rehearsal: the men repeatedly take it in turns to fail to penetrate the female, who then fellates only one male while the others masturbate and urinate. Thus, in a scenario of multiple possibilities, itself created as a form of obscure ceremony, gesture and 'conformity' (the one, heterosexual act between only two people) are 'perversely' re-enacted. Elsewhere, the happenings recall aspects of religious ceremonies – in the case of *Leda and the Swan* (Muehl and Kurt Kren, 1964) and *O Sensibility* (1970) mixing the erotic and the religious (the woman, soaked in blood from the freshly decapitated swan, is then penetrated with the swan's neck). For these reasons, Durgnat is able to see a 'qualif[ication of] the happenings as the creation of a Symbolist reality, equivalent to ecclesiastical ceremony' (Durgnat 1972: 310).

It is possible to find a correlation of praxis between the 'effect' of the surprisingly new and different aspects of *A Bout de Souffle* and the same in, say, the *Scheisskerl* episode of *Sodoma* (co-directed with Hanel Koeck), in the group sex, sadomasochistic practices, enemas and coprophilia, or in *O Sensibility* (a bizarre erotic ballet in the manner of *Swan Lake*) in the bestiality. Both Muehl and early Godard share a sense of actualité as confrontational and attainable in the mise en scène. But whereas, in the nature of *A Bout de Souffle*, confrontation was circumscribed within a notion of film itself, Muehl confronts bourgeois notions of civilised behaviour 'head on', via 'happening'-like occurrences. Muehl's critique is not a MacMahonist equivalent but conceptual, in relation to the nature of the viewer's reaction to the films. Muehl ignores the critique 'at one remove' possible with intertextuality in order to engage with the 'system of order' itself, at the point of contact. All buffers to such a direct access – Gruppo 63-style structuralism (as targeting the microcosmic systems of order), the trance-like happening as filmed by Philippe Garrel (as attaining the 'heightened' vantage point from which society can be observed in a complete fashion) – are 'naively' junked, as if little more than irrelevant distractions. Yet the reaction of the viewer is seemingly one that actively seeks further qualification; that rapidly finds new buffers, so as not to be naked before the events shown. And the conceptual framework that then comes to offer protection is that of revolutionism; these

events, as seen, are the common currency of bourgeois society – the acknowledged unseen-familiar rather than unseen-alien. So it cannot be argued that
the films work in a reformist way (sniping at the unacceptable); they offer a
total critique. Thus Vogel's reaction is one that connects Muehl's work to the
immediate times; the happening as a statement that lays bare the hypocrisy
of imperialist bourgeois society: 'Defecation, as a human activity, must also be
demystified and made public, if the prevailing "order" (which sanctifies violence
and genocide but denies the body and its functions) is to be destroyed' (Vogel
1974: 253). In this 'prevailing "order"' lies the continuation of historical fascism.
And such an approach to this on Muehl's part 'liberates' from bourgeois notions
of, in this instance, monogamy or sanctity of one's own body (through scenes of
self-mutilation or the constant covering of bodies with excrement and food).[25] In
their 'point blank' presentations, Muehl's films seek to eek out, from the viewer's
own bourgeois mores, their individual residual of fascism. The films demand an
account for the nature of the disgust the viewer feels, as in Vogel's reaction. And
the return of form to the presentation of content marks Muehl's radicalism: the
materialisation of the concepts made abstract in the critiques of the Brechtian
New Waves. In this way, Muehl's referent is not the hard 'outside' of found reality
– and the subsequent extension of an invitation to find points of contact for the
viewer, as with *Zabriskie Point* and *Performance*, which seem typically bourgeois in
their 'readings' of the social in the light of Muehl. Rather, the tenor of the events
Muehl renders via a realigned, renewed ontological-real demands – as in Vogel's
reaction – the very abstraction of the hard 'outside' of found reality, to the point
of a 'spirit of history' of the shameful episodes of human behaviour; history as an
ongoing 1968 convulsion, in respect of being a '"festival of the oppressed"' (Hall
and Critcher et al. 1979: 241). So Muehl's zone of liberation does not liberate the
viewer from such shameful episodes, seeking to de-alienate or achieve psychic
wholeness or healing in this age of neurosis. Rather, from the comforts of the
viewer's bourgeois or encroaching bourgeois society (a society shared by Muehl
too), Muehl seeks to 'liberate' the viewer 'towards' such shameful episodes. This
project represents the opposite of the co-opted Reich (the neo-Reichianism of
the libertarian element of a cinema of permissiveness): the breaking of sexual
repression cannot but occur in tandem with a grasping of the horrors of historical
fascism or totalitarianism that imposed such a mass psychology of repression.
And the praxis of this radical project is entirely dependent on the tradition of a
post-Bazinian ontological realism in which the veracity of reality, the actualité of

'the real', can confront the viewer even to the extent of an attempted raising of his or her consciousness.

Artaudian Radical Film

At this point of confrontation to the ends of consciousness-raising, the matter of achieving an act rather than articulating a critique – affect over effect – may be identified as a logical step for the radical film. Such thinking was already in operation in the idea of a Third Cinema as a counter-attack on the hegemonic First and Second (that is, the imperialist) cinemas; thus *La Hora de los Hornos* had been described, by its makers, as 'an act, before being a film: an act of liberation' (quoted in Channan 1983: 3). The expanded critiques apparent from the mid 1960s onwards are qualified by an ever further questioning of the progressive use of critique, even within the same film: its ineffective and unaligned nature, its personal rather than critical quality, its bourgeois-like tendency to yield the removed 'reading' of the found situation, its acquiescence to a limiting confinement within the fictional constructs of the film. And, it must be added, at the point of 1968: the failure of the critique to match the revolution outside the cinema – as one slogan of the time had it: 'Structures do not walk the streets!' (quoted in Žižek 2004: 131). So, within the field of the conceptualisation of film as outlined, and at the crucial point of a seeming pre-revolutionary situation, the onset of a dialectic of praxes is inevitable.

This progression and these questions are to be found in sharp relief in Kluge at this point. *Abschied von Gestern* (*Yesterday Girl*, 1966) with its New Wave freedoms to roam widely, to interrogate faces in close-up, is an Oberhausien, Brechtian dramatised exposé of the lot of an East German immigrant, honing in on the workings and workers of the bureaucracy she encounters, so as to investigate questions of a social nature. This, as a possible direction (and the achievement of the film is such that, in 1966, it is highly suggestive of a New German Cinema to come), is soon abandoned – a methodology supplanted not only by *Rote Sonne* and its import of Godardian intertextuality, but by Kluge himself in his subsequent *Die Artisten in der Zirkuskuppel: Ratlos*. Here the found reality under investigation is removed to make way for a densely allegorical, somewhat fantastical tale (Elsaesser goes one further – the film is a 'fable' with a 'moral' (Elsaesser 1989: 98)), one given over to Artaudian spectacles (indeed, the film is set in the

milieu of the spectacle: a circus), and one that continually undermines the position of the viewer (the sympathies and empathies that the narrative and concerns
of *Abschied von Gestern* had supported are now difficult to place). Kluge's 'moral'
is here readily redirected to the questions of engagement and commitment that
had assumed unspoken answers in *Abschied von Gestern*: the film dramatises the
difficult evolution of praxes of engagement and commitment for the radical artist.

In the films associated with Muehl, a praxis of critique moves towards a praxis
given over to, or towards, 'action'; the films both identify and seek to erode the
same concern: the repressions of bodies. Such a materialisation of the concepts
previously made abstract, in the critiques of the Brechtian New Waves, is clearly
accommodated within the conceptualisation of a post-Bazinian realism. Thus
this startling, albeit logical, step for the radical film is not one that steps out of the
ontology of radical film-making of the 1960s. In fact, this remaining within such
coordinates could be said to be a defining characteristic: when confronted with
the radicalism of the 'formally' radical films of this period – Muehl, the Zanzibar
films,[26] the Dziga-Vertov and Medvedkine groups – one is struck by their failure to break with post-Bazinian realism. *A Bientôt, J'Espère* (Chris Marker, Mario
Marrett, 1967–68), despite its concerns, is straight reportage from 'behind the
scenes' of the strike – and then mostly a straight mix of the public (marches,
addresses) and the private (interviews in workers' homes). *Classe de Lutte* (Le
Groupe Medvedkine de Besançon, 1968) adds a variety of opinions (from interviews, graffitied slogans, as expressed in popular-style songs of revolutionary
intent, and via voice-overs), and extends the critique to an analysis of news cov-
erage and photographs, and addresses, directly, the making of the film itself. This
reflexive gesture, compared to Godard's work (although he himself is credited
among the many directors of film), is limited to the extent that it merely qualifies, rather than disrupts, the film's form; the film opens with a shot of an editing
machine, operated by two women (the film concerns the lot of women in 1968),
beneath verses written on the wall beside it (*'Le cinéma n'est pas une magie – /c'est
une technique, et une science'*).

Thus even *Le Lit de la Vierge* (Garrel, 1969) refuses to countenance supernatu-
ral effects for its miracles (the 'special effects' remain obvious in the way in which
they are executed; that is, as grounded in a familiar reality), and seems to require
a post-Bazinian realism to lend a veracity, and gravitas, to its rituals and happenings. The extreme of stylised and gestural acting in *Marie pour Mémoire* (Garrel,
1967) requires a post-Bazinian realism, so as to encase and 'frame' such goings-on

– rendering the act of filming as that of creating a window for the viewer, to look into the 'actually existing' bohemian-countercultural environment and scrutinise its subjects. Post-Bazinian realism here enables the imagining of radical cinema, by allowing it to circumscribe itself, 'simply', within the limits of realism. And post-Bazinian realism becomes, therefore, the correct vehicle for the communication of such consciousness-raising events; no further precision is necessary. This phenomenon is particular to the convulsion of 1968; when reality itself is overtaken by expressions of a seemingly inexhaustible radicalism (any number of events spring to mind, in addition to those listed by Vogel, above (Vogel 1974: 306)), then an alignment of form to content, where content may simply be drawn from that reality as encountered, is enough. Yoko Ono, revising McLuhan's famous maxim, articulated such thinking: 'the *message* is the medium' (quoted in Wenner 2000: 117, her italics). Time and again, the confrontationism of the Zanzibar films – the high tide of a revolutionary avant-gardism – does not extend to a questioning of the nature of the long takes that are so provocatively used 'against' the viewer. Rather, questions of a consciousness-shifting purchase are understood to flow from these moments of absolute veracity. Simply put, the radicalism of much of Zanzibar seems to reside in a straight documentation of arresting goings-on or objects, presented without contextualisation. To give two examples: the endless shots of the moon in *Vite* (Daniel Pommereulle, 1969; the tactile 'revelation' of the moon forced via these many shots, as suggestive of an existence away from the earth and its failing revolutions, or the given locale of the next commune – now fully removed from state and society), and the strategies used to engender viewer frustration or boredom in *Détruisez-Vous: Le Fusil Silencieux* (Serge Bard, 1968): characters who stare directly at the viewer for long takes (to the point of, for Shafto, 'a veritable call to action' (Shafto 2000: 12)), naked couples who embrace rather than make love, the lengthy blackouts between shots. The Zanzibar films, in such uninterrupted stretches of concentration, are driven to a fetishisation of difference for the radicalism of their images – in *Vite* the unapologetic, obscure hippie rituals, the expansiveness of the uninhabited sub-Sahara desert, the fullness of the unimpeded sunlight, the celestial concerns. And difference here signals the radical consciousness, the revolutionary intelligence behind the structuring of the film, in that the viewer – remaining in the cinema, and as experiencing the film – seeks to tune into such an intelligence, as the focus for a now transcendental cognitive mapping. (Zanzibar, in this respect, and Garrel, as noted below, therefore represent the 'Messianic' quarter of the counterculture

Figure 4.3 Massed technologies of reproduction as failing to satisfy the search for the meaning of cinema: Jackie Raynal in her *Deux Fois* (1969)

of 1968.) So, although Jackie Raynal announces in her Zanzibar film *Deux Fois* (1969) that 'tonight will be the end of meaning', as if targeting the stunted and limited 'meanings' that one expects from conventional films and their conventional narratives, conventions that are roundly rejected in the text of *Deux Fois*, Raynal's meaning itself resides solely in, and creates itself from, a straight Bazinian ontology. Indeed, the stakes are upped considerably in this respect in one of the film's many long takes: 360 degree pans from the middle of a road, with oncoming traffic. With such a seemingly dangerous shot, the very presentness of the real in the frame, and the necessity of absolute interaction between the mise en scène and found reality, remains paramount. Likewise, *Acéphale* (Patrick Deval, 1968) melds intimacy with materiality: the film opens with extended close-ups of a face, a naked body, and amplified heartbeats and breathing.

Therefore the acknowledgement must be made: post-Bazinian realism remains, here, sufficiently radical in itself – its depth and potential matches the revolutionary project, indeed is, for these instances, the revolutionary project. And the question must be raised: how can this be? The answer is to be found in the continuation of Bazin's 'transferred reality' – the reproduction that is also the remnant of Bazin's Shroud of Turin analogy, as discussed above. So the coin of the film aesthetic is, and remains, that of found reality. Now newly realigned and correlated, one speaks to the other, goads it on, intervenes directly – in short, the aesthetic of post-Bazinian realism allows for, in the above-mentioned 'real connection', a crossing into found reality in order to assume the affective role of agent of revolutionary change (rather than court jester, as in the satire of the Czech New Wave, or undercover observer, as in the British New Wave, or exuberant polemicist, as in the French New Wave). This crossing represents a distinctive difference, in intention, from the strategies discussed so far: the critique in radical film seeks to illuminate and lay bare structures and society for the viewer, pace Brecht; the achieving of an act in radical film seeks to step into the moment, and be a decisive element of that moment, in which the viewer takes to 'the streets' for militant-revolutionary purposes. So a methodological qualification must be made: the seeming proposal, in the films, of an intention to achieve an act, is the key that is to be used to unlock these texts. Other approaches, predicated from a 'critique' reading of such films, often fail to respond to the completeness of the texts (as noted in passing below); their selectivity tends to preclude sympathy for these otherwise difficult texts. Therefore, it is with the acknowledgement of the triple esotericism of these texts (firstly, the dynamics of a 'naive' revolutionary intent of yesteryear; secondly, the destabilising lack of theoretical rigour and historical analysis, in the texts, in respect of, thirdly, this action-orientated revolutionism – elements of which are even then often eclipsed by sloganeering, polemicism, or an easy avant-gardism), as enabled in the context of post-Bazinian realism, that a restorative approach can now be taken.

The radicalism of the Muehl films points to the way in which post-Bazinian realism remains the foundation of such a revolutionary project. The critical distance between the subject and the presentation needs to be dissolved, as in the happening. The film-event needs to envelop, not distance, the viewer; to be the occurrence in itself, not just 'as' a reproduction of an occurrence. Were this methodology to stop at this point, however, there would be no need to move beyond the ill-defined radicalism of the neo-Reichian films, or the exposé-critique of Late Modernist film – all of which partially incorporate such an approach. Here the evolved forms of subjectivity were eminently suitable for sexual concerns, for a phenomenological recreation of found and intimate reality, as it is experienced. And it was at this juncture of the world encountered through the subjective frame that political concerns had been formerly discovered too, both in the areas of sexuality and interaction with society – the forms of subjectivity aesthetically rendering experiences to be interpreted as insights into the human condition under societal duress. To now transform such material for interpretation into an act – to 'transmutate' such sentiments into a palpable and galvanising effect – would require not so much a methodology of evolving Verfremdungseffekt (as a making strange of the norms, of language and content), but an expanded Verfremdungseffekt writ large across the very radical methodology itself (as a making strange with the norms, of language and content). The former engenders reflection and critical and emotional distance, the latter prompts a re-evaluation from a position of critical and emotional intimacy. The former circumscribes its estrangement within the proscenium arch of the cinema screen and the begin-ning and end of the film, so revealing the film to be at best merely a reflection of, or indicative of, or a token or embodiment of, the superstructure all around, 'outside' the cinema. The latter 'liberates' the estrangement from the proscenium arch – it is carried not in the faculties of critical inquiry, once outside the cinema (the brain of the filmgoer, as it were), but in the physiological effect it exacts (the eye of the filmgoer). In terms of the bodies of theoretical work that lend them-selves to the conceptualisation of film at this point, the notion of a utilisation of Verfremdungseffekt for Artaudian ends seems apt.[27] Barber's description of Artaudian cinema as a narcotic (Barber 2001: 29) is correct from the position of biological intent: the alteration first of the physical state so as to bring on an alter-ation of the mental state. This affectiveness draws on a tradition better associ-ated with (and instigated by) the Living Theatre than the Berliner Ensemble – the idea of a raised consciousness, arising from and giving succour to, a revolutionary ecstasy or trance. As the 1968 street song 'The Commune's Not Dead' put it: 'We were in ecstasy amongst the cobblestones / Seeing the old world go up in flames' (quoted in Viénet 1992: 139).

In programmatic terms, the Artaudian radical film offers the situationist ges-ture, within an experiential narrative, as its methodology. Many such films exist on the cusp of outright action, as reflected too in the abandonment of contrived (in any sense) film-making for the underground news service of *Ciné-tracts*: snap-shots of the events raging across the country (occupations and protests, police and policing, strikes and street battles), with rousing slogan intertitles (graffitied on walls and roads, and written on blackboards; 'short and cryptic messages which stick in the memory', as Chris Marker described the slogans of 1968 in his 1977 documentary on the events, *A Grin without a Cat*). In reality, most films

Figure 4.4   Film-making from, and for, the front line: reportage and critique on the pre-revolutionary situation in the anonymously directed *Ciné-tracts* of 1968

placed in this category ultimately 'back down' in the face of such aspirations, finding solace in renewed metaphorical critiques, vague gesturalism (one *Ciné-tract* shows the words 'film tract' on a palm, which is then clenched into a fist), the grotesque, the absurd, satire, or dissipate their radicalism into obscurantism. (As aspirant non-bourgeois films, they were obliged to advance a new methodology, a new perspective – each film had to exist as a manifesto for the films to come, an easier task than direct revolutionism.) While there are traces of Artaudianism in films discussed thus far, particularly in the previous section, the films considered in this category are those for which Artaudianism is the main component – even if not carried through to the final degree.

While the films of sexual liberation have been read in terms of the happening (as inclusive and consciousness-raising events), the Artaudian radical film suggests an isolation of the viewer, a forcing of the viewer into a position of prostration before the breaking of bourgeois mores (of film language rather than sexual behaviour). Equally problematic is that the radical political context for these films is clearly not one of limited criticisms, or protest or reform; the methodology indicates an outright rejection of the helplessness of the anti-bourgeois bourgeois film. And the tenor of above-quoted comments from *Vent d'Est* and *La Hora de los Hornos* suggests the kind of result this literal cinéma-militant had in mind. This is the milieu in which, for example, the Soviet invasion of Czechoslovakia was greeted, in France, by 'a small group of ultra-left cinéastes [who] welcome[d] the invasion on the grounds that it would "put an end to the petit-bourgeois films of Miloš Forman"' (Ali and Watkins 1998: 149). Such films seek to exemplify a contagious sensibility of breathless despatches from the near fronts of the ongoing revolution, with the time for measured reflection, or even individual and localised actions (*Nicht Löschbares Feuer* advises workers to disable armament-producing industries by insubordination and stealth theft) as rapidly fading.

Bertolucci's *Partner* embodies such aspirations and their lineage; it shares elements common in both Artaudianism[28] and Godardian Brechtianism, reworking the notion of the happening as a radical event into filmic situationist gestures. And, in relation to Bertolucci's oeuvre, as with Kluge's, this development represents the step into cinéma-militant after the limited scope of *Prima della Rivoluzione* – the step from critique mounted to radical intent. The space for sentiment and the time for reflection that so preoccupied the protagonists of *Prima della Rivoluzione* has now been abandoned; *Partner* is a film made in, or emanating from, a time of crisis – the very opening credit sequence is designed around the colours and pattern of the Vietnamese flag (which itself becomes a recurring motif in the film).

Far from chasing after that quality of 'vulgarité' that Bertolucci found in the ontological-real of Godard's methodology (Bertolucci 1967: 29), *Partner* constantly evacuates such a 'real' from its mise en scène. It is a film of closed spaces, deliberately artificial environments (constructed as if a set on a theatre stage – often literally so), and mostly consists of the schizophrenic monologues of Pierre Clémenti's two Jacobs. Such a direct, and literal, realisation of a 'theatricalized space' (the term Hedling uses to describe elements of *If . . ..* (Hedling 1998: 98)) now becomes an arrested state-of-being of evolved anti-illusionism – a radical form that now no longer defines itself in relation to its breaks with or negations of the conventional (that tendency that represents almost all major aspects of the New Waves up to this point). The film exists 'after' intertextuality, where its status as a film is a given – and acknowledged not so much 'in' but indeed 'as' the mise en scène from the outset. Here the methodological openness to found reality– the radical praxis of only a couple of years before – is disregarded in its entirety, with the concomitant engagement with that found reality as clearly an insufficient end in itself. Thus the mise en scène can only be a literal construction, and so *Partner* shares a preference for enclosed spaces and claustrophobia with *La Chinoise* and *Le Gai Savoir* (1967–1969). The way in which the central charac-ters (the two Jacobs) are unambiguously played by the one actor structures the narrative of the film around a similarly self-conscious fantasticism, also born of anti-illusionism.

The mise en scène demands, and the film cannot progress without, the reten-tion of disbelief. And this strategy in furthered by Bertolucci's utilisation of an anti-ontological film language. Early on in the film Jacob visits Clara's (Stefania Sandrelli) house for a party. As he argues with the servant regarding his invitation, the camera pans away from the doorway in a movement exactly, almost mechani-cally, the reverse of the camera movement that had initially followed Jacob up the steps. The camera stops for a few seconds until Jacob's double arrives, and then follows him up the steps. Such a pre-emptive visual anticipation of the nar-rative development of the film via camera movement (not to mention the visual order necessitated by it) is the antithesis of a sense of an organic response to the fleeting reality all around the camera. Here, reality is arranged to unspool for the camera – not vice versa. It suggests that the film exists for the camera and by the camera, and the world choreographed in relation to the camera's gaze – a step beyond Godard's acknowledgement of the camera 'in' the film (or, in relation to the methodology of *Pierrot le Fou*, 'that of an army advancing through a country and living off the inhabitants' (Godard, Milne and Narboni 1972: 224), the camera located in the found reality filmed, and as filmed). In *Partner* there is no such pre-rogative towards accommodating a sense of immediate reality, manipulated (lit, arranged, re-enacted, framed and so on) for the purposes of the film. In the con-text of the New Waves, Bertolucci's impulses are paradoxical and ontologically perverse or contrarian.

In *La Chinoise*, and particularly *Le Gai Savoir*, this tendency allows for an aspir-ant microscope view of protagonist-specimens: the radical cell, temporarily dragged back inside (from its preferred location: the streets – that is, the locus of militant agitation) is examined as embryonic – the microcosm of the society of 1968 to come. Wollen finds the praxis of *Le Gai Savoir* as one of a "'return to zero", to de-compose and then re-compose images and sounds' (Wollen 1982: 99): an examination, testing and prodding, of the young radicals presented – a progression along the lines first seen in *Masculin-Féminin*. In post-Bazinian terms, this can be aligned with the idea of reality coming to the film (rather than the film apparatus being taken to reality); a stripping bare of the nodes of the real for a forensic inspection. But Bertolucci, in the situationist mode, scuppers such thinking for his 'theatricalised' world. The film is one of meaningless language; sets overrun by books, and dialogues of nonsensical words and sentences. And this resultantly inconsequential rhetoric is taught in the theatre department of the University of Rome by Jacob, and seems to have infected the other lecturers. This suggests a methodological collapse in the representational nature of all mediums of art in the face of the ideological crisis (to which 1968 is seen, it may be inferred, as one response): the inability to communicate, to voice the debate – that is, for these mediums to have become infected with the 'unreality' later diagnosed as an 'evil' in the film.

This tension is personified in the protagonist(s). Jacob (a lecturer in Brechtian theatre, at one point seen spraying spiderwebs over scenery, a literal 'laying bare' of the mechanisms of theatre) meets his double, also called Jacob. This second Jacob is an anarchic political activist who may be read as a reflection of the first Jacob's repressed desire to put his theories into practice, the desire to engage with reality rather than remain stuck in unreality (the realm of the act rather than the realm of the critique; the streets rather than academe). This tension suggests itself as a resonation of the debate over the disputed role of film at this juncture, and organises the film along the lines of such a debate: the quasi-adapted Dostoevsky source provides the material for a Late Modernist-like bleak world view (the anti-bourgeois critique), while Brechtian method here gives rise to a series of radical happenings centred on notions of unreality and theatre; a critical realism of, and towards, aspirant action. The next progressive step, the utilisation of such happenings in the context of reality, ultimately fails to occur; the two Jacobs remain locked in confrontation and the theatrical experiments never move beyond impasse. The use of Artaud in this endeavour is introduced in a scene in which one Jacob reads from Artaud's manifesto, *Le Théâtre et Son Double*, in a declamatory, Brechtian manner while the camera pans about the dark theatre set-like room, illuminated by flashes of light from a lamp. Artaud, and the Jacobs, remain imprisoned inside – their revolution stalling on the theatre, rather than world, stage. (Alternatively, this might be read in relation to the

Artaudian plague; the Brechtian theatrical environment as the incubator for a revolutionary praxis of a higher order – a plague primed for release on the world stage, as with the Living Theatre, with the envisaged militant viewers of the film to come to realise their task in this respect.)

Even when such claustrophobic recreations break out into the 'real' world, Bertolucci attempts to keep this real world at a distance. Jacob's and Clara's bus journey uses Rome, seen through the bus window, as a stand-in for a cinema screen (an experiential sequence 'quoted' in the film – a long take in front of the sitting characters). And Jacob's Brechtian theatre students stumble through the streets of Rome blindfolded as for an exercise – in isolation from the reality suddenly all around them. The final reality spectacle, a continual 360 degree pan across the Rome skyline (that is, the camera movement of the Godardian ontological-real) is accompanied by Jacob's declamatory monologue, seemingly seeking to sublimate this cinéma-vérité moment into the self-conscious fictional constructs of the film; an anti-illusionism assuming authority in the face of the ontological-real:

> *Our subject is life. But if you find that life lacks something, steal a camera and try to give style to life. Do long panoramic shots of life in colour and 'Scope if your views are broad. Make fixed-angle* [i.e., from a stationary, 'locked off' camera] *shots of death in black and white if you like Godard and Straub makes you cry . . .*

This monologue talks of the need to filter reality through the falsifying medium of cinema – and not only through the medium of cinema as exemplified through the visual allusions to Eisenstein, Murnau and Cocteau in the film, but through the cinema of Godard and Straub and Huillet. Earlier in the film, Jacob advises his students:

> *The world is not as we see it, nor as we experience it most of the time, nor as theatre shows it. The world is a prey to evil, that is, unreality. The theatre is one of the roads that leads to reality. In the beginning, things were true. The world in its infancy was real.*

Such sentiments, which self-consciously speak of the methodology of *Partner*, represent a variation of the New Wave use of anti-illusionism: these sentiments

suggest that reality is to be found in, rather than tempered by, the very processes of anti-illusionism. Therefore any fundamental methodological acknowledgement of the existence of a palpable reality via film form is a passing off of
'unreality' as the real thing. As an anti-illusionist strategy in itself, such a sentiment informed *Deux ou Trois Choses* and *Made in USA* in their ontological-real
approaches to stylised unrealities. Now, while 'quoting' an example of film form
derived from such a methodology, the film suggests that reality must be rewrit-
ten via Godardian and Straubian mannerisms – as if their methodologies also
fail to correctly 'place' reality in their films. That is – those very elements that are
highlighted as the non-real, their anti-illusionist qualification of the actual-real
elsewhere in the films, should be reassessed. Two directions are apparent from
this point. Firstly, to then manipulate the non-real in a Brechtian fashion, resulting
in a self-consciously fabricated film form that highlights the artificial nature of
the complete film – a direction that would be fully taken up after the 1968 films
of revolutionism. This first option can be said to represent a break with post-
Bazinian realism – and *Partner* indicates that such a break is 'in the air', not least in
the work of Straub and Huillet. Or, secondly, to then channel the actual-real into
the realm of the non-real, to re-present reality in and with – jarringly – the 'wrong'
film form. This second option, which represents the perception-shifting method
of the happening, seeks to highlight the problematic nature of the real, exposing
the fictional or spectacle nature of a society 'outside' that arises from, and in the
realm of, that real – for situationist effect. (Such a conclusion parallels Debord's
theorising at the time; both Debord and *Partner* implicate a society of spectacle
as the condition of Western late capitalism.) Here, rather than subscribe to post-
Bazinian assumptions that unmediated reality in the mise en scène and anti-
illusionist gestures could effectively 'lay bare' the mechanisms of film-making and
provide a context for a truth content, Bertolucci posits the anti-illusionist film
as a film that mounts an attack on itself in relation to these tendencies. The film
implicitly rejects the assumption that by presenting reality film can be seen to be
of reality – that its relationship to reality can be that direct. Reality is constantly
forcibly 'degraded' in the film; in the theatricality, in the scene in which shots of
buildings are 'crossed out' in red, in extreme stylisation (the rotating shadows of
chandeliers – once again stylisation equated with the highly contrived Ophülian
aesthetic lexicon) and with the use of inaudible dialogue.

Bertolucci takes this point up to the 'moment' of the ontological-real, so as
to illustrate the limitations of the mise en scène. This occurs in the sequence in

which Jacob teaches his students how to make a Molotov cocktail. He lights the fuse and repeats three times that for every five prepared one bomb will work – the question is unavoidable: will this instance be one of the five? As Bertolucci then cuts to another scene, the fuse is effectively 'snubbed out' by this exit. In this way, Jacob's instructions for political theatre (in this context, violent revolution; the theatre lesson is introduced as a 'moral')[29] remain in a state of impossibility on the screen, stuck within the parameters of the fictional mise en scène. Bertolucci must, therefore, stop before 'theory' becomes 'practice'; the bomb cannot detonate, since the explosion would have ended the theory and begun the practice – moved from the revolutionary gesture to the revolutionary act. In the meanwhile, Bertolucci's mise en scène must retain the tension of an unexploded bomb – to imagine film as a potential 'bomb'. To hammer this point home, the Molotov cocktail is then strapped to the camera tripod for a duration as it pans. (And Jacob makes his theatre class restore the desks to the classroom floor before beginning to teach, since he teaches theory, not practice.) These moments are examples of Verfremdungseffekt writ large across the very radical methodology itself; the film is alienated from the New Wave precepts and devices that are also present in the film; it remains critical of them and actively works against them, and finds a Brechtianism, without precedent, in this position.[30] One can surmise that the final act of this process (the launch of the cocktail) is left to the radicalised viewer; Bertolucci refines post-Bazinian realism to a more modest point (a more complete concern with its fictionality over bourgeois concerns with its ontological-real) from which he can recalibrate the relationship between the revolutionary mise en scène and the revolutionary cohort in the audience. Likewise, the black/blank screen of *Détruisez-Vous: Le Fusil Silencieux* seems to prompt the viewer to 'complete' the project of the film; the black/blank screen cannot be read exclusively either as an admission of the failure of the film, or the triumphant last work in negation of cinema with certainty – the onus for the completion of the project of the film (and the film is programmatic in its revolutionary intentions) is left in the lap of the viewer.

Such questions, at base, are timely: how one is to grasp, interpret and master the 'reality' all around – particularly in times of change and crisis? The emblematic use of the Molotov cocktail focuses such questions: how is one to protest, or to intervene in the sociopolitical situation? This is not only a theoretical speculation – it is the question raised in the moment of action, on the barricades, with the lit fuse of the Molotov cocktail burning down (as in the earlier

sequence). Yet the point at which Artaud is called in to revolutionise the practice of Brechtian Verfremdungseffekt in *Partner* cannot but fail. The revolutionary
idea of the breaking of the spectacle of society as a decisive and consciousness-
raising occurrence, growing from the essence of the happening (as the 'marriage
between theory and praxis' (Lebel 1968: 100)), now demands that Rome is theatricalised. The first steps are to be taken in destroying the boundaries between
theatre and audience and opening the environment of the performer, of which
there are several examples in the film (the blindfolded students, Jacob 'performing' as a customer in a cafe and so forth). Then a situationist gesture is proposed:
capturing Rome's electricity supply – gaining the power to make a revolutionary anti-illusionist gesture on a citywide scale – a demonstration of the 'unreality' that oppresses those held by it (a kind of process of, in Lebel's terminology,
'transmutation' (Lebel 1968: 100)). The earlier switching on and off of the lights
(during the reading of Artaud's manifesto) indicates the kind of action that would
be taken. The plan is less sinister than the mythical 'capturing of the water sup-
plies', with a mind to spiking the water with massive infusions of hallucinogenics
– 'the now infamous threat' of 1960s radicals (Stephens 1998: 36); a strategy of
'psychedelic rape', as Doyle terms it (Doyle 2002: 95, note 28). The plan recalls
a slogan of Lotta Continua (a New Left group with whom Pasolini was affiliated;
they collaborated on the 1972 documentary *12 Dicembre*): 'Let us seize the city'
(Katsiaficas 1987: 54).

   Partner is clearly not content to present its revolutionary spectacle as an end
in itself but to retain equivocation. The film attempts to take one step beyond
remaking the world with excessive dissonance: the dialectical processes of the
film remain ongoing (so that the actual remaking is left for action on the streets).
This moment of equivocation is common to the cinéma-militant films that seek
to shift perception, and is therefore characterised by a rejection of any one reading (a frustrating of the desire to make sense of the film – as with *Sedmikrásky*
(*Daisies*, Věra Chytilová, 1966), which, for Eagle therefore, has 'the spirit of a Dada
happening' (Eagle 1991: 233)), while presenting a didactic approach to the revolution to come or upon us. Thus *Détruisez-Vous: Le Fusil Silencieux* ends with a
lengthy lecture on society and revolution from Alain Jouffroy – with the camera
assuming the position of a student at the back of a University of Nanterre lecture theatre (and filmed in April 1968; the campus is largely empty since it had
been closed by the police). It can also be said that the moment is characterised
by a rejection of the one reading – identified earlier in relation to the impasse

– that automatically presents itself: the suspension of meaning arising from an inability to present a sustained reading of the crisis so close at hand. Pasolini and Anderson both broke free of this direction prior to the end point apparent in Antonioni; their suspension of meaning does not preclude – indeed, seems in part to arise from, in an equivocal way familiar to Bertolucci's and Bard's hanging conclusions – an inclusion of the Artaudian revolutionary moment.

Such a moment, in Bertolucci and Bard, can be said to be a tipping point, or the chipping of flints to cause the spark that ignites the action outside the cinema. It is radically ambiguous, a zenith of experientialism, with an Artaudian fervour for change grafted onto a Brechtian response to the systems of organisation that underpin the making of meaning in film. It is often beyond, or after, opening gambits of confrontationism; a delirium-revolutionism of non-bourgeois articulations that dares to go beyond the impasse and imagine a revolutionary cinema. Garrel, in *Le Lit de la Vierge*, for example, conjures up a bohemian-countercultural phenomenology in his latter day mystery play, with a wandering Christ (Clémenti) revisiting the contemporary world and finding poverty, war, devastation and disinterest. The hypnotic pace of the film, the obscure rituals and Cocteau-like dream imagery observed, often from afar via long takes, results in an experientialism that looks towards a 'higher consciousness'. (Conversely, the same effect is achieved in Clémenti's own films, such as *Visa de Censure* (1968): a rapid non-narrative barrage of images, from pop to political, that suggest a countercultural subjectivity, to be imbibed in tandem with the hallucinogenics often present at their informal screenings.) *Le Lit de la Vierge* demands passivity on the part of its viewer, even as the dreadful events unfold (Christ arguably commits suicide as he, finally, 'returns' to nature – walking into the sea). But elsewhere (and most notably in *Week-end* (1968) the moment stumbles – the high note that eventually cracks as the abilities of the singer come under scrutiny. And the nature of the stumbling points to the nature of the conception of 1968 and a revolutionary cinema.

Anderson's *If . . .*, for example, flunks the answer, and this is particularly illuminating, since the film is an exemplary example of the forms and concerns of revolutionism. *If . . .* defies fixed narrative meaning (making for a 'richly suggestive ambiguity' (Taylor 1975: 91)) through a number of provocative devices: the switching between colour and black and white, seemingly at random ('[a] rather unwieldy pastiche of Brecht' (Porton 1999: 211)[31]); equally randomly imposed 'chapters' on the material; the switching between reality and fantasy sequences; a proliferation of surreal images; and a final scene of 'actual' revolution. Thus normality is continually disrupted, problematising narrative meaning – as in one moment of surrealism with the appearance of the supposedly dead school chaplain in a cupboard drawer in the headmaster's study, now alive. For Hedling, this renders the reality, as presented, as questionable (Hedling 1998: 101–2), and for Lambert, 'negotiable' (Lambert 2000: 166).

Since such an approach, on the face of it, erodes the possibilities of engagement and so is vastly at odds with a sense of 'committed' film-making formally associated with Anderson, it would seem reasonable to assume that Anderson initially sought to critique, in an abstract fashion, institutional power. This was true of Anderson's picaresque and anachronistic *The White Bus* (1966), where it is the experience of institutional power comes to the fore, with the protagonist's encounters with the bizarre and absurd manifestations of the civil state. This could be said to be an eminently Brechtian device; any sense of a totality of society is constantly 'off screen' – the lineaments of society only occasionally 'visit' the film, manifesting themselves at one remove (in civil ceremonies, for example). A similar operation is in evidence in Anderson's documentary *Raz, Dwa, Trzy* (*The Singing Lesson*, 1967; directed with Piotr Szulkin). Here the Brechtian form is more literally engaged with, via songs, a stage and audience, theatrical performance 'in rehearsal', as well as the occasional disassociation of sound and image. Anderson loads actualité onto this exposition of the making of theatre while turning the images of Poland in 1967 (the setting of the documentary) into a fantasy. Such a contrarian reversal of forms represents a critical realism familiar from Godard's use of intertextuality and the ontological-real and false[32] and, in the Cold War context of a consideration of 'freedom of expression' (a point of hysterical propaganda in the West), illustrates an absence of state interference in the day-to-day experience of life in Poland. With *If . . .* the desire for a critique of institutional power remains but now Anderson finds an actual example of institutional power at work (in the setting of the film, the school), which also functions as a metaphor for wider institutional power; society in microcosm. In terms of this actual example, Anderson is then obliged to show revolution in answer to 'what is to be done?' – the film ends with the pupils gunning down teachers. But in terms of the wider metaphorical aspirations of the film, this revolution is necessarily countermanded, rendered as 'universal' and sentimental rather than actual – how could it be otherwise, in terms of, at the moment of culmination, addressing a spirit of revolutionism in the context of wider society? So this spirit itself is manifest by rendering the sequences of revolutionism as utopian (fantasy-like and stylised, even intertextual[33] – the culmination of the 'negotiable' realism of the film). Such a calculation gives rise to a situation 'in which superficially militant sentiments are ultimately defused by essentially conservative trepidations' (Porton 1999: 207). When Taylor claims – identifying the reversal of forms also apparent in *Raz, Dwa, Trzy* – that *If . . .* 'works as only cinema can, on the indistinct border between fantasy which has the solidity of tangible experience and reality which seems as remote and elusive as a dream' (Taylor 1975: 91), he outlines the structure co-opted for further 1968 circumnavigation. Revolutionism can be safely confined to the realms of fantasy, as the film primarily illustrates a desire to rebel, or revolutionism as presented as an outgrowth of the satirical element of the film. Anderson only intimates that the scenes of revolution do not belong entirely to the fantastical. This could be said to be the 'acceptable' face of 1968 – one that sublimates revolutionism into radical ambiguity; that relocates class struggle to an ultra-bourgeois milieu while all the time presenting revolutionism as a noble enterprise (even to the extent of locating its emanation to within nascent bourgeois circles). And yet, from that same milieu (this time a wealthy Milanese industrial family) with a similarly radical ambiguity (that of the suspended meaning), and with, effectively, the same reading of rebellion 1968 as an internal matter for the bourgeoisie, Pasolini's *Teorema* achieved the absolutely 'unacceptable' face of 1968.[34] Whereas the problem of the anti-bourgeois bourgeois film has been diagnosed in relation to Chabrol, Pasolini reverses this formulation to equally vexing effect: now the Artaudian language of the anti-bourgeois film form (experientialism, the consciousness-raising happening) is used to criticise the anti-bourgeoisie. Thus *Teorema* both embodies the 'spirit' of 1968 (Schwartz terms the film 'one of the symbols of the European '68' (Schwartz 1992: 517)) and articulates a class-based perspective against it. And this perspective is not via a checklist of concerns for art from the Left, but that of re-identifying the ideological crisis in the light of the failure of the left to identify that crisis. The film therefore 'lands' on the above-mentioned blind spot: radicalism and the radical gesture in relation to the lack of historical analysis, theoretical rigour and an engagement with sociopolitical realities. So the criticism exists within the evolved framework of interjection identified above as a literally critical realism, often taking the sophisticated form of 'a speculative, essayist cinema' (Aranda 1975: 230),[35] and is expressed via a film form of revolutionism located firmly in the bourgeois milieu. Thus in a wider sense *Teorema* anticipates the debates and positions that would occur over education and culture in the Sorbonne and the

Théâtre de l'Odéon in May and June 1968. It is from this position that Pasolini examines sexual liberation in relation to radicalism.

The film deals with the shifts in consciousness (an 'awakening') of individuals in a bourgeois family after encounters, mostly sexual, with a charismatic young man, the Visitor (Terence Stamp). His sudden presence, and effect (the scales that fall from their eyes), speaks of a divine intervention – but his amoralism (the emotional devastation he leaves in his wake) suggests the opposite of a benevolent being. In the world of the film, described by Greene as 'a highly stylised universe that banish[es] any trace of spontaneity, any hint of naturalism' (Greene 1990: 131), the Visitor's presence, and then absence, becomes an ambiguous occurrence that cannot be absorbed within the parameters of the bourgeois family. After the encounters, of a human and sexual communication outside (that is, un-co-opted by) the bourgeois norms (thus, in Pasolini's words, encounters of 'a love without compromise, a love which provokes scandal, which destroys, which alters the bourgeois' idea of themselves' (quoted in Stack 1969: 158)), each character makes a radical gesture that can be seen as analogous to the dissenting positions during the crisis of 1968. (So the 'theory of theories' of the film's title is that the bourgeois family is held together by sexual repression.) In this respect, the film works like the index of dissident positions visited in *Jag är Nyfiken – En Film i Gult (I Am Curious (Yellow)*, Vilgot Sjöman, 1967), as well as introducing a Christ-like figure into the ruptures of the times, seen as rejecting the bourgeois (as Christ had with the Pharisees), as would the Zanzibar films, and *Leo the Last* (John Boorman, 1970). The son, an aspiring artist, shifts into experimentation with anti-illusionist-type creations, with expressions of authenticity and spontaneity over the inauthenticity of bourgeois tastes – paintings that exhibit the nature of their own creation: he urinates on or blindly spills paint onto his canvases, talking of the ambiguous nature of 'signs', defacing the canvases he considers beautiful, refusing to revise mistakes (presumably since this would allow for the implementation of beauty, a bourgeois conception in this context).[36] The mother treads a line between sexual liberation and a will to prostitution, picking up street boys resembling the Visitor at random, before stumbling into a church. The daughter becomes catatonic and is eventually institutionalised. The father asks 'What would happen if I stripped myself of everything?' and does just that: he gives his factory to the workers (a clip, shot as a cinéma-vérité newsreel, as if a *Ciné-tract*, that disconcertingly opens the film) and literally strips in Milan Central Station. The Visitor also awakens or inculcates homosexual feelings in both the son and the father. The Servant returns to her village, performs an inexplicable miraculous cure on a small boy, levitates above a house and is finally partly buried in a crater on the outskirts of a farm. Viano finds in this a gesture of hope for the future (Viano 1993: 206), while Rohdie resists such a reading, noting the apparentness of the cinematic trickery used in creating the miracles – they are 'representationally false' (Rohdie 1995: 160), something Viano finds to be a deliberate strategy of aesthetic naivety. Ambiguity can be read elsewhere too; the son continues to paint, the factory is surrendered without logic or explanation, and the mother's story suggests a breaking free of the repressions that previously held her, or something within her, in check. In this way, Pasolini offers more hope for the project of 1968 than Kluge.

So the encounters with the authentic or divine, in the figure of the Visitor, give rise to a series of contradictory liberations: the negations of anti-bourgeois artistic expressions (the son), nihilistic sexual promiscuity and religion (the mother), sexual 'transgressions' (the father and son; in the context of the times, and particular in bourgeois Italian society, sexual freedom via a preference for sexual marginalisation), dropping out of society and into institutional imprisonment (the daughter), religious reverence and martyrdom (the Servant) and using authority to surrender all authority (the father and his factory). Such ruptures are readily mapped onto the revolutionary endeavours of the soixante-huitards (and suggests the limited nature of radical civil dissent as originating in unavoidable tremors within bourgeois order) – and all ruptures speak of incomplete revolution, of helplessness before (and within) bourgeois society, and are ultimately without hope. Hence for Rumble the film is an 'allegory of disempowerment' (Rumble 1996: 140) – even at this time of seeming empowerment for the dissenters. The same logic is apparent in the trials and 'hunting down' of dissidents in *Punishment Park* (Watkins, 1971) (dissidents are allowed their say before being eliminated) – both as a grim variant of Marcuse's 'repressive tolerance'.[37]

The narrative of the film consists of vignettes that follow the family members. Each member is wrenched out of their malaise and forced into the present through the encounters; their subsequent actions make little sense in terms of a possible or projected 'future' – something jettisoned as the particulars of their bourgeois existence are given up (the factory, heterosexuality, dignity – in the father's stripping, and so forth), and even the compliant lot of the family's servant falls apart. Thus the film is locked firmly into Pasolini's sense of the present and, with regards to their actions, into the futility of 1968; the revolution is not seen to be tenable – cannot exist 'beyond' itself; its methodology offers no perspective for dealing with the immediate future, its praxis has no awareness of the true nature of the present. The vignettes are experiential in style, even to the extent that long stretches lack dialogue altogether. The very use of dialogue becomes part of the experiential – silence reins during the Visitor's stay, but with his absence comes incessant talking, as if an attempt to make sense of or explain the ineffable. Pasolini forces this presentness 'into' the characters, and into the mise en scène; the viewer can only look at the characters as they, like Michel in *A Bout de Souffle*, experience the world as it goes by. Pasolini removes psychological depth – there is no character development, only a series of conditions or afflictions that overcome the protagonists and their fumbling dealings with them. So their alteration of consciousness – their individual crises – occur in the 'here and now'. Other than a moment of jubilation or release associated with the breaking of expectations and bourgeois mores – the unshackling from one form of alienation – the characters are soon confined to the empty and mostly pleasureless gestures that represent the reactions to their crises; the son's art remains gestural, the father's abandonment of the factory meets only with confusion, the mother seemingly derives no pleasure from her brusque sexual encounters, and the maid remains sullen. The liberations, despite the formal optimism arising from their progressive results, are overtaken by a growing sense of a wider ambiguity, so that the film fails to reach a conclusion at the point of a final ambiguity – the 'Artaudian' howl from the naked father on the Mount Etna slopes. Thus the film consciously breaks off at the point of the future (when some kind of further development is required), with the revolutionary happenings as little more than nuances in the 'limbo of increasing despair'.

Mount Etna functions as this limbo, embodying the same ontological ambiguity as the setting of *Il Vangelo Secondo Matteo*. At all points, the film cuts to shots – both brief shots and long pans – of the volcanic slopes; such shots are ambiguous, recurrent and 'mysteriously intercut' (Greene 1990: 133). These shots sometimes function as cutaways, sometimes as new sequences; sometimes as POV shots (that is, following a shot of a character markedly looking); sometimes as, seemingly, associative montage (for example, the juxtaposition of an Etna shot with the clenched fist of the catatonic daughter); as akin to an intertitle, as a punctuating episode between narratives or time lapses; and, finally, as a physical location (particularly with the presence of the naked father on the slopes). The Etna shots remain in a state of inexplicability in terms of the narrative, suggesting

Figure 4.5   Endless discussion but the answer remains absent, stretching from the immediate present (back?) to the atemporal, prehistoric limbo (*Teorema*, Pasolini, 1968)

everything from flashbacks to a sightseeing trip, from an 'inner landscape' to the fantastical psychologised space in which the id can run riot,[38] and as a counterpoint to modern Milan. Greene relates the Etna shots to a Third World aesthetic, a 'zone of prehistory' (Greene 1990: 147) in relation to the sustained reprise of this technique in Pasolini's *Porcile* (*Pigsty*, 1969).

Porcile alternates between two narratives: a *Teorema*-esque caricatured tale of a German industrial family – the son engaging in bestiality with pigs and eventually consumed by them – and a young cannibal, who wanders across a volcanic landscape and, when captured, rebels against attempts to civilise him, with fatal results. *Porcile* reversed the order of *Teorema* in several respects: *Porcile* begins with the prehistory and only occasionally cuts back to the present; the vital young male is now the cannibal, banished to such a zone of prehistory; the children of the bourgeoisie now bemoan their inability to create meaningful revolution – bemoan a feeling of being aware but of being suspended, unable to act; thus they initiate their own 'happening' (or anti-happening) via the deviant act (bestiality) rather than such an event being brought to them.

The analysis offered – indeed, demanded – by these two films stretches across the year 1968 and Pasolini's critique remains formally unswayed by the civil disruptions. The experiential narratives, and the idea of the consciousness-raising 'happening' in *Teorema*, ensure that the films directly 'intervene' in the experience of 1968 rather than exist as interjections about 1968. Thus the film exists more 'in' the situation than 'of' the situation; its form places the viewer in the same position as the protagonists, locked into a sense of the present; its language is that of the radical aesthetic of 1968. The 'crisis in ideology', as identified by Pasolini (quoted in Stack 1969: 157), determines the unsettled nature of the content – the crisis giving rise to a series of questions (on revolutionary action in the face of a perva-sive bourgeoisie) that must be answered before narrative progression, before an ending or narrative closure can occur to a satisfying degree. Such questions are posited at the point of the film's stopping, in the radical ambiguity of *Teorema*'s close, as a direct rupture in experientialism – a halting of life itself in the face of the assumed regrouping of the bourgeoisie. In the narrative of the film, the radical gestures do not disrupt bourgeois society in any final or fatal sense, nor does the religious miracle or the recovery of the factory by the workers. For Pasolini, such pessimism indicates a belief in the continuity of the bourgeoisie over 'local' dis-turbances such as 1968 – while seemingly retaining a belief in the emancipatory nature of action against the bourgeoisie in itself.[39]

Godard's use of 'happening'-like moments, as expressed in terms of an aspir-ant revolutionary film form (indeed, it is the element that here revolutionises film form), suggests a more favourable reading of 1968; more space is afforded to anti-bourgeois occurrences (in the film and in the form). With the absence of rounded characters, or even slight character development, and the investigation of char-acters more typical of Godard, *Week-end* (*Weekend*, completed October 1967 but only released after May 1968) consists almost entirely of spectacular set pieces. And such set pieces are often spectacular in their narrative redundancy (the 360 degree pans around a farmyard as a pianist plays Mozart to baffled and bored workers) and their confrontational form (the extended tracking shots of grid-locked and smashed cars, the lengthy monologues about the Third World), and are exaggerated to the point of the ridiculous (the long opening monologue of *Week-end* describing, when not drowned out by music, almost a parody of sexual acts; the existence eked out by the cannibalistic rural commune at the film's close). *One Plus One* (shot in June and August 1968) offered a problematised 'spectacle' of the Rolling Stones in rehearsal. This provocative act of retaining a concentration on the state of rehearsal throughout (and, even more frustrat-ingly, a rehearsal of an endless re-embarking on the same track), while avoid-ing any substantial encounter with the members of the band – the very apogee of Wollen's Nouvelle Vague 'un-pleasure' (Wollen 1982: 79) in Godard's work – 'culminates' with the anticlimactic absence of a performance of the finished track in the film. As noted above, this absence ensures that no narrative concerning the creation of the track can retrospectively account for these lengthy sequences; they remains open-ended, inconclusive – an action against the viewer. Such moments, spectacular and redundant, suggest a kind of pure Artaudianism in intent in their state-of-assembly of the provocative spectacle (or insights into the making of, or unfinished, spectacle) but barely register the desire for a progressive shift in consciousness. Rather, the death and destruction in *Week-end* – an apocalyptic vision of society collapsing into barbarism – can only be taken to be a savage anti-bourgeois parody, in the manner of the Godard of yesteryear. Any situationist gesture within these sequences merely becomes a further element of satire. How else can the gridlock sequence be read? It cannot be surmised that this is the situation on the outskirts of Paris, nor does the sequence say anything beyond showing the technological facilitation of man's inhumanity, and his seeming ability to accommodate such inhumanity. The long take form works as the ironic comment (in the manner of the 'wrong' ontological approach) on the fantastical content – as in *Made in USA*. Since Godard's Artaudianism occurs without resort to the ontological-real, it becomes a Hitchcock-like exercise in pushing the limits of form. There is no sense of a palpable reality in the film from or with which the conscience can be stimulated.[40] Therefore, Godard's dialogue is no longer just with French, or popular, cinema (the MacMahonist element), or just with the expansion of film form for progressive-artistic Bazinian reasons (the Nouvelle Vague element), but with the viewer: the question of the effect of form, pushed to extremes with this content matter, renders the form as revolutionary in intent. Other matters (the formal concerns of former Godard; the exploration of protagonists and their interactions with the world, the interpellation of ideology and politics, and so forth) are somewhat marginalised with this new dynamic.

Thus *La Chinoise, ou Plutôt à la Chinoise* similarly utilises an Artaud-informed 'realism of spectacle', and also in relation to an equally theatrical/fantastical 'doubling' of the world, and reassigns the spectacle against the student protagonists of the film, the group with whom Godard's sympathies (and indeed the audiences') would formerly have been found. The student 'groupuscule' laboratory of revolutionary debate and expression – the communal flat of a revolutionary cell – resembles agitprop theatre with its garish primary colours and constant 'set dressing' (the graffiti-ing on the walls). It is frequently transformed into an anti-university-like lecture theatre (readings, often loudly declaimed in a Brechtian-manner, from Mao), thus formally establishing a performance and audience within the same space. This full gamut of revolutionism, ever on display in the film, is now undone by the heightened theatricality of the mise en scène, with the flat as at an unnatural remove from the real world in itself, a 'theatricalised space' as with *Partner*, and then – in this privileged space away from the real world – the further remove of the agitprop theatricality. The result suggests the creation of a framework for gestures and posturing on the part of the protagonists rather than a 'real' and revolutionary engagement with the world. Their theatre/spectacle of revolution is merely a theatre/spectacle for – that is, to contain – revolutionism; the playpen pastime for the young middle classes. When, towards the end of the film, Guillaume (Léaud) attends an actual theatrical happening, jarringly outside the claustrophobic confines of the flat, he wanders through demolished houses and piles of rubble (the messy and 'hard' detritus of un-theatricalised space), as if the numb child protagonist of *Germania Anno Zero*, and passes the graffiti 'Théâtre, anneé zero'. This cannot be read but as an ironic comment on the self-sufficiency of the spectacle generated inside the cell/flat; contemporary revolutionism as bred in such a theatrical and unreal environment, as with *Performance*. And yet – unfairly, in relation to this schema – when the students attempt to engage with the real world, in another such foray into reality (this time for a political assassination; the least gestural of all revolutionary activities – for the would-be assassins, at least), the film itself immediately and consciously 'falls foul' of an awareness of its limitations. As with Bertolucci's un-detonating Molotov cocktail, Godard's loaded gun cannot 'really' be fired by the students – their revolutionism necessarily, and organically, remains gestural rather than actual. And so slapstick (as high unreality) now rapidly overwhelms the momentary realism of the sequence: the number of the victim's room is mistaken and the wrong person shot as the whole sequence degenerates into broad physical comedy.

Figure 4.6 Crosshaired cinema: the camera as bomb, and student radicals, in Bertolucci's *Partner* (1968)

These revolutionaries aspire to radical action but, like the film itself, have no certain mechanism for dealing with or moulding (rather than simply reflecting) reality. Earlier on, Guillaume recounts with approval a political action by a Chinese student who had unwrapped the bandages that covered his head in front of journalists ('Look what these revisionist swine did to me!'): his face was un-bruised and so that action, for Guillaume, was 'something like Brecht or even Shakespeare'. Here the 'high' approved praxis of gesturalism is discussed, finally, in relation to theatre practitioners, looping back on itself. And further proof of the futility of their revolutionism is provided by the disaffected commune member – termed a revisionist by the others – who notes the insignificant amount of money the French government spends in relation to terrorism; proof that terrorism in itself is of little consequence to the bourgeois state. Likewise, via pop art-style montages, Godard renders the cell members' 'politics' as personality-driven, as in the realm of the comic book, and as superficial and newly fashionable (as are the members themselves: attractive, constantly smoking, dressed in the correct attire, renouncing their bourgeois families, permanently leaving to attend protest marches and planning to shut down the 'puppet universities'; the actors who portray them iconographically convey various caches of revolutionary/avant-garde cultural strains). The look of the film is one drawn from its era, utilised to 'make revolution glamorous, a pop event' (Dixon 1997: 83). Likewise, the inter-views – 'dialogues' – much like those in *Masculin-Féminin* (but here with an added anti-illusionism: the camera is seen in reverse angle shots) – concentrate on the biographies of the protagonists. The film concerns itself with revolutionaries over revolution – as if a tract against the errors of bourgeois individualism.

Despite this the film was generally misread and then condemned accordingly – along with those who misread it; for example, Régis Debray: 'In France, the Columbuses of political modernity thought that [in] following Godard's *La Chinoise* they were discovering China in Paris, when in fact they were landing in California' (quoted in Jameson 1984: 189). Thus the film has become emblematic of all that was perceived to be wrong-headed about '68 revolutionaries – perhaps in the context of its seminal, or anticipatory, status in relation to the events of 1968, as noted in relation to Rosenbaum's comments (Rosenbaum 2000: 32–33). To paraphrase Debray's thoughts elsewhere, the film was not a revolution in the revolution, but a revolution in and against the revolution. So without first acknowledging the precision of the resultant 'qualification' of the subject matter now provided by Godard's theatrical/fantastical mise en scène, and the alteration of the expected meanings that arise from the narrative's concerns, the film becomes difficult in the extreme; Morrey, for example, feels obliged to note any number of possible readings of Godard of this period (see Morrey 2005: 76–79).

In this respect, Godard's reading of student militant action was as unfashionable as Pasolini's. But Godard also errs towards the equivocal rather than the condemnatory, aligning his film form with the radicalism of the proclamations within the films, as illustrative equivalents of the idea of insufficient radicalism – and then following both through to discover that neither is able to deliver on their promises, proving this point. To put it another way, the films cannot just be tracts against the errors of bourgeois individualism when they spend so much time with their bourgeois individuals. As a film of a seemingly pre-revolutionary situation, *La Chinoise* suggests a methodological remnant of critical realism – that the 'acts' contained in the film are open to self-criticism, implying that there is a dialectical hope for a better understanding and adjustment on the part of would-be revolutionaries, a 'primer' for the tests to come. How else could this 'catalogue of errors' otherwise be read? And, unlike *If . . .*, the film accepts the existence of a real will to actual, militant rebellion. *Week-end* illustrates rather than explains the nature of the bourgeoisie; with such exposé over analysis, the proletariat would be galvanised into action. And the major themes of *Week-end*, violence and destruction, criminality and barbarism, are the same charges levelled against those engaged in civil unrest in 1968 – but here they are placed firmly within the sphere of the bourgeoisie; such ills are the preferences of bourgeois society. Thus the film pre-emptively 'lobs back' the slanderous charges to come. Likewise, the charges made against the bourgeoisie by discontents – out of touch, isolated, self-important and narcissistic, failing to comprehend the implications of their actions – are first seen in the revolutionaries of *La Chinoise*. Under the microscope of his non-bourgeois film form, Godard thus finds a revolutionary perspective as hobbled by the continuation of tropes from, and of, the oblique presence of the bourgeoisie. In this penultimate 1960s stage of the reimagining of film, in film, as a flux of anti-illusionist gestures, Godard denotes an awareness of the chasm between gesture and act. Godard's militants remain blind to the chasm – and through the avoidance of such an awareness the revolutionary cell turns into an otherworldly sect. The would-be militants and revolutionaries are not able to move from gesture to act, or indeed to distinguish between the two in their rarefied environment. This is finally apparent in the irony of the title, *La Chinoise*, and in the way in which their weapons are literally harmless toys. The suggested reading of this revolutionary stratum of students is one of infantilism. In their squabbling the students fail to see the limitations of their actions. Bellocchio, for the squabbles of his revolutionary cell of *La Cina è Vicina* (*China is Near*, 1967), divided between Catholicism, socialism and Maoism, finds a different context; he maps the interpersonal tensions straight onto an extended family. Political ideals seem to be symptoms of mental instability, or are subsumed by sexual tensions, and terrorist activity descends into farce. Likewise, the revolutionary intellectuals of Bellocchio and Tattoli's contribution to *La Contestation* (1967, 1970), the section 'Discutiamo, Discutiamo' (Let's Talk, Let's Talk), seem engaged in playacting. Their bickering remains confined to a lecture theatre – cut off from any interaction with the world outside. For Godard and Bellocchio, the idea of 'China' carries two doses of irony – both the distance of these neophytes from their political destination, and the closeness of their behaviour to a 'Chinese' political reality (the intrigues and factionalism of internal power struggles).

However, their radical will and revolutionary motivation – and Godard's, as expressed in the film – are real enough. The cell members name class stratification, living and working conditions and the Algerian situation as reasons for revolt. Godard outlines this context, in voice-over, at the beginning of the film:

> On the one hand the French working class will not achieve political unity nor stand on the barricades to obtain a 12 per cent rise in wages[;] there will not be in the foreseeable future a crisis so dramatic for European capitalism that the mass of workers in order to defend their vital interests will pass to a revolutionary general strike or armed insurrection . . . on the other hand the bourgeoisie will never give up power without fighting and without being forced to by the revolutionary action of the masses. Thus the principal problem of a socialist strategy is, henceforth, to create the subjective and objective conditions from which a showdown with the bourgeoisie can be entered into and won. (As quoted in MacCabe, Eaton and Mulvey 1980: 54–55)

The latter sentiment identifies the need for the application of a revolutionary sensibility to all aspects of contemporary life. But the following year, with the infantile gesture sudden overtaken by the actual manifestation of this revolutionary sensibility (and not necessarily in the way Godard envisages in the above monologue), the essential problem seems to have remained. It is in relation to this precise moment that Pasolini finds fault in the real-life counterparts of Godard's and

Bellocchio's 'Chinese'. And this now throws the lesser-revolutionary excursions of radical consciousness into a sharp relief; subjectivity is all too readily occupied by individualist-hedonist-predicated attempts to unshackle oneself, biopolitically and economically, from the state and its mores. This makes for an 'ideological deficit', as it were, in the burgeoning revolutionary subjectivity; psychedelia over Marx, marijuana over Lenin. At this point, criticisms made by Godard, Pasolini and Bellocchio become entirely constructive – the attempts to halt or stave off the dissipation of revolutionary will. And the precision of this type of criticism resides in the 'altered' film form: the doubling of the world – a new world of illusionism, fantasy, interpersonal tensions (of the Milanese family of *Teorema*, of the flat-cell of *La Chinoise*, of the theatre of *Partner*, even of the school of *If . . .* and the bohemian pad of *Performance*) that necessarily rejects the ontological-real in, and for, its expression. The post-Bazinian real remains, by default, the method of the articulation of the 'truth' – outside these environs, on the streets, in an ethnographic and reportage sense.

Therefore, until the moment of the shift from pre- to actual revolutionary situation occurs, the warnings of the endemic plague of fantasies – to paraphrase Žižek – must remain, grounded aesthetically in the routing of the ontological-real of post-Bazinian realism. This may not have been a conscious praxis or intended didactic strain on the part of the practitioners – aspersions have already been cast, above, on Anderson's revolutionary perspective, and Bellocchio, as well as Pasolini, would have won few friends among student radicals at the time – but the tendency towards stylisation at the end of the New Wave points to a dawning awareness. In this formation, film – in its halting journey from a site of cultural resistance to resistance itself – stops, with the promised land in sight, and begins to implicate itself; a deliberate degeneration that seems better able to accommodate equivocation over the project of 1968.

Thus for *Week-end* (for which filming began five months after the release of *La Chinoise*), which deals explicitly and entirely with revolutionary-like civil and social upheavals, Godard returns completely to the world of the bourgeoisie via a grotesque tableau vivant, now anything but oblique, and drawing on Brecht via Grosz for bourgeois types, as with *Porcile*. In the expansive horizon of *Week-end*, seemingly a fleeing from the hothouse claustrophobia of *La Chinoise*, the former abstractions of the everyday (of the notion of prostitution in *Deux ou Trois Choses*, for example) become the ferocious manifestations of a sustained macro-system – and to the nth degree. Hence, as MacBean finds in *Week-end*, the

> . . . *juxtaposition of the bourgeois ritual of consumption with the hippie ritual of consumption* [that is, cannibalism, which] *points to a dead-end in which the only movement is in vicious circles of endless exploitation and destruction. The hippies feed off the bourgeoisie and the bourgeoisie nourishes within itself future hippies. . . Moreover, the hippie way of life ironically seems to attract the most blatantly fascist of the young bourgeoisie, as is illustrated in the fact that the mod girl . . . who invokes class priorities, and who indignantly berates and despises the peasants early in the film, eventually turns up as a member of the hippie band engaged in guerrilla warfare against the bourgeoisie.* (MacBean 1975: 52)

As in *La Chinoise*, Godard's polemical position still maintains that civil revolution and militant action is useless where it is still tolerated by, and assimilated into, bourgeois society; one could add the term 'hippie bourgeoisie' to the lexicon that includes 'red bourgeoisie'. Unlike Pasolini, Godard reaches this sentiment from the position of, in this film, an anti-bourgeois statement – the provocation, in the manner of creating the 'subjective . . . conditions from which a showdown with the bourgeoisie can be entered into', which structures *Week-end* in its entirety – with Grosz-like portraiture lodged within Godard's 'happening'-like spectacles, taking the place of the 'critical' position once occupied by the postmodern unreality of Godard's contemporary Paris. This accounts for the gusto and vitality of the film; the bourgeoisie presents endless fodder for caricature while the more overtly Brechtian films tend to pick over one or two aspects of bourgeois existence. *Week-end*'s happenings concern bourgeois sexuality, pastimes (the mass mobilisation of Parisians in search of a rural weekend break) and culture (the irrelevance of the Mozart, here performed for farmyard animals). In its scope and its concentration on the bourgeoisie, together with its refusal to follow through any one theme or vignette, *Week-end* represents the sewer rather than the sewage. The lineaments of bourgeois existence are to be discerned, and viewed with distaste.

Week-end's strategies of confrontation are drawn from an expanded and one-note expression of Verfremdungseffekt – the desire to revolt and frustrate the viewer. At all points Godard spoils or negates the elements of aesthetic beauty within the film; the colours are harsh and overbearing and the sound cacophonous. The film continually courts boredom as its narrative foundation (specifically, in the Mozart scenes, the seven minute gridlock scene and the rubbish collectors' monologues). This suggests a degree of difference from the Zanzibar films, where boredom is a narrative device and remains a rewarding experience, and one conceptually necessary for the films. Godard maintains a narrative, of sorts, but one frequently extended to the point of tedium, and often 'just' for the sake of tedium.

Such a confrontational approach is apparent from the outset of *Week-end* when an undressed Corinne (Mireille Darc) describes, at length, a ménage á trois. Godard backlights the scene, presenting almost a silhouette of the actress. This represents a double negation since the viewer sees neither the orgy Corinne is describing in laborious detail, nor this notable model of the day in her underwear. In this way, the dialogue, for lack of any visual interest, becomes the principal aspect of the mise en scène. And yet the music (itself a sort of pastiche of portentous Antonioni-esque scores) swells up over the dialogue from time to time, rendering Corinne's words inaudible – and usually at the most climactic points of her narration. Similarly, later in the film, with Corinne's breasts only just obscured by bath bubbles, Godard places an archaic painting of a female nude above the bath tub as a poor compensation for the viewer. The frustration that Godard elicits springs from the usual listless acceptance of naturalism (unity of sound

Figure 4.7   In deflecting the voyeuristic gaze, Godard substitutes aesthetics for aestheticism in his exposé of the bourgeoisie in private. *Week-end* (1968)

and image, clarity of image) as, here demonstrated, the vehicle for the voyeuristic expectations of bourgeois cinema. The film suggests its (i.e., the film's) shame-less 'bourgeois' double: Darc, as fully visible, talking luridly and animatedly, and with 'arty' music mixed correctly into the background so as not to break a unity of sound and image, and offset any perceived exploitation with high art gestures. Such an invited counterfactual reimagining of the film brings Bergman instantly to mind – particularly in relation to just such a scene in *Persona* (an attractive woman talking at length about sexual encounters). Godard's indicated bourgeois double results in the film of the aforementioned ideological deficit: the radical consciousness that titillates rather than galvanises.

Once out of Corinne's apartment, the narrative is picaresque, but with little or no plot development; all vignettes seem without purpose or reverberation, with characters picked up and dropped at a whim. Godard refuses sympathetic fram-ing, predominantly remaining at a distance with long shots. The image is flattened, which is achieved by the eradication of depth-of-field cinematography (not using depth-of-field lenses or placing characters against walls, so preventing depth of field); Henderson finds this to be a technique 'Towards a Non-Bourgeois Camera Style' (in his 1970–71 *Film Quarterly* article):

> . . . [such a] *reversion to a cinema of one plane is a demystification, an assault on the bourgeois world-view and self-image . . . That space in which the viewer could lose himself, make distinctions and alliances, comparisons and judge-ments, has been abrogated – the viewer is presented with a single flat pic-ture of the world that he must examine, criticise, accept or reject . . . infinitely thin, absolutely flat bourgeois substance that cannot be elaborated but only surveyed.* (Henderson 1976a: 424)

In and with this flux of negations comes the eradication of the sense of an infinite experience of the world that underpins Bazinian ontology.

Godard offers no diegetic intervention or formal comment on the events of the film to temper these strategies, as identified by Henderson; the commentary that has been a constant in all his films, from Michel of *A Bout de Souffle* onwards, is now absent. Such a confrontation demands that the viewer recoils from the grotesque world presented. The film exists, therefore, as a radical happening: a spontaneous statement that confronts and destroys preconceived bourgeois ideas, and undermines certainties. Such sentiments are suited to the Artaudian presentation – which allows for a frisson of revelling in the disgust – but in this form, as merely a vehicle for the verification of the level of hatred towards its subject, the film avoids political sophistication. Its constructive criticism, as the revolution in and against the revolution, becomes easily co-opted. Most problematically, therefore, the portrait of the alternatives that emerge (even accepting a 1968 Dada-esque context of, as one slogan had it, 'I have something to say, but I don't know what' (quoted in Priaulx and Ungar 1969: 153)) chimes exactly with de Gaulle's slanders (of a June 1968 televised speech): 'This explosion was provoked by groups in revolt against modern consumer and technical society . . . groups, moreover, which have no idea at all of what they would replace it with, but who delight in negation, destruction, violence, anarchy, and who brandish the black flag!' (quoted in Viénet 1992: 95). To return to the opening statement of *La Chinoise*, as a 'socialist strategy', *Week-end* may work towards provocatively 'creat[ing] the subjective and objective conditions from which a showdown with the bourgeoisie can be entered into', and in this sense 'recovers' and normalises barbarian practices such as violence and rape for its portrait of society,[41] but there is little about victory in relation to such a showdown. In the final analysis, *Week-end* is a product of the vacuum of theoretical rigour and historical analysis.

Critiques of 1968

Despite the lack of an ideological perspective beyond the grotesque carnivals that Godard presents in his revolutionary films – or, indeed, because of such a lack – their radical reformism and confrontationism implicitly suggests hope. Godard indulged the revolutionary gestures, in his characters and in his methodology (in *Week-end*), that Pasolini denied or derided. The very juxtaposition of the two sets of 'rehearsals' in *One Plus One* (the literal rehearsal of the Rolling Stones and the revolutionary 'rehearsal' of the agitprop sections; the black militant cell and its weaponry, the political graffiti and so on), for example, suggests the 'actual event' is only waiting to occur. The lesson of the film is that the viewer is in the position to bring together both rehearsals, the one plus one of the cultural and the political, in and through the undertaking of the revolutionary act; the films seek to galvanise and prime the proletariat. So, despite Godard's satirical bent, the idea of a use of revolutionary action remains – in fact, it remains the only reasonable course of action in the midst of the contemporary France that he presents. The joylessness of the films (the functional couplings of *Week-end*, the puritanism of the youth in *La Chinoise*, the lack of the completed song in *One Plus One*) closes off any sense of decadence, diminishing revolutionary jouissance; the world denies even jaded pleasures. Thus Godard's apocalyptic vision of con-temporary society was of the 'late capitalism' phase (or model) – the grounds on which revolutionary action is possible. Such a sensibility, in relation to 1968, is even identified, as 'apocalypticism', by Hewison (Hewison 1986: 145) – a fin de siècle degeneration; a noting of the end of old times, not the origins of new times; the crumbling of the old empire, not the consolidation of the new empire. Here the inevitable socio-economic collapse is visible; the seeds of capitalism's destruction have long since sprouted. Silverman and Farocki find this to be true of *Week-end* itself, as a self-identifying artefact of this phase, through Godard's use of intertitles such as 'A Film Adrift in the Cosmos' and 'A Film Found on a Scrap Heap'; (Silverman and Farocki 1998: 84). The film is announced as a con-sumable product of a society in the process of falling apart, of a society over-whelmed by its own refuse.[42] For this reason, refuse and revolution are the 'end points' of Godard's films at this stage. Despite the formal innovations of *Week-end* and *One Plus One*, the films ultimately offer a critique of late capitalism akin to that offered by the Late Modernist film: presenting that which Lukács found in Rosa Luxemburg: 'In her work we see how the last flowering of capitalism is transformed into a ghastly dance of death' (quoted in Geras 1973: 17).

Ironically, such articulations – or such a reading, which 'recovers' these films – then arises from the very films that favour intervention over analysis; action over thought. The revolutionary moment that stumbles, as noted above, articulates not only the failings of the revolutionary imagination, but catches a glimpse of its own reflection in the process: self-critique, even self-implication. Such doubts, as voiced accidentally or otherwise, jostle with the Molotov moments of the militant cinema of 1968. And the non-accidental voicing of such a critique represents a tonic for the 'ultra-', 'far-' revolutionary or militant left: the scrutiny of a false, contested or impossible revolution.

Pasolini's films of this period decline the level of hope found in Godard. Thus even the most strident political action in *Teorema* is seemingly pointless (the father giving the factory to the workers; met with bafflement),[43] and even the most strident example of personal rebellion in *Porcile* (cannibalism) fails to ward off the world of the bourgeoisie (that is, the processes of civilisation). The lesson of these films concerns the failure of such revolts against the bourgeoisie, and so questions the nature of the leftist radicalism undertaken in vain (hence for Pasolini '[t]he point of [*Teorema*] is roughly this: a member of the bourgeoisie, whatever he does, is always wrong' (quoted in Stack 1969: 157)). Pasolini's would-be revolutionaries are doomed from the outset, and it is on this presumption that the critiques are formed. The pre-'evénéments' *Teorema* denies revolutionary hope and this denial is reprised, re-enforced even, in the post-'evénéments' *Porcile*, in the way in which the contemporary half of the film is set in 1967. Pasolini presents the young revolutionaries prior to their day on the streets of Paris and so anachronistically forces the focus onto (or, rather, returns the focus to) those initial debates about militant action, in an abstract, anticipatory way. The year 1968 is thus bracketed by these two films, and rendered as little or nothing more than an internal battle within the bourgeoisie.

Porcile is emphatic in the way in which it reasserts the predominance of the bourgeoisie through a dense allegorical approach to the internal battle. And, as with Godard, cinema itself is called to the dock as a facet of both the revolutionary milieu of the time and as a willing or unwilling apparatus of state. Those personal and societal revolutions that are tolerated by society, in Pasolini's vision of the times, are to be found in the revolutionary cinema too. Such an interjection is communicated in an intertextual fashion via the iconographic cast of the film: Léaud (a regular of Truffaut's), Italian film-maker Marco Ferreri, Clémenti (the sullen young man in *Belle de Jour*, avant-garde auteur, Zanzibar's Christ and Bertolucci's Jacobs) and Godard's then partner Anne Wiazemsky. In addition, Purdon notes the characters' names (and performances) as Brechtian (Willemen 1977: 52) and in this the critique could be said to extend to the Brechtian aspect of New Wave film-making. Pasolini presents New Wave images, appropriately populated with New Wave personnel, but now stripped of their original sentiments.

The contemporary protagonist of *Porcile*, Julian (Léaud) is unable to engage in revolutionary action, since he is unable to resolve his feelings towards his industrialist father – that is, his revolutionism is held back as it is in hock, in a familial sense, to the bourgeoisie. He can only assault or debase himself, since he recognises within himself the bourgeois element that he detests – as if a missing character from the Milanese family of *Teorema*. He is consumed, literally, in this moment of self-criticism (eaten by the pigs that he sexually desires), while his father enters into a pact with a rival industrialist, prompted by threatened blackmail over the scandals surrounding his son's wayward behaviour. As the son flounders over his own 'perversion' (so that the bestiality might also be viewed as

a metaphor for his alienation – a desire to run away from his own race, the bourgeoisie, and associate with the swine instead), neo-capitalism asserts its dominance by renewing an acquaintance with its fascist roots. The rival industrialist is
a grotesque caricature and the ambience is that of Visconti's *The Damned* (1969):
the Germanic military-industrial pact of the Right, and great powers behind
closed doors. For Greene (1990), the setting, Godesberg, links the two 'fascisms'
– historically, of Nazism (this was the location from which Hitler delivered an
ultimatum on Czechoslovakia), and of the contemporary (Godesberg is a tourist
town favoured by West German businessmen).

In the non-contemporary half of the film (the pre-history narrative), which is
intercut with the contemporary narrative, a young cannibal (Clémenti) is lured
into a trap by the pre-industrial representatives of capitalism (the army and the
church) and, when he refuses to repent his ways, is fed to wild dogs. The cannibal
mouths a revolutionary sentiment, 'I killed my father, I ate human flesh, and I
quiver with joy' during this process (thus equating civilisation with Oedipal suppression; a timely blending of Marx and Freud). Such consumption readily represents the dramatisation of the idea of assimilation and 1968 – the 'consumption'
of the dissidents by bourgeois society, of which the post-1968 'march through the
institutions' was also a part. And, in the cannibal's fate, is the brutal elimination of
truly revolutionary anti-bourgeois elements (the killing of the father, the sense of
jouissance from 'unacceptable' acts – the eating of human flesh in this instance).

The juxtaposed narratives, as with *One Plus One*, demand a synthesis in the
mind of the viewer. The foundation for any such synthesis is introduced as *Porcile*
opens, with shots of stone tablets – as if a second Mount Sinai moment, now
with a 'new law' to replace the old – and a voice-over, which intones '[a]fter
having properly interrogated our conscience, we have decided to devour you
on account of your disobedience'. The new law, and the new societies that it
underwrites, threatens an assimilation/annihilation of disobedients. Both Julian
and the cannibal adopt the mode of disobedience (that is, they have the appearance of hippies), and both are consumed (by pigs and dogs respectively). But
now it is the narrative of the film that is shattered, not stone tablets – and this
allows for a number of readings that seek to mediate between the prehistoric
and contemporary halves. Viano find an interconnectedness between the two
in terms of personification; that the cannibal is 'a visual dramatization of Julian's
unconsciousness' (Viano 1993: 234). This could be said to place the will to rebel
in an ancient context – as with Antonioni in *Zabriskie Point*, as argued above.

Alternatively, the juxtaposition of the old and the new could be said to suggest a reading of the movement of history over several thousand years: the ever-present forces of bourgeois civilisation, of which neo-capitalism is but a recent phase, now reassert themselves over the upheavals of the 'revolutionary' period, just as surely as the Stone Age radicals were eradicated.[44]

Such a final critique of the events of 1968 is thus to be found in the films of revolutionism themselves – this discreet strain that now addresses (rather than stumbles over, in the manner of the Artaudian films) the conception of 1968 and a revolutionary cinema. Radical methodologies aside, it is notable that these films are mostly allegorical, picaresque and lack historical specificity. After a decade of attempts to engage with found reality, these late New Wave films failed to find a wider perspective in the unfolding events, taking refuge in caricature, the radical gesture (political and sexual) and techniques of alienation themselves, retreating from Bazinian ontology to remake and examine the world at one remove. Implicit in this tendency is a sense of the difficulty of attaining a satisfactory analysis of the moment while 'in the field'; this cinema's a- or even anti-historicism flies in the face of the orientation to the ready and available 'history in the making'. It is telling that the *Ciné-tracts* ultimately leave their orientation towards front-line reportage (which included, via montages of still images, the sense of placing the viewer in the crowd, in fear of the massed police) in favour of analysis of news media and image-making, anticipating the methodologies of the Dziga Vertov Group: rostrum work on still images, the writing on/defacing of newspapers, advertisements and pornographic magazines, and even an attack on insufficiently revolutionary film-makers.[45] And the force that propels this flight from the streets (of which only the beginnings have been identified, above; the full flowering is considered below, as the characteristic of a post-1968 cinema), unavoidable at the point at which revolutionary activity is scrutinised critically, must be said to reside in the lack of theoretical rigour and historical analysis mentioned above. It is not the failing of the soixante-huitards to smash the system, but their failing to address, or comprehend, the system they seek to overturn. Of this failing, Foucault commented in 1977:

> The way power was exercised – concretely and in detail – with its specificity, its techniques and tactics, was something that no one attempted to ascertain; they contented themselves with denouncing it in a polemical and global fashion as it existed among the 'others', in the adversary camp. Where Soviet

socialist power was in question, its opponents called it totalitarianism; power in Western capitalism was denounced by the Marxists as class domination; but the mechanics of power in themselves were never analysed. This task could only begin after 1968, that is to say on the basis of daily struggles at grass roots level, among those whose fight was located in the fine meshes of the web of power. (Foucault 1980: 115–16)

And of the coming and unavoidable comprehension that Foucault here posits as a necessary 'coming of age', in and for subsequent leftist sensibilities, Eagleton notes that post-1968 thought is marked by an almost a priori acceptance of the 'system' as found, that '[it] could be disrupted but not dismantled' – and that this is the field and scope for struggle, for better or worse (Eagleton 2004: 51). For Deleuze and Guattari, 'May '68 Did Not Take Place' since its demands, unable 'to be assimilated by French society', had to be ignored instead: 'Every collective enunciation by a new existence, by a new collective subjecticity, was crushed in advance by the reaction against '68, on the left almost as much as on the right' (Deleuze and Guattari 2001: 210). The consequences of such suppression, in the cultural and social spheres, would give rise to the nihilism of punk and post-punk: 'situations of abandonment' (Deleuze and Guattari 2001: 211).

This turn could be termed a de-utopianisation of radical politics, or de-radicalisation of utopian politics – the beginnings of the reverberation of which, in the persistence of radical Western European films, through and after 1968, is discernible.

In the absence of such an analysis of the specifics – the 'mechanics of power' – it is unsurprising that films supposedly from the epicentre of the power struggle took refuge in caricature, the radical gesture, techniques of alienation themselves and the field of analysis (found reality, and the Bazinianism that reproduces it). And, equally, that those films that critiqued 1968 did so by engaging on these levels too – problematising the assumed radical import of gestures, offering a new series of allegories, as if speaking the language of 1968 against 1968. Although Foucault's tone is critical, there is an implicit acknowledgement that these errors and oversights themselves paved the way for a reconstituted leftist theoretical challenge beyond 1968. Such an orientation was understood as central to Semiotext(e)'s Schizo-Culture conference of 1975: the press release opens by identifying their assembled 'representatives of a movement which since 1968 has produced a break-through', 'a revolution in desire', 'a strategy for dissolving and questioning systems', a 'new analysis of capitalism', and so forth (press release reproduced in Lotringer and Morris 2013: 7). And such a reconstitution of the left-ist theoretical challenge is also apparent in the beginnings of post-1968 directions in film.

The formal defeat of the nominal revolution came in the fall of the bastion of liberalisation, and the utopian model, with the Soviet and East Bloc invasion and occupation of Czechoslovakia in August. The clock was 'set back' to the Hungarian October of 1956; this was the end of the hope for a leftist theoretical challenge to communism. The reverberations of the crushing of the Prague Spring were such that, in his post-mortem of 1968, Young opens with the observation that '[i]t is perfectly understandable why the NL [New Left] was pronounced dead even by its own supporters and sympathizers during the early seventies' (Young 1977: 364).[46] And in its wake came the Croatian Spring and other bouts of 'normalisation' in East Bloc countries (including the ending of the Czech New Wave, for Škvorecky, 'the *finis Bohemiae*' (Škvorecky 1982: 7), and the 'Black Film' movement in Yugoslavia) – a reassertion of Soviet hegemony that would ulti-mately prove to be untenable. These blows to the conscience of the European left (intellectual, dissident, revolutionary, orthodox), the re-elections of de Gaulle and, narrowly, Nixon, the full militarisation of Spain, and even the beginnings of the formal end of the fledgling 'permissive age' (see, for example, Weeks (1994: 276), and Hall and Critcher et al. (1979: 250ff)) meant that the optimistic talk of an 'October revolution' in the United Kingdom (Farren and Barker 1972: unnum-bered), or more general revolutions to come (see Viénet writing in 1968; Viénet 1992: 122), unsurprisingly came to nothing.[47] Regardless of its disputed status, any 1968 revolution was over, not least in the fading of 1960s liberal political tolerance; in the West a 'counter-revolution had begun … The slogan under which this counter-revolution advanced was "law-and-order"' (Hall, Critcher et al. 1979: 241–42). Renewed Cold War brinkmanship and imperial adventur-ism (most brutally manifest in Chile in 1973), and violent authoritarianism in the face of industrial unrest and as a reaction to worldwide economic depression characterised the new decade. The further betrayals by the Left and trade union bureaucracies marked their behaviour in 1968 as the norm, not the exception; their concerns remained founded on the survival of capitalism during this period. It was in this context, and that of the success of the Tet Offensive against U.S. forces in Vietnam in February 1968, that the '"hot Autumn" militancy of 1969'

(Eaden and Renton 2002: 143) gave rise to the era of 'la strategia della tensione' in Italy. Katsiaficas places the multiple fronts of such extra-parliamentary militant groupings, including ETA (Katsiaficas 1987: 55), in the context of Guevara's 'Foco Theory' (Katsiaficas 1987: 36ff). And it is at this junction that a number of issue-driven political initiatives arose: ecology and environmental groups, in some respects swallowing peace movements (as in Greenpeace), gay rights and women's liberation (which Young contextualises as 'a sort of antibody' (Young 1977: 367) to New Left sexism), squatting campaigns and rent and anti-eviction fights, and revivals of regional nationalism and secessionism. However, these mostly found accommodation within parliamentary democracies (as did their leaders, including notable soixante-huitards), often with ease; they represent the essential failing of the post-1968 'task of the revolutionary party [which] is to prolong the period of abnormality, to preclude any return to normality' (*New Left Review* 1968: 3).

Immediately after 1968, a sudden and palpable strain of pessimism, joining the strain of defeatism, is evident in those films that seem to reverberate with the aftermath. This seems true of the unhappy endings of *Le Lit de la Vierge* and *Vite* where, in Shafto's reading, the 1968 revolutionary is now reduced to 'a mad shaman, making one last desperate effort ... to provoke the true revolution' (Shafto 2000: 27), and *Acéphale* (shot in July 1968), where the hippies live an underground, marginalised existence, living among abandoned ruins, even at one point as if cast back in time, to the time of cavemen. Herzog's *Auch Zwerge Haben Klein Angefangen* (*Even Dwarfs Started Small*, 1970), via an experiential and confrontational 'meaninglessness', as Franklin puts it (Franklin 1983: 114), represents an 'hallucinatory attack on half-baked revolutions', for Farber (Farber 1998: 303). The film follows an insurrection by dwarfs on an abandoned volcanic island housing the institution in which they live. The film assembles a catalogue of familiar revolutionary occurrences (destruction of property, some wanton free love, comradeship among the rebels), all inconsequential. The use of dwarfs for revolutionaries suggests the possibility of a variety of unflattering readings of 1968 upon which the film resolutely refuses to elaborate (nor is it entirely clear if the film is absurdist in intent).[48] The constant laughter suggests the revolution is nothing more than a puerile, hedonistic endeavour. The hippies of Baratier's documentary *Eden Miseria* (1967) have dropped out of society, which has led them to Kathmandu. They seem miserable, uncomfortable and aimless; drugged into a stupor and unable to articulate a clear view of the actions they have taken.

Schroeter, for *Der Bomberpilot* (1970), audaciously presents an epic narrative for his three female protagonists that takes them from Nazi-era Germany to countercultural/bohemian West Germany, and locates elements of each era in the other so as to establish a continuum. The communal living, and naked exercising and dancing in nature, coded here as aesthetics typical of Nazi-era film, resonate in the countercultural/bohemian milieu. And the self-empowerment, manifesto-writing, and general interest in questions of breeding and procreation, which figure largely in the countercultural/bohemian milieu, in turn hark back to the preoccupations of the Nazi period. To have made such connections, in 1970, would have been nothing short of scandalous both to those who maintained the dream of 1968 through a continued status of dropping out, and those engaged in the march through the institutions. In this context *La Sua Giornata di Gloria* offers reason for hope, even in its vision of a dystopian near future in which soixante-huitards have gone underground to escape the death squads of a totalitarian government. The film opens with outtakes from *Partner*, in which the utopian and revolutionary will to usurp the city now suggests the bygone 1968 that is being forcibly suppressed. Here, the revolutionaries have been forced back into the enclosed spaces familiar from *La Chinoise*, and continue to debate those currents that found free reign in both 1968 and 1968 cinema (specifically Brecht and alienation, utopianism and communism, and dialectics). In *Necropolis* (Franco Bracani, 1970) they simply seem to exist underground, as if now banished to a realm of unreality to prevent further insurrectionary activities. The film seems given over to listless theatrical stagings, and is Zanzibar-esque in its rituals, obscurantism and slowness, suggesting that the loss of life 'in the open' is a dehabilitating punishment for the residents of this society of the dead (a society populated by several familiar faces from the films of 1968). In this imagining, those whose desires for reality had aspired to the remaking of reality were to find themselves exiled from that reality altogether. The nature of this shift in sensibility is acutely apparent when considered in relation to *Lettera Aperta a un Giornale della Sera* (*Open Letter to the Evening News* (Francesco Maselli, shot in 1968 and 1969, released in 1970): here the radical assembly of artists and thinkers is awash with new technology and naked younger women (one radical flirtatiously boasts of his 'dialectic energy'), and their collective actions have immediate reverberations on both the Italian Communist Party and the wider capitalist world. But the problem of action remains the same: the assembly find themselves actually invited to fight alongside the North Vietnamese resistance, with the Partito Communista Italiano

(PCI)'s blessing, as the 'international cultural brigade', which engenders a series of existential crises and sharper questions about effective militancy. They identify themselves as essentially helpless, 'screwed and gratified by our contradictions, sleepily proud with our well-oiled conflicts' and yet, once they do decide to depart for North Vietnam, are stood down at the last minute.

Pessimism found a more palpable subject in those films that suggested the advent of a new police state – Watkins's *Privilege* and *The Gladiators*,[49] and *Z* (Constantin Costa-Gavras, 1968), clearly modelled on recent Greece – and the futility of revolution from the outset. *Z*, in a jarringly straightforward fashion, illustrates police state machinations as the moral of its story and suggests that working against the state within its legal parameters is a worthless activity. A political assassination is vigorously investigated and those responsible (a shady nationalist-monarchist organisation, operating outside the law) brought to justice. This results in a military coup, so that the entire judicial process comes to function as little more than a casus belli against the working class. In Bergman's *Skammen* the utopian life of a small island is routed with the outbreak of war, presented in an entirely absurdist way (rape and torture notwithstanding) – as if visiting the onslaught against the North Vietnamese on the secluded Northern European bourgeoisie. The post-apocalyptic setting of *I Cannibali* (*The Cannibals*, Liliana Cavani, 1970) suggests that the upheavals of 1968 have been met with state violence: public spaces are strewn with corpses and ignored by order – now the street posters proclaim 'death to anyone who touches the rebels' bodies'. *Le Lit de la Vierge* takes the state of war as the norm for civilisation from the outset; here there is no idyll to be broken. Such a pessimistic sentiment might also be extended to Bertolucci's *La Strategia del Ragno* (1970) and its failed assassination attempt of Mussolini, a history uncovered in the present by the son of the chief conspirator, local hero and fascist mole. In terms of an aestheticism and exuberant style – the very opposite of Verfremdungseffekt – this film and Bertolucci's *Il Conformista* (1970) mark a substantial distance from, arguably even a refutation of, New Wave aesthetics. This distance is also apparent in Bertolucci's concerns with a 'psychoanalytical' approach to Italian fascism; the psychology of the protagonists as representative of the collective psyche of Italy during the years of fascism. In Fellini's work beyond 1968, typified by a critical anti-illusionism (set pieces of the most grandiose kind; ships sailing by and vast historical panoramas and so forth would consciously be presented as mock-ups),[50] such a stance continually equates illusionism as inextricably entwined with the existence of historical fascism. Fellini and Bertolucci, after 1968, concerned themselves exactly with a historical examination of, as Foucault put it, the 'fine meshes of the web of power' (Foucault 1980: 116).

A new methodology can be said to be apparent in Pasolini's work too, beyond 1968 – even to the extent of a dissolution of (or attempts at resolving) the 'suspension of meaning' stasis. Rumble argues that Pasolini's move into the mainstream of film-making for the *Trilogia della Vita* in the early 1970s,[51] facilitated via representations of sexuality, denoted an understanding on Pasolini's part that the schizophrenic aspect of Western cinema (that is also characterised in Pontecorvo's quoting of Lenin in relation to the 'inner contradictions of capitalism') was a fault line that could be exploited. From the outset, Pasolini's films beyond *Porcile* are marked by the acceptance of 'the perhaps inherently compromised character of the new medium' (Rumble 1996: 5). Such a stance, in assembling a new aspirant anti-neo-capitalist perspective, implicitly discounts many of the radical directions of film in the period 1966–68.

A Refounded Radicalism

The fallout of the failure of 1968 would have been unavoidable in leftist film culture. In an inevitable phase of self-criticism, whether private or public, a conclusion that the revolutionary phases of film-making up to 1968 had, along with most facets of the revolutionary scene of 1968, failed to galvanise or sufficiently agitate the proletariat would have been particularly apparent. Yet whatever local failures were evident at the time, the idea that the 'task could only begin after 1968' (Foucault 1980: 116) suggested that a resultant 'May of film theory' in Harvey's description (Harvey 1980: 117) would be concerned with the way ahead as much as the mistakes or excesses of the cinéma-militant. This upheaval occurred via re-engaging with the very nature of representation, something that extended beyond just film-related concerns, fired by a desire to reappraise the revolutionary or dissident potential of the original Bazinian model of the ontological-real – 'a rigorous reevaluation and deconstruction of the old Bazin aesthetics of ontological realism' (MacBean 1975: 314). This in itself constituted a sustained self-criticism; a questioning of praxis and an overturning of methodologies. And a reapplication of Brechtian method, or a method within that lineage, would invariably follow. In an overview of this period of transition,

Beasley-Murray found:

Without necessarily positing any casual relation, the withering of neorealism can perhaps be compared to the fate of Bazinian theories of realism in the twenty years from the late sixties to the late eighties. With Christian Metz and the first wave of linguistically-based semiotic film criticism, it became almost ritualistic to denounce the naiveté with which Bazin had claimed to find in The Bicycle Thief [*Ladri di Biciclette*, Vittorio De Sica, 1948] *the paradoxical non-discovery of "no more cinema". As Phil Rosen put it in 1989, "Since the 1960s . . . Bazin-bashing has become fashionable in film-theoretical discussion". Thus even Jacques Aumont . . . reprimands Bazin (and his evaluation of neorealism) in stating that "Bazin's enthusiasm for this 'new' film form pushed him to an excessive stance".* (Beasley-Murray 1997: 42)

Beasley-Murray's use of the term 'withering' recalls Marx's, suggesting that, as an exemplary model of Bazinian cinema, and then model for post-Bazinian realism, neo-realism was emblematic of this false religion – something whose time would invariably pass. Rosen, with more circumspection, suggests that Bazin was an easy target for the 'familiar breakthrough tendencies in post-1968 film theory', since such breakthroughs, radical in intent, could all then be defined in negative correlation to Bazin's conservative model of cinema (Rosen 1987: 30, footnote 1). Belton, in his article 'Bazin is Dead! Long Live Bazin!' confirms this thesis, positing 'these romantic notions' as under siege, in the 1970s onwards, from '[c]ontemporary film theory, especially that articulated in the pages of *Screen*' (Belton 1987: 75).

Two discernible new directions are apparent at the beginnings of a post-1968, post-leftist theoretical challenge, regenerated political cinema.[52] Yet despite a breaking with the radical and revolutionary films of the 1968 period, these directions are evident, in embryonic form, prior to 1968. As if still propelled forward by the momentum of their sheer activity, Godard and then the Dziga Vertov Group continued to turn out films with an unabated frequency, in which a renewed dialecticism, particularly in relation to the idea of representation, flourished (regardless of the precision of the critique). This consolidation of revolutionary concerns across and after 1968 represented a final gasp of the leftist theoretical challenge in the ongoing attempt to expose and interject the mechanisms of the creation of meaning in both Left and right spheres in the bourgeois West.[53] And, wiping the slate clean altogether through the rejection of a realism founded on a notion of the ontological-real, aspects of the early years of the New German Cinema represent a second direction. In Straub and Huillet's films, a new state of discontinuity was established in film form, in the formulation of a modus operandi beyond the provocations of Godard. Fassbinder's early films suggest a new approach to, or rethinking of, Brechtian method – a blueprint for a political cinema of the 1970s. These films of the post-1968 directions work from the assumption that the nature of representation is itself of political import, ultimately rendering any ontological status to the image as irrelevant (so that, as Douchet simply puts it, Fassbinder 'rejected presentation for representation' (Douchet 1999: 297).[54] This is an intervention in the Foucault-identified 'fine meshes of the web of power' (Foucault 1980: 116) – although it was not necessarily understood as such at the time – and will be here briefly summarised, in these two new directions, so as to note the nature of the ending of the 1968 revolutionary phase in its principal characteristic: the routing, from film-making praxes, of a post-Bazinian realism.

The Dziga Vertov Group, in their ultra-leftism, could be considered in relation to those films that represented a critique of '68 revolutionism. In *Pravda* (1969)[55] this critique is aligned with the Group's investigation into the generation of meaning, as mounted on the premise of 'the need to analyse the basic processes of representation in the media seen as a capitalist institution' (Britton 1989: 180). This occurs within the frame, in the analysis of the footage of and from post-invasion Prague; an isolation and critique of bourgeois modes of representation that aspires to ascertain the nature of contemporary Prague.[56] The documentary *Pravda* excludes sympathy for any reformist revolutionaries or dissidents, and so formally finds a place in the post-1968 'accusations of "petit-bourgeois revanchism", [echoing] both Russian propaganda and pronouncements by the non-pro-Russian, but hard left sects' (Young 1977: 220).

The film utilises a dialectical voice-over conversation (an imagined dialogue between Lenin and Luxemburg), substantially on the reformist tendency. Dubček is accused in this respect, as is Chytilová, interviewed and described as 'like Arthur Penn' (a then modish Hollywood film-maker whose work – such as *Alice's Restaurant* (1969) – seemed vaguely countercultural). The students are accused of 'suicidal humanism, not revolutionary determination'. The film finds a dictatorship of a revisionist proletariat; the workers are newly enslaved. To illustrate this, the film utilises wordless fixed shots of workers at machines[57] – an attempt to alienate the viewer in an experiential context (a communication or taste of the sense of their imprisonment, achieved in the length of these sequences). The conclusion is essentially the same as *Ucho* (*The Ear*, Karel Kachyňa, 1970): revisionism in and through the institutionalisation of the Stalinist bureaucrats. But, with the enhancement of the Dziga Vertov Group's Maoism, this conclusion now includes a bitter critique of the Soviet accommodation of the West in this revisionism.[58] The Western consumer presence in Czechoslovakia (so that 'the streets of Prague have become like those of London', seen in the presence of Western car hire companies, for example, as noted by (MacBean 1975: 149)) is presented as evidence of the reformist desire for coexistence. The streets have become a battleground in terms of conflicting 'advertisement' images that – under the Group's scrutiny – come to represent the truth of the sociopolitical situation.[59] And, as well as the actual and incongruous advertisements for Western consumer goods, the presence of Soviet tanks also only works to 'advertise'. Czechoslovakia of 1969 is effectively like a Western country, awash with neon advertisements, pop music, pornography, hippies, wire fences and 'workers [who] would rather wash their cars than fuck their wives'. Even intertextuality has been commodified; the Group cut to a blank screen on more than one occasion, saying that they cannot show the required image, as Czech television has sold it to a German, Japanese or American media company.

The representations of post-invasion socialism are treated with equal disdain. Against a shot of the red side of a tram, the voice-over posits: 'There was fighting between different kinds of red – between the red which comes from the Left and the red which goes off towards the right'. In such ways, the Group find and present visual evidence for the political struggle that had become, post-invasion, a theoretical struggle over types of 'Red'. It is in this context that the 'neutrality' of *Vent d'Est*'s use of genre is apparent. This 'epic form' (the western) comes to be a 'scientific' environment in which the theoretical struggle can occur, across both East and West (a critical space that allows for comments such as 'I killed the sheriff of West Berlin', made in the midst of a discussion of the police state), as well as being identified as a genre given over to 'just an image, rather than the appearance of a "just image"' – an approach not dissimilar to Leone's.

However, the development of the film consciously halts at this point as much of the film then consists of a collective discussion concerning what images and sounds are to be in the film. Yet even this is an advance on the confusion of *One Plus One*, the dead end in which revolutionary gestures are circumscribed within a sense of aspiring to create revolutionary gestures. What is to be usefully made of the long sequence in which a film crew and interviewer follow Wiazemsky, asking her sometimes lengthy questions (to which she replies with either 'yes' or 'no')? A caricature – that the supposedly objective interviewer imposes his words, his interpretation of the debate and of the subject, on the subject? An instruction to the proletariat that attempting to discuss such issues within the parameters of bourgeois debate is to be avoided? That there is no real discussion between the media and the subject? Does Wiazemsky's formally smart appearance suggest that the well-attired (and well-spoken) hippies of the film crew are to be considered as essentially conformist to the 'required' dress codes of the bourgeois media? The self-questioning nature of the Group's films implicitly indicates an abandonment of such gestures and the political naivety of Godard's pre-1968 films – a naivety that Godard himself dismissed as 'bourgeois'. Godard dismissed his pre-1968 films thus:

> *- At what exact point in time did the break from bourgeois to revolutionary film-maker occur?*
> *Godard: During the May-June events in France in 1968*
> *- Are there any of these earlier films that you now consider to have any positive merit?*
> *Godard: Perhaps* Week-end *and* Pierrot le Fou. *There are some things in* Deux ou Trois Choses Que Je Sais d'Elle. *Some positive things in those films.* One Plus One *was my last bourgeois film. I was very arrogant to make that, to think that I could talk about revolution just like that – just to take images thinking I knew what they meant.* (quoted in Carroll 1972: 61)

Of *One Plus One* Godard said, 'the whole thing was a mistake' (Dixon 1997: 107). After 1968, for Godard, the concept of the revolutionary film is readdressed with the maxim: 'The problem is not to make political films but to make films politically' (quoted in MacCabe, Eaton and Mulvey 1980: 19). In this respect, the Group's work is a continuation and intensification of directions, and explorations of cul-de-sacs, encountered during Godard's 1960s auteur period.

This is the basis for the self-questioning noted above: an awareness of the evolved processes of the creation of meaning as the root of all progressive film-making, an advance on anti-illusionism (which only sought to problematise the suspension of disbelief). For Godard, this awareness occurred simultaneously to the making of those films he then dismissed as lacking in such self-questioning.

Godard's *Le Gai Savoir* was shot in 35mm between December 1967 and January 1968 and edited in 1969 (Dixon 1997: 93; MacCabe, Eaton and Mulvey 1980: 20),[60] so that it could be said that, for this film, Godard finds a post-1968 sensibility in the pre-'68 material. The film consists of dialogues between two radical students (surrounded by darkness, mostly shot in long take), documentary footage and interview/word association games with a child and worker. Alienating devices come in the form of technological assaults, such as audio barrages (including as a way of 'censoring' bursts of bad language and instructions for bomb-making, via audio pitches on the soundtrack)[61] and absent images (the same reasons given as in *Pravda*). In the manner of *Partner*, the film flees from reality, finding shelter in a laboratory-like TV studio. The experiment at hand concerns the analysis of images through a questioning of their implicit meanings – that is, an attempted rupturing of the fixed bourgeois 'reading' of images. In the first instance, Godard ruptures by removing the sounds from the images; words are spelt out, and then reduced to meaningless sounds. The film announces this endeavour as 'Let's start from zero' and 'First we have to get back there – back to zero' (recalling the 1968 slogan 'Forget all you have learnt' (quoted in Harvey 1980: 12)). This becomes a constant refrain and applied to all aspects of life (sexual, political and technological spheres), a Maoist-tinged critical realism in an attempt to implement a cultural revolution of film form.

The September 1968 issue of *Cahiers* placed at the head of its table of contents a quote from Barthes concerning the idea of a return to zero:

> Since Marx, Nietzsche, Freud, criticism, the tearing away of the ideological wrappings with which our society surrounds knowledge, feeling, behaviour, value, is the great work of the century. We must not each time begin again from zero. (quoted in Harvey 1980: 33; their emphasis)

Almost as an echo of this, *Le Gai Savoir* ends with, in voice-over: 'This is not the film that should be made, but if a film is to be made, it must follow some of the paths shown here'. This is a substantial revision on an intertitle in *La Chinoise* – 'a film in the process of being made' – and a leap forward in respect of the pastiche of radical consciousness offered, counterfactually, in *Week-end*, as noted above; the text's double is now suggested as that of a maturely revolutionary form. *Le Gai Savoir* occupies a very tenuous position – caught between phases of Godard's work, both pre and post 1968, and only able to gesture towards the new analysis that was deemed necessary. The very setting, the television studio, denotes an era of mass communication and disposable images, broadcast once and then forgotten, rather than images as the precious vessels of the ontological-real, and film-making as a channelling of the intrinsically revolutionary 'real'. In part, the film represents the coda to the ambiguity of *Week-end* and confusion of *One Plus One*; *Le Gai Savoir* is the tentative way ahead – and this is the 'good knowledge' of the film's title. And, in part, where the film retains pre-'68 traits, this makes for a rather schizophrenic mix; the protagonists frequently leave to attend demonstrations and engage in terrorist activity and then return for further deconstruction. As they talk, they illustrate a desire to analyse the situation – but the nature of the situation itself remains uncertain (which finds a visual resonance in the way the protagonists are surrounded by an impenetrable darkness). The film ends with an acknowledgement of its own uncertain status; *Le Gai Savoir* remains anticipatory in the manner of *La Chinoise* – pointing to the directions just 'around the corner'. The protagonists acknowledge that Bertolucci, Straub, Rocha (of the *Cinema Nôvo*) and Skolimowski will film the scenes 'not in' *Le Gai Savoir* in a way that will be suitable for the masses (*Le Gai Savoir* is firmly within Godard's 'unwatchable' period – that of the 'aesthetic disaster' (Ali 1987: 253)). At the point of 'Year Zero' in *Le Gai Savoir*, Godard calls for a complete rethinking of the nature of political film, as mouthed by the protagonists: '*Pas représentation, présentation pas spectacle, lutte!*'

Un Film Comme les Autres (Godard, 1968)[62] is a product of this interzone – a film born of a direct engagement with the political struggle, utilising alienation in an extremely confrontational manner, and is a shunning of spectacle or, indeed, anything that might be considered to be 'bourgeois'. The film consists of two one hour reels: a tight, near static shot of an almost anonymous group of students and workers sitting in tall grass and discussing revolutionary topics on 'an extremely elemental level' (Roud 1970: 148), frequently intercut with documentary footage of 1968 insurrection. Much of the footage (from both strands) is reused in each reel, indicating that the live sound that is at first suggested with the obscured images of the discussion may be nothing of the sort. Such intercutting seeks to forcibly present the 'situation' for analysis (early on someone comments in relation to the civil unrest '[t]his wasn't a complete failure – we did learn a lot of things . . .') in a way that remained unclear in *Le Gai Savoir*.[63] And yet the connection between the two strands remains vague; the documentary footage is barely more than illustrative, and the two narratives, in the manner of *One Plus One*, possess little direct connection. Yet this very project represents the closest filmic equivalent to the 'counter-universities' and 'alternative courses' operating at this time, not least in the Sorbonne; one comment alludes to this – '[t]he task of the student is to open the university to the workers'. The radical negation of the film is such that even the construction seems haphazard.[64] Rather than the implementation of the models of deconstruction proposed in *Le Gai Savoir*, the film may be seen as an extended *Ciné-tract* on revolutionism as it evolved – or a prolonged version of the word association interviews in *Le Gai Savoir*, as if presenting types of contemporary people to be analysed by the viewer. The sunny mise en scène of *Un Film Comme les Autres*, in direct contrast to the oppressive darkness of *Le Gai Savoir*, suggests a dialectical relationship between the two films.[65] Regardless of Roud's comment, watching either or both of the reels of *Un Film Comme les Autres* would leave the viewer in a clearer position as to the events, and, in this respect, the film is one identified by Godard at this time as 'no more than a blackboard offering a concrete analysis of a concrete situation' (quoted in MacCabe, Eaton and Mulvey 1980: 58) – a film for the immediate aftermath of 1968, raw material for the process of self-criticism. The film contains pre-'68 sloganeering ('The weapon of criticism cannot replace the criticism of weapons') but also indicates an awareness of language and representation; the collapse of the ORTF (Office de Radiodiffusion Télévision Française) strikes is attributed to the way in which the workers were 'unable to . . . speak with their own voice, in a language other than that of the government that they had rejected', so that the task, articulated earlier in the film, is an 'organisation of language'.

Arguably, the context of ultra-left sentiment is not the most fruitful for the beginnings of a sustained consideration of the nature of representation. In heading straight for '68 hot spots or nodes of crisis (the television studio in *Le Gai Savoir*, the car factory workers in *British Sounds* (Dziga Vertov Group, 1969),[66] the cell of student radicals in *Un Film Comme les Autres*, post-invasion Czechoslovakia in *Pravda*, the radical commune/terrorist cell in *Vent d'Est*, the Palestinian militants of *Jusqu'à la Victoire* (1970)), these films tend to find the material to illustrate the political readings advanced. However, this impressive catalogue of locations – unrivalled in film-making at the time – seeks to lock a consideration of representation, at the outset, into contentious political situations. This occurs not least in the identification of alienation, in the Marxist sense, at all levels of society, and a continuation of the Maoist analysis – in *British Sounds*, for example, political (the neo-fascist monologues), personal/professional (the workers' discussion) and sexual (the naked woman).[67] This results in a film that consists of little more than a series of provocations. In this respect, the questions of representation occur within the horizon of the re-education of an ideal proletariat.[68] Subsequent academic considerations of representation (the 'textuality' aspect of cultural studies) tended to void such formal political considerations, severing the connection so forcibly made in this cycle of films – and confirming the progressive use of locating this project within such concerns. Indeed, this apoliticism is often attributed to the 'march through the institutions' of disillusioned, turncoat soixante-huitards, 'proclaiming the futility of the pretence of communism to reappropriate social wealth. Today these same philosophers cynically deconstruct, banalize' (Hardt and Negri 2001: 158; Hardt and Negri critique this attribution).

This turn to questions of representation, although far from new in respect to Godard's work, was new – here, in the wake of 1968 – in respect to the extent and degree of the turn. The deconstruction of processes of generating meaning, through the pulling apart and reassembly of constitutive elements of that process, does indeed represent a return to zero. And this return to zero discounts, or eradicates, all that has gone before – not only in respect of Godard's reproaches to his own early work, as noted above, and Leone's dismissal of the militant fervour of the radical-revolutionary populist project, and in the about face of Bertolucci's praxis, but also in respect to the underlying conception of progressive cinema. Werner Schroeter's *Maria Callas* film cycle seems to make a fetishistic ritual of this new approach: endless gazes at (and camera movements into) images of the singer, scrutinised in minute slow-motion detail, as if searching for, or meditating on, an emotional truth in the snapshot or newspaper reproductions, accompanied by old, tinny opera recordings.[69] And this search then becomes the portrait of the singer. In all, it is the process of an import of reality – the ontology of a post-Bazinian realism – that is also eradicated.

And that which Harvey then terms as a 'post-'68 assault on realism' (Harvey 1980: 107) was not based on evidence of a general shift in film-making methodologies; the conceptualisation of film from critical theory quarters had followed suit. Deleuze and a number of others attacked the foundations of Bazinian and neo-realist assumptions.[70] The advent of Metz's work on film and the re-reading of film imagery in a psychoanalytical framework, possible 'after' the discounting of an ontological connection to the reality from which the imagery is drawn, may be placed in this context. This is discussed in post-1968 terms in MacBean (1975: 285–311) and Harvey (1980: 34), who dates this 'new' sensibility from spring 1969 with the publication in *Cahiers* of a two-part article, 'La Suture' by Jean-Pierre Oudart (where Oudart reconfigures the relationship of film and viewer along psychoanalytical, specifically Lacanian, lines). Nicholls notes that '[i]n the wake of 1968, the *Cahiers du Cinéma* abandoned the politique des auteurs in favour of supposedly political semiological theory', which he terms a '"Maoist" period' (Nicholls 1993: 50).[71]

The resultant 'heady and sometimes unstable blend of semiotics, psycho-analysis, and various schools of Marxism (particularly the work of ... Althusser)' (Williams 1992: 389) can be described as a reengagement with radical directions of 1960s cultural thinking. In the light of the failure of 1968, a reassessment of that project would have been unavoidable, with post-Bazinian realism discarded so as to allow for a return of a questioning of the nature of representation. To have retained a Bazinian realist position (which certainly would have been a temptation in terms of the Third Cinema) would have been to be guilty of a 'singular semiotic naiveté' (Van Watson 1989: 40) – a criticism Eco had made of Pasolini before 1968.[72] These developments, which had been in the air prior to the 'evénéments' of 1968, needed the formal failure of 1968 and the routing of post-Bazinian realism in order to come to the fore. Indeed, the failure acts as a catalyst in this endeavour.

One indicator of the dawning of a new semiotic 'sophistication' was the reap-praisal of the work of Douglas Sirk; in Sirk was to be found a 'correct' (that is, achronologically, a 'post'-Godardian) Brechtianism. Specifically, this was achieved through a subtle and subversive application by Sirk of a Verfremdungseffekt-like quality.[73] Sirk's images spoke of North American life of the 1950s, embracing the fantasmatic foundations of that society, as mirrored in the 'garishness, the pastel tackiness' (Kolker 1983: 241) of the aesthetic. In relation to the terminology above, much of Sirk's Hollywood work could be said to be a model of the bourgeois anti-bourgeois film: the ills of society isolated and identified from the vantage point of the bourgeoisie. Yet once Sirk had formally isolated the inherent sociopolitical conflicts within that bourgeois sphere (sexual conflicts, racism, the foolhardi-ness of materialism, the nihilistic impulses behind hedonism, the refusal of love), these conflicts were themselves made abstract, as if only the symptoms of a deeper malaise in that society – achieving a sense of something 'not quite right' in this shift from micro- to macrocosmic reading, of insincerity in the emotions of the one-dimensional characters, and so forth. Thus, unlike Hitchcock in his Hollywood work, Sirk was seen to be able to propagate a pervasive sense of aliena-tion, to the point of anti-illusionism, but also from the position of the mainstream;

both subversion and a rejection of the marginality of the avant-garde praxis for this endeavour. So, from a position that held little or nothing in common with Bazinian precepts of realism (and that predated (and so discounted) the 'degeneration' of a post-Bazinian realism phase) and that self-reflexively embraced a 'false' system of representation so as to access more abstract societal concerns, Sirk's work suggested a progressive possibility. In this way, Sirk was 'recovered' as an earlier progressive model, and one that then inspired and could be updated (in the case of Fassbinder, in the reappraisal of Brechtian method that can be found in his work; Willemen goes so far as to identify a 'Fassbinder's Sirk' (Willemen 1994: 244)), that lent credence to fledgling avant-garde directions already apparent (in the work of Straub and Huillet and their Brechtianism), and that was therefore in keeping with the post-1968 thought about film that seemed to colour the emergent New German Cinema. Now alienation was the viewer's initial point of entry into the film, as it were – as with Schroeter's listless party/'happening' of *Neurasia* (1969), consisting seemingly of drugged partygoers, silent and near-motionless, in spartan surroundings – and not the critique to be found at the heart of the film, or the state that the film was to finally achieve.

In the work of Straub and Huillet the viewer encounters a Brechtian mode rather than praxis: films of an emotional deadness, and non-acting, as Verfremdungseffekt. The forms represent an acceptance of a fragmented or shattered totality, formally a process of the Brechtian New Wave films, now as the norm. *Chronik der Anna Magdalena Bach* (*Chronicle of Anna Magdalena Bach*, shot August-September 1967 and first seen in February 1968) seems mostly unedited, as if an assembly of dailies yet to be put into an order of narrative sense, or an order that sheds light on the life of its subject, Bach. The structure forces out continuity, even from the characters presented (they are given no space to 'develop', or to achieve characterisation). Their emotions are only available in the music seen in performance – not in the flat voice-overs of Bach's wife concerning relatively minor and un-illuminating aspects of his life – or the assortment of period documentation filmed. In terms of a conceptualisation of 'history', this period drama consciously undoes two bourgeois facets: historical figures over the sociopolitical, and a 'psychologising' of such figures. The figures are present, but remain empty and 'unfelt' in the texture of the film: they do not represent an entry point into a sense of the time and place. The structure suggests a file of historical research – the raw materials that Straub and Huillet have yet to put into order, presented to the viewer for that task.

The 'shock of the new' of this approach is evident in Roud's writing about *Chronik*; he attempts to force continuity and narrative development back into the film – using whatever elements he can extract from the film to do so (Roud 1972: 73–86). Another telling early mistake in relation to Straub and Huillet's work is in Andi Engel's attempt to explain Straub's comment that *Chronik* is a 'contribution towards the liberation fight of the Vietnamese people' (Cameron and Chabot et al. 1970: 129), itself prompted by a comment from Godard that the film lacked contemporary relevance (Roud 1972: 71). Engel is obliged to find a common denominator of purposefulness and self-autonomy in Straub and Huillet's work and the Vietnamese (as does Roud, both Bach and the Vietnamese reject inertia (Roud 1972: 71)). Neither can see that Straub and Huillet's starting point of a fragmented totality is an attack on bourgeois norms of communication – a rupture aligned to the insurgency against the Americans in Vietnam, in the shattering of the notion of American hegemony that informs, underwrites and maintains such norms of communication.

For *Der Bräutigam, die Komödiantin und der Zuhälter* (*The Bridegroom, The Comedienne and the Pimp*)[74] Straub and Huillet adhere to the 'unedited' techniques of *One Plus One* – juxtaposing narratives with seemingly little in common – resulting in an 'unmade' film. Roud finds that this 'makes the viewer a party to the process of creation. '[Straub and Huillet have] preserved the Bruckner text [fragments of a play, in this film] so that we can, as it were, follow the same path he [i.e., Straub and Huillet] did' (Roud 1972: 99). Yet regardless of thematic connections and resonances between each section (which Roud discusses at length (Roud 1972: 87ff); they are existential rather than revolutionary) the film shifts jarringly between different methodologies and styles. At one point a filmed play, shot from a fixed position outside the limits of the stage scenery (one long take of ten minutes), is followed by relatively rapidly cut action sequences, shot on location and with medium close-ups, so that Roud can identify in this short film an 'edifice of contrasts of styles, techniques, and textures' (Roud 1972: 97). Such an edifice is only possible if the styles, techniques and textures mean nothing in themselves; if they do not carry the narrative 'weight' of any Bazinian ontological truth.[75]

Straub claimed *Der Bräutigam* was, in part, 'born out of the impossible May revolution in Paris – all the final scenes and the music at the beginning and end refer to it' (quoted in Roud 1972: 87). While this may be true of the final destination for the protagonists (marriage and a rural suburb), the lack of any sense of engagement with the ontological-real aspects of the film provides (again) the final 'impossibility': the implication is that such imagery does not carry with it any meaning or import beyond itself, cannot determine the film. Thus the formal avant-gardism (juxtaposed narratives, the edifice of contrasting styles) is lacking in galvanising intentions or gestural radicalism. Whereas even at their most extreme the films of revolutionism indicated a will to radicalise or to radicalism, here such a film is overwhelmed with a sense of passivity in the face of petty-bourgeois surroundings. Those characters who rise above passivity are only those who seek to capitalise on the ills of society – the Pimp (Fassbinder), for example; their awareness is of their imprisonment within such a society and the limited chances of alleviating that imprisonment (such a configuration could be said to give rise to a Foucaultian anti-hero). And yet Straub and Huillet refuse decaden-tism; they do not dwell on passivity but, rather, remove everything from the film other than key isolated moments in mostly unseen vistas of action and human interaction. These are the moments in which the protagonists surrender, accept-ing their unhappy lots in life – the minor defeats in their day-to-day lives that embody an entire philosophical approach to life. (Such moments are of even greater dramatic import than a shooting at the end of the film, which mostly goes unheeded.) Thus 'little is left save behavioural patterns, little nodes of action, dramatic constellations. The story-line . . . is almost impossible to work out from a single viewing . . . Nor can one work out the quotation from Mao which is painted on the back wall of the [theatre] set . . .' (Roud 1972: 91). The same might be said of Bach; Straub and Huillet wipe out almost all traces of the person and life, leav-ing only 'nodes' of music. Such violence against the norms of narrative structure, and the removal of a context in which avant-gardism might take on a radical import, suggests the absolute pervasiveness of alienation. The films are subject to it, and can only hope to reflect something of the truth of it, even if via indica-tions of the extremely limited possibility of 'revolt' in the medium of film, or via a nonchalant shrug in the face of the ills of society and those who embrace such ills. Thus Straub has 'naturally been rejected by the stupider left-wing critics, especially in France, because his artistic honesty has kept him from caricature and from over-simplification' (Roud 1972: 9); presumably the same critics Herzog mentions, and who did not take to *Rote Sonne*. But it is telling that Roud terms Straub's direction as one of 'honesty', indicative of a scaling back of the perceived possibilities of film in the wake of 1968. Also gone is outright anti-illusionism, which Straub would have perceived as mannerist; of early experiments with direct sound, Straub claims 'In *La Voix humaine* [presumably the Cocteau section of *L'Amore* (Rossellini, 1948)] you can hear the dolly. That's beautiful. But you should not pursue that idea systematically, like some bloody intellectual who would say: "I'm going to let the audience hear the noise of the dolly, so that they realize that they are seeing a movie"' (quoted in Cameron and Chabot et al. 1970: 130).

Fassbinder's early films, also from this period, utilise comparable strategies of alienation from the outset. Here narrative structures are intact and indeed 'classical' – Fassbinder's alienation does not detract from his formal reworkings of North American genre films; 'homages, pastiches or parodies' (Elsaesser 1996: 267). In the first instance, Fassbinder nominally turned to the gangster genre with his early shorts and *Liebe ist Kälter als der Tod* (*Love is Colder than Death*, 1969), *Götter der Pest* (*Gods of the Plague*, 1970) and *Der Amerikanische Soldat* (*The American Soldier*, 1970). Such reworkings represented an automatic 'critique' of the genre and the ideals it represented – and in a more sustained and less oppositional fashion than the gestural intertextuality of the New Waves; Fassbinder did not place distance between his films and genre films but, rather, found in their formulation recognisable moments of human interaction.[76] In this respect, Fassbinder's Brechtianism is akin to that of the Sirkian model: both emotional engagement and a distance via an aesthetic 'at one remove'.

Fassbinder formally rejected Brecht[77] and noted that his concern with an idea of alienation was not aligned with the methods of the Brechtian New Waves – unlike Kluge's Brechtianism, which Fassbinder termed 'intellectual' (Shattuc 1995: 87) and seemed at pains to distance himself from (see Kardish and Lorenz 1997: 88). Fassbinder's use of alienation occurs in relation to a literal distanciation, that 'not quite right' element within the frame; his alienation was 'stylistic' rather than achieved structurally. Thus Fassbinder's approach evidences a filmic equivalent of the theoretical re-evaluation of Brecht and film – a post-New Wave Brechtian method.

Such a post-1968 Verfremdungseffekt was first apparent in Fassbinder's *Katzelmacher* (shot in August 1969), which was possessed of a 'Brechtian logic' of dramatic construction (Elsaesser 1996: 33), of a resemblance to 'the young Brecht' through Fassbinder's 'knowing how to take sides against himself' (Elsaesser 1996: 246) and whose 'avant-garde status was [in part] based on the impression that Fassbinder was following Bert Brecht's anti-illusionist precepts' (Elsaesser 1996: 45). Vogel describes the film as characterised by: 'stylized, proscenium-type acting by non-emoting stereotypes against chalk-white backgrounds [which] creates a Brechtian attack on the German petty-bourgeoisie' (Vogel 1974: 88). The post-war petty bourgeoisie, in the German context of the 1960s, is still represented by the squabbling, apolitical and hierarchically minded workers, which Fassbinder presents as motivated solely by racism. Everything else remains in the realm of the non-emoting – mechanical and automaton-like; walking, eating and drinking, sexual intercourse, playing cards. Occasional acts of violence, usually against women, momentarily break the utter indifference the characters possess towards the world around them, to which they contribute 'stupefyingly mundane talk' (Farber 1998: 310) and 'absurd, inane conversations' (Farber 1998: 339). Thus with *Götter der Pest*, the boundary between generic 'types' and actual portraits blur; both jostle for the sole dimension Fassbinder affords to his characters. And the reworking of genre is here entirely minimal; only the bare bones of a plot, a minimal use of genre 'types' (where the detectives are little more beyond the raincoat, the gun and the cigarette), and a languid pace replaces the otherwise strong narrative drive of the gangster genre. This contrasts starkly with New Wave intertextuality and genre pastiche, which piled as much genre business as possible into the frame to overwhelm the viewer with the absoluteness of the embrace of a foreign code.

Fassbinder imposes a rigorous, even ascetic, visual order on the film: tight framing, an often completely immobile camera (and tableau-like compositions for it) and a studied lack of imagination to the framing. This underscores the emotionless lives of the protagonists, presented in a brutal, unflattering and over-lit fashion, in a grainy black and white often rendered with little or no depth of field. The sets are barely dressed (*Liebe ist Kälter als der Tod* consists of white rooms, a couple of chairs and a table) – and even when outside the streets and cafes are deserted, as if cleared of people for the filming. No attention is paid to anything beyond the immediate sphere of the characters. This suggests an anthropomorphic strategy, if only by default, as there is little else to hold the viewer's attention. But this in turn forces the viewer to consider the non-acting and non-interaction (eyelines often do not match, characters tend to gaze off-screen), and the characters are rarely presented centre-screen (an area often kept vacant).[78] Indeed, Fassbinder's early aesthetic was indebted to the 'cheaply made porn-films . . . [which] began to surface in the early 1960s' (Elsaesser 1996: 348, footnote 14). Confronted with as much, Farber identifies a barrage of alienating devices in such anti-aestheticism (see Farber 1998: 307–12), ultimately confirming that '[h]is strategies often indicate a study of porn movies, how to get an expanse of flesh across the screen with the bluntest possible impact and the least footage' (Farber 1998: 312). Such a 'porn' aesthetic depreciates the film, locking the entire mise en scène into a poverty aesthetic, so as to speak of the paucity of even the exploitational nature of contemporary film-making from which it is drawn. In this context, the invisible editing and conformity to elements of classical Hollywood film grammar seem all the more stagy and false; it registers that the gun shots in *Liebe ist Kälter als der Tod* make no body wounds in a way that would not register in the genre films to which it nominally looks.

At first glance, Schroeter's *Eika Katappa* (1969) would seem to present the very opposite of asceticism and the poverty aesthetic; the film mostly consists of colourful and highly stylised dramatisations of fragments of baroquely staged operas, sometimes 'on set' and sometimes relocated to outside surroundings. But the stagings are strangely presented: the lip-syncing is often way out, Schroeter films in a 'naive' and frontal way, the performers seem drugged or genuinely distressed, or, as if a misuse of neo-realist technique, amateurs are dragged onto the set and display confusion. The hippy-like company makes for an aesthetic that is typical of 1969, and would potentially suggest the notion of an alternative community that arises from the Zanzibar films. And yet the pummelling exaltation of operatic excesses across the film's considerable length (including stretches that seem like unedited rushes), and specifically endless death scene arias, seem to bury any resultant contemporary sensibility beneath the psychology of previous centuries, as expressed in the music. Even the contemporary settings, in this sonic recontextualisation, are recast as ancient times. Much the same operation is true of the domestic scenes of Schroeter's *Argila* (1969), which are seemingly mythologised as they are reworked as opera, and *Aggression* (1968), where scenes of sexual violence against a woman, accompanied by intoned critiques of patriarchal structures, are framed by a dream-like, Cocteau-esque interlude, aestheticising the woman in a composition complete with flowers, and so seemingly vastly at odds with the agitprop, proto-Second Wave feminist nature of the film. These films are defiant in their suppression of any expected contemporaneity, and idiosyncratically present death and tragedy as part of a continuum that stretches back millennia rather than to the frustrated hopes of only a year before.

Such rigour prompts a second consideration of Godard; even at his most anti-bourgeois his films retained the spirit of a bourgeois realism in their lush colours (regardless of the blocking of deep focus and depth of field), in the inventiveness of the agitprop sequences – their vitality and jouissance – and the freedom of his

Figure 4.8   Hippy death throes in operatic baroque: Schroeter's *Eika Katappa* (1969)

performers to move and interact within them, and in their intellectual invention. They did not deny an exuberance. In this respect, the presentation of the Rolling Stones in *One Plus One* is not an aberration but a logical conclusion to the vibrant aestheticism that, under the guise of an intertextual romanticism, added a seductive element to all his films, even in the Dziga Vertov Group. When compared to early Fassbinder, in Godard's words of 1959, Godard's France remained 'look[ing] good, cinematographically speaking' (quoted in de Baecque 1997: 155), even up to and after 1968. The 'un-pleasure' (Wollen 1982: 79) Godard achieved through narrative strategies had not been extended to the visual surfaces.

For early Fassbinder, any sense of a dynamic interaction with the world on the part of the camera, as with the New Waves, is eradicated. *Götter der Pest* barely ventures outside – let alone acknowledges the existence of a world beyond its claustrophobic confines; Farber notes that 'people have a captured-inside-a-doll's-house feeling' (Farber 1998: 311). Fassbinder 'engages' with the world he pins down in front of the camera, and finds nothing there other than 'the fascist potential of people without jobs, education or social prospects' (Elsaesser 1996: 270). For such reasons, Hayman terms the film 'an aggression against the audience that applauded it' (Hayman 1984: 44). Such an approach dissolves the distinction between anti-bourgeois and non-bourgeois film cited above as the foundation of the political spectrum of New Wave films; Fassbinder presents anti-bourgeois sentiment from a non-bourgeois form. Is this not an eminently recognisable realisation of the aspirations of radical film aligned with 1968, albeit one that implicitly rejects the excesses of the cinéma-militant and the position from which those films were predicated – that of post-Bazinian realism? Indeed, in this brief overview of the new directions apparent on the cusp of 1968, as pushed to the fore with the post-mortem of 1968, and as first evident, in embryo, prior to 1968, it becomes apparent that the paradigm shift necessary for a refounded radicalism in European film occurs with, and through, the abandonment of post-Bazinian realism. Such a maturation of revolutionary cinema, which results in a phase comparable to the modesty of Antonioni's position of *Blow-Up*, comes at the cost of revolutionary zeal; the foundations of such maturity, compared to the revolutionary cinema prior to 1968, seem distinctly defeatist. For Fassbinder, Schroeter and Straub and Huillet, alienation is ultimately turned against the bourgeois elements, or latent bourgeois elements, within their films. It is in the condition of representation that is attained that alienation now functions in a progressive manner. Such a state of self-criticism can only occur after the removal of Bazinian precepts of realism and with the establishment of an ability to engage with the artificial rather than the ontological nature of film form, a recreation rather than transference of reality – isolating and rejecting those elements of film form that function as bourgeois discourse. An anti-bourgeois sensibility that had degenerated to a level of confrontationism through caricature in the militant phase of the Brechtian New Waves now determines the materialist context for the characters presented.

Notes

1. *Loin du Viêt-nam* was released in the October and November of 1967 in France and the United Kingdom respectively. Bertolucci recalled that the belated Paris success of *Prima della Rivoluzione* can be attributed to the way in which the film 'was seen as a criticism of the PCI coming from the left' (Gerard, Kline and Sklarew 2000: 86), something endemic among the activists of 1968, and that it 'expressed fears concerning the Communist Party which were later to be expressed in '68' (Gili 1998: 139).
2. This tendency in film distribution – termed 'The Cinema Rises in Rebellion' by René Micha (Cassou et al. 1970: 151–74) – is the context for the impulse to disrupt film festivals. The desire to establish new networks was manifest in film collectives, assembled to produce auteur-less films, such as the Société pour le Lancement des Oeuvres Nouvelles (SLON) collective behind *Loin du Viêt-nam* (later reformed as the Groupe Medvedkine), Dynadia, Zanzibar, Cinéastes Révolutionnaires Prolétariens and the post-1968 Le Groupe Dziga Vertov (the Dziga Vertov Group, whose members varied from film to film but included Jean-Pierre Gorin and

Godard). Distribution networks were also reconsidered, giving rise to The Other Cinema, and the attempts to radicalise both production and distribution with Etats Généraux du Cinéma Français (for a full history of this organisation see Harvey 1980: 16–27, 121–25 and Hartog 1972/73: 58–88). The practices of the Etats Généraux, such as showing films in factories, wrested film showings away from the bourgeois environment of the commercial cinema. The Etats Généraux aspired to a semi-militant 'Fifth Column' of film distribution; the films were uncertified and so technically the showings were illegal too.

3. Neo-capitalism denotes a more active version of that which is more commonly termed 'late capitalism'. While the latter was theoretically given over to floundering on its own internal contradictions, moving from one crisis to the next, neo-capitalism marked the resurgence of an aggressive, all-pervasive, ideological (in Althusser's definition) capitalism. Pasolini saw this as true of the economic boom in Italy in the 1960s, and neo-capitalism as brazenly manifest (particularly in First World imperialist endeavours) after 1968. Wall, writing in 1969 in relation to the Italian use of the term, notes its transnational organisation and technocratic nature, which he reads as a bulwark against the East Bloc in relation to industrial competition and quality of life for the worker (Wall 1969: 22).

4. Some future members of the Angry Brigade appeared in One Plus One (MacCabe 2003: 219).

5. The Union Nationale des Étudiants de France (UNEF) was a militant left-wing group initially associated with protests against France's presence in Algeria.

6. Hence Diederichsen distinguishes between 'a left and a right wing of the psychedelic experience' (Grunenberg 2005: 87), and the 1970 Playboy publication The Sexual Revolution is able to advance permissiveness in entirely apolitical terms: 'Today, it is obvious that many in America are adopting a new romanticism. Their thrust is anti-intellectual, anti-ideological and is toward the eroticization of practically everything' (Kaiser 1970: 6).

7. The writings of Reich were co-opted as a theoretical foundation for the notion of sexual liberation as an act of revolutionism by some at this time. Reich simply became a badge of radicalism, used to legitimise otherwise regressive sentiments. Such 'neo-Reichianism' was present in the prison manifestos of John Sinclair (associated with the White Panthers movement), which Caute terms 'imbued with the mindless male chauvinism of the counterculture: [for example] "Fuck God in the ass. Fuck your woman until she can't stand up . . . Our program of rock and roll, dope, and fucking in the streets is a program of total freedom for everyone"' (Caute 1988: 274). Such sentiments (which Hale qualifies as 'tongue-in-cheek' for those in the know (Hale 2002: 142)) informed the concerns over the 'anti-intellectualism of student activists . . . their slide towards a book-burning, slogan-shouting nihilism' (Young 1977: 62), and such concerns were ammunition for those smearing students in revolt, such as Beloff (Beloff 1969: 66–77). Weeks notes that 'Neo-Reichianism'

was far from Reich's own (Marxist and Freudian) reading of the relaxation of moral attitudes, which, for Reich, occurred at the behest of 'necessary adjustments by capitalism to its changing demands . . . no more than a corrupted use of sexual libido' (Weeks 1994: 250), a reading that tallied with Marcuse's (see Hall and Critcher et al. 1979: 257). Ollman is explicit about the misuse of Reich in such ways – 'To avoid the kind of misunderstanding that had [sic] bedeviled most discussion of Reich's ideas, I would like to emphasize that Reich's strategy is not a matter of 'advocating' sexual intercourse . . . Reich does not expect everybody to be "screwing" everybody all the time (a fear Freud shares with the Pope), though such relaxation would undoubtedly lead – as it already has in part – to people making love more frequently' (Ollman 1979: 166).

8. The use of Marcuse's writings at this time is as contentious as the use of Reich's. Young notes that it was in Marcuse's work that the Marxist notion of alienation was brought to the fore (with an anti-capitalist rather than anti-industrial spin) (Young 1977: 19–21). Such an identification of the contemporary societal dynamic allows followers of Marcuse, and Marcuse himself, to perceive all strategies or activities of jouissance as a progressive and revolutionary de-alienation, so that – as a Sorbonne slogan had it – 'The society of alienation must disappear from history' (quoted in Roszak 1971: 22), and imagination, in all its radical potential, is freed. Marcuse writes:

> The new sensibility has become, by this very token, praxis: it emerges in the struggle against violence and exploitation where this struggle is waged for essentially new ways and forms of life: negation of the entire Establishment, its morality, culture; affirmation of the right to build a society in which the abolition of poverty and toil terminates in a universe where the sensuous, the playful, the calm, and the beautiful become forms of existence and thereby the [sic] *Form* of the society itself . . . [and at this point] the hatred of the young bursts into laughter and song, mixing the barricade and the dance floor, love play and heroism. (Marcuse 1969: 25–26)

Such inclusiveness, which for Marcuse transcends diversionary and sectarian questions of individual and collective freedom, entryism, socialism and militancy (Marcuse boils revolt down to psychological fundamentals, for example 'the human sensibility which rebels against the dictates of repressive reason, and, in doing so, invokes the sensuous power of the imagination' (Marcuse 1969: 30)) redeems all 'youthful' preoccupations as eroding the ossified old order. Marcuse, in this respect, provides the foundation for the very lack of theoretical rigour and historical analysis that characterised many of his 1968 followers. However, Marcuse's role in this respect was more often than not assumed, or given, by student activists at that time; in retrospect, Marcuse is more appropriately regarded as the theorist of 1967 and the radical potential of the Summer of Love.

9. Young defines 'confrontationism' as a Marcusian impulse to 'delineate, through praxis, the contours of repression . . . provoking corporate liberalism to show the limits of even the most flexible "totalitarian" consensus' (Young 1977: 283).
10. Alan Kaprow defined the 'actual' (that is, theatrical/performance art) happening in 1959 as 'an action that cannot be transported or reproduced' (quoted in Dorléac 1997: 40). In relation to Kaprow's work (and other happenings), Croyden offers this definition: 'Happenings are a juxtaposition of diverse elements and occurrences, performed in any environment by an audience who are at once spectators and participants' (Croyden 1975: 79). Lebel, an exponent of the theatrical happening, describes the occurrence as a collective event that represents, and is seen to represent,

> our only chance to have done with this exploiting society, with its slave-owning mentality and its irremediable culture. Art is in full and fundamental dissidence with all regimes and all forms of coercion, but especially with those regimes which use it for their own ends. To this mercantile, state-controlled conception of culture, we oppose a combative art, fully conscious of its prerogatives: an art which does not shrink from stating its position, from direct action, from transmutation. (Lebel 1968: 92–93)

The happening thus turns sentiment into action – the 'transmutation' – a 'marriage between theory and praxis' (Lebel 1968: 100). The happening can also function as a 'collective exorcism' (Lebel 1968: 99) and represents 'the renovation and intensification of perception' (Lebel 1968: 104). Experientialism in film may therefore be read as a filmic equivalent of the happening sensibility; the viewer becomes a 'participant' by allowing the film to become an 'experience' for him or her (usually via sequences that jettison narrative in favour of effects, longueurs, atmosphere, often expressing subjective impressions – a visual mimicking of an individual's 'experience'). *The Trip* (Roger Corman, 1967), a prolonged recreation of the protagonist's hallucinations and experiences while under the influence of LSD, represents the very structure of experientialism, while *The Invasion of Thunderbolt Pagoda* (Ira Cohen, 1968) recreates LSD aesthetics in the liquidity of its mise en scène, as surfaces blur and melt into other surfaces. More typically, and elsewhere, as in *HWY: An American Pastoral* (Jim Morrison et al., 1970), for example, such liquidity, as a kind of expressionist effect achieved via spatial distortions of an otherwise recognisable reality, occurs via the use of a fisheye lens. The experiential seems to determine the very structure of Carmelo Bene's baroquely psychedelic *Hermitage* and *Nostra Signora dei Turchi* (*Our Lady of the Turks*; both 1968). Both could be dismissed as little more than sequences of nonsensical events, and so labelled as surrealist, but the films invite new ways of perceiving thematic concerns 'after' the idea of a linear narrative has been jettisoned. They could be said to demonstrate the freedoms of imagination by seeming to exist in a place (or emanate from a place) from which all rules of narrative expectations have been put to one side. While experientialism is more often utilised to the ends of a passive reception, even in the nominally politically radical Zanzibar films (as discussed below), active and confrontational experientialism is also possible; Michalka notes one extreme in relation to Peter Weibel's 'action films', with a physical assault of the audience by the artists participating in the screening/happening (an assault returned by those in the audience who had not fled) (Michalka 2004: 99).

11.   This mostly unexplored area may be seen as lending, in part, a theoretical 'catch-all' that underwrites the above-mentioned lack of theoretical rigour and historical analysis. Derrida found in Artaud a position against 'all ideological theater, all cultural theater, all communicative, interpretive . . . theater seeking to transmit a content, or to deliver a message' (Bürger 1996: xxii), so that Artaudian method, as such, allowed for the possibility of a 'transcending' of the particulars of aesthetic strategy, even with regard to the concern of forging an anti- or non-bourgeois film form. Artaud figured at the time in film culture; when, in *La Chinoise*, the most radical member of the revolutionary cell claims his father worked in theatre with Artaud, which invites the conclusion that the Brechtian method of political film has an equivalent, or even a variation, in the Artaudian experiential film (or the filmic equivalents of happenings or situationist gestures; writing in 1969, Thoms, for example, sees Artaudian praxis in the multimedia environment of the consciousness-shifting liquid light show (Thoms 1978: 238)).

There was perceived to be a direct correlation between the two approaches; indeed, the Living Theatre, exponents of theatrical happenings including free love, drug use and stand-offs with authorities, worked from the notion of a correlation. The common denominator between Brecht and Artaud was founded on the shared objective of artistic expression (in the widest possible sense): to raise the consciousness of those present. The blurring of the boundaries between sexual liberation and radical political commitment meant that even the most hedonistic of happenings could be claimed as radical anti-bourgeois expressions, and, indeed, in a time of bloody imperialist adventures abroad, the very act of love represented a force of opposition. Yet, at this time and in the context of the counterculture, the Artaudian film or play was one of inclusiveness rather than cruelty; it sought to redirect the idea of a Brechtian 'critical realism' outside the communalism between film or play and audience, so creating a critical distance from society at large and thus exposing its police state-like mentality and unmasking its totalitarian nature. This vortex of methodologies could be said to include ideas from Althusser, Mao, Marcuse and Reich in the framework of a combined Brechtianism and Artaudianism. Artaud's actual writing about film, in *Scenarios on the Cinema* (see, for example, Artaud 1999: 59), was as unspecific as Brecht's; Barber finds that

> Artaud's film theory . . . [essentially] espouses a violent unleashing of the spectators' senses – those spectators remain alertly grounded in the tactile

world, aware both of what the film is subjecting them to, and also incited to react, in simultaneously physical and revolutionary ways . . . For Artaud, the cinema was literally a stimulant or narcotic, acting directly and materially on the eyes and the senses. (Barber 2001: 29)

In this respect, Artaud represents the theorist for the transformation of critique and gesture into the actual action: the priming of the audience for physical interaction with the world. Greene provocatively concludes her study of Artaud (1970) with the claim that his work was only really being understood, for the first time, and acted upon, in the milieu of the then contemporary counter- and bohemian cultures. The qualification lent to this position, in this study, is that the understanding was certainly enthusiastic, but often haphazard. The later use of Artaud by Deleuze and Guattari (for *Anti-Oedipus* and *A Thousand Plateaus*, first published in 1972 and 1980 respectively), who are at times near forensic in their analyses of Artaud's writings, may be considered a corrective to these earlier uses.

12. Situationist gestures function in film in the same way as happenings; they represent a moment intended to 'shift' the consciousness of the viewer (so revealing the false spectacle society mounts to mask the alienation of its inhabitants from them), a record of an action that would suggest an idea not previously conceived of, a gesture made 'against' the situation of the film. In *Partner*, for example, the 'crossing out' of images of buildings seems to suggest such an attempted shift (the negation of the palpable, ontological-real of the film in favour of the artificial theatre environment in which the protagonists reside); in the BBC drama *Year of the Sex Olympics* (Michael Elliott, 1968) a renegade artist has such an idea in mind when he exposes his painting via live television, rupturing the viewers' complacency in relation to the media-driven 'Big Brother' state of the future. The Situationist per se is one who 'engages in the construction of situations' (Sussman 1989: 198), (Situationists disavow the very term 'situationism'; Sussman claims 'situationism' is '[a] meaningless term improperly derived from [situationist]' (Sussman 1989: 198), a tendency that Viénet sees as a media-driven attempt to rewrite situationism for the purposes of a 'doctrinal establishment of an ideology' (Viénet 1992: 16 note 2)). The happening and the situationist event are possible in a theatrical environment, since the audience can participate, even if only by dint of their physical presence, as Croyden notes. Such participation is impossible with film – rarely, if ever, a 'one off' situation, and the cinema is not generally a 'theatrical' environment in this manner. The film-maker therefore resorts to gestures towards the happening, achieving a 'situationism' conceptually (so that the viewer's acceptance of the physical interchange of the protagonists in *Performance* (belatedly released in 1970) can be understood to be situationist by MacCabe (for example, MacCabe 1998: 76). Just as experientialism can be a filmic equivalent of the spirit of the happening, the situationist gesture represents a filmic equivalent of the debated term 'situationism'. (Therefore, gestures evidently perceived to be, or presented as, situationist on the part of

the film-maker in the context of such films are taken as such; whether 'correctly' situationist or otherwise.)

13. Lebel noted, at the time, a breaking of the preoccupation of material accumulation via drug use: 'The era of hallucinogenic drugs ushers in a new state of mind, breaks with industrial preoccupations, in order to devote itself to the revolution of being' (Lebel 1968: 94). This was literally the case in Italy, where 'marijuana smoking was equated with factory absenteeism as an emblem of struggle against capitalism' (Drake 1989: 91). Roszak offers a more precise reading; drug use as a 'reformulation of the personality, upon which social ideology and culture generally are based' (Roszak 1971: 156, see also 168) – something that is impossible when such a personality has yet to be fully formed, as is the case with – Roszak implies – would-be revolutionaries (Roszak 1971: 159). Roszak's contextualisation of drug use is effectively that of biopolitics; a radical refusal to work via a deliberate degrading of a physical and mental ability to work. At this point, a reading that diverges with Lebel's hedonistic revelry is possible: for Austin '[p]sychedelia's social project . . . [was] to retreat en masse and wait for the status quo – already wobbling under the pressures from social changes and revolutions on almost every front – to fall under its own weight' (Austin 2005: 190). For Hardt and Negri this refusal of work and authority means that '"[d]ropping out" was really a poor conception of what was going on in Haight-Ashbury and across the United States in the 1960s' (Hardt and Negri 2001: 274): the contours of the new society become visible with the standing down of the requirements of the old – even if such a standing down results in an addled and immobile proletariat.

14. The success of *Easy Rider* (Dennis Hopper, 1969) in North America, an experiential film par excellence that utilised a particularly European New Wave approach to film-making, is often seen as marking the beginning of an auteur-driven anti-establishment period of American film-making. It was in this context that Antonioni came to shoot *Zabriskie Point* in the United States. The youth market in North America had an established commercial tradition of revolutionism, with films such as *Head* (Bob Rafelson, 1968), *Wild in the Streets* (Barry Shear, 1968), *The Trip*, and *Hell's Angels on Wheels* and *Psych-Out* (Richard Rush, 1967 and 1968 respectively). Thus *The Strawberry Statement* (Stuart Hagman, 1970), concerning student radicalism and campus unrest, was able to utilise fairly confrontational New Wave techniques but otherwise remained an entirely conventional film. Godardian critical realism was more evident in films that aspired to serious political statements, such as *Medium Cool* (Haskell Wexler, 1969), *Ice* (Robert Kramer, 1970), *Sweet Sweetback's Badasssss Song* (Melvin Van Peebles, 1971), and a Godard-like utilisation of pastiche in *Beyond the Valley of the Dolls* (Russ Meyer, 1970).

15. In *The Function of the Orgasm* Reich posits neurosis as a condition arising from a lack of 'orgiastic potency'; in *The Mass Psychology of Fascism* (first published 1946), Reich notes 'The Social Function of Sexual Repression' (Reich 1997: 24 and ff) as taking on

the 'chief social function [which] is to secure the existing class structure' (Ollman 1979: 165).

16. For a discussion of the ill-fated attempt to repeat *Woodstock* (Michael Wadleigh, 1970), see Sanjek and Halligan (2013).

17. The status of this object is more than arbitrary; a subplot in the film involves housing developments in the desert. This house could be said to represent just such a hope for the future – the next stage of technological progress – something that provokes the Lawrencian reaction from the proletariat closer to nature, as discussed above.

18. Lebel noted such an association at the time: 'Recent experiences have shown that the ingestion of certain hallucinogenic substances [such as those seen taken by the protagonists of *Performance*] create a mood in which each person dreams the dreams of others' (Lebel 1968: 98).

19. In *Performance*, the bohemian and semi-derelict Powis Square 'pad' in which Jagger conducts burnt-out and Byronic rock star experiments with hallucinogenics recalls the lurid stories of the goings-on in Redlands (Keith Richards's country house) that were leaked to the media at the time of the police raid. *Wonderwall* (Joe Massot, 1968) seems to capitalise on the same ambience.

20. These films, termed 'materialaktion' by their makers, were principally shot in Austria with Muehl and members of his commune, the AA-Kommune (Aktionsanalytische Kommune), as the Vienna Action Group; the role approximating director was usually taken by Kurt Kren (associated with the Austrian Film-makers Cooperative), when present. Barber notes that Muehl and his associates were 'strongly preoccupied with Artaud's work in the mid-1960s' (Barber 2001: 31), and this was particularly so for member Günter Brus, who worked with Artaud's texts in his own publications (see Barber 2004: 27). The films are mostly experimental shorts, some of which have been grouped into cycles. Legal screenings of these works remain difficult in many countries, but they have been shown in galleries, cellars, nightclubs and on campuses in Europe and North America (see Barber 2004: 58). In this respect, the redress of content necessitates a step away from the major studios who backed Roeg and Cammell, and Antonioni.

21. Although the films are often associated with underground and experimental film happenings, they remain confined to the screen, unlike most other multimedia/liquid lightshow 'happening'-orientated films/installation works. Gottfried Schlemmer's 1969 film *The Time for ACTION has come*, for example, culminated with the director himself ripping through the screen on which the film is projected, from behind, and then leaping into the audience (whereupon he reads the text he is seen writing in the projected film, which 'calls on the cinemagoers to actively intervene in social processes and to understand the world as one that can be transformed' (Michalka 2004: 109)). In this context, the Muehl films seem conservative in their rejection of such an 'expanded screen', in favour of documentation, ritual and passive experientialism. The 'assault' originates in radical content alone, not

radical, 'expanded' or assaulting form. This point is particularly visible if the films are compared to *Belle de Jour* – despite the extreme differences of approach, both Muehl and Buñuel are concerned with, and take as their primary object of attention, that which Reich identified as, in Rycroft's summary, an 'insistence that much of what passes for normal sexual activity among European adults is really a compulsive, neurotic symptom, impelled by anxiety and sadism, not by genuine sexual desire' (Rycroft 1971: 60). The trauma of this discovery, as sublimated into form, results in Buñuel's radically ambiguous mise en scène, whereas in the Muehl films, with an un-ambiguity to their form so as to contain the trauma of this discovery, a radically confrontational documentation of the actualité of such sexual practices arises. The same might be said, arguably to an even more extreme extent, of the anarcho-/ utopian-Green bestiality documented in *Bodil Joensen "A Summerday"* (*Bodil Joensen – en sommerdag juli 1970*, Shinkichi Tajiri and Ole Ege, 1970).

22. Such an 'act'-based nature to these films remains the case in relation to their legality where screenings remain outlawed.

23. Muehl was not the only exponent of extremity in respect of 'happenings' – various Situationists also presented startling happenings at this time (see Dorléac 1997: 44).

24. Although it is possible to reject or deflect the question altogether; Robert Jungk, in *Die Zeit*, reported on a 1968 happening seemingly conducted by an associate of Muehl's (of a 'Maoist splinter-group of the Austrian Socialist Students') and winds up considering the reasons for the conduct of the main participant as a way of finding a context to comprehend the event:

    The argument of those who dared to object at the end of this miserable Orgy-in-Academe had no chance against the pseudo-Freudian dialectic of the "Partisans" . . . Did the organisers of this Happening know that the "artist" they had persuaded to take part in their demonstration had been under psychiatric observation for several years in a Vienna mental hospital . . . Were they aware that they were, in effect, providing a public platform for the private satisfaction of sexual neuroses?' and so forth. (Jungk 1968: 93)

    This may have been the University of Vienna 'Kunst und Revolution'/'Art and Revolution' action of 7 June 1968, discussed by Barber (2004: 49, 99 and ff) and documented in Faber (2005: 62–63, 178–79).

25. This can be read in terms of a breaking of Reichian 'character armour', made explicit in Makavejev's *Sweet Movie* (1974) when the commune's activities are contrasted with archive footage of Nazi 'baby athletics'. In this respect, the anarchic force of the orgasm is not equated with a conventional display of 'fulfilling' sexuality (pornography) – something which, by its very absence in these non-bourgeois films, is suggested as a construct of bourgeois society – but retains a gleefulness, as Barber puts it, in respect of 'acts of sexual and excremental furore' (Barber 2004: 56).

26. The Zanzibar Group were (and remain; some of the films are lost, and credits for the films were suppressed at the time) an obscure loose collective of film-makers, primarily based in France, that was disbanded, as the group dispersed soon after 1968. The members, as much bohemians as revolutionaries, and often technical amateurs in relation to film-making, straddled the worlds of fashion and conceptual art, and acknowledged a debt to situationism. Their films were privately funded, eradicating the necessity for a distributable, or even showable, product – a necessity that not even Godard, at his most avant-garde prior to circa 1970, could completely avoid. The Zanzibar films revolved around May 1968 – as member Patrick Deval put it: 'before, in a prophetic manner, during in a documentary and historical way, and after in a melancholy way' (quoted in Shafto 2000: 6). On the former count, the early Zanzibar film *Héraclite l'Obscur* (Deval, 1967) casts the titular protagonist as a proto-hippy on the margins of (ancient) society.

27. Such a lending is evident in terms of shared intent and structures, but also acknowledges the anecdotal evidence of an integration of Artaudianism at this time. In addition to the above-noted instances, it is telling that Godard, interviewed shortly after completing *One Plus One* and asked about Garrel, informally associated with the Zanzibar films ('After seeing a private showing of a film by . . . Garrel, Godard was heard to say he felt "depassé"'), praises him as '[a] young Antonin Artaud'. Such praise was not extended to the "hippies", who, Demoriane suggests shortly after this comment, 'could be a force to purge Capitalism [sic], as the Red Guards purged Soviet Communism . . .', since, for Godard, 'The hippies will do nothing until they are politicised' (Demoriane 1968: 4). Artaudian praxis, so it would seem, was not perceived to be a lesser concern, for those unwilling to embrace formerly ideological concerns in their film-making.

28. The visibility of Artaud – thematically and in terms of form – is such that Kline can offer a far-reaching reading of the film under the sign of Artaud. Even the act of adaptation on Bertolucci's part (of Dostoevsky's *The Double*) is declared to be an aspiration to the Artaudian 'double': 'Socially, politically, psychologically, and aesthetically . . . *Partner* proposes a reinscription of cultural artefacts operating like (and unlike) Artaud's plague, seeking to test and arrest our notions of reality and replace them with that double of reality Artaud dreamed of' (Kline 1987: 54).

29. Bertolucci's debt to the Living Theatre is apparent here – or, more accurately, the initial role of the Living Theatre in the imagination of radical Europeans of the time (as noted by Tytell 1997: 223); Lebel's own book on the Living Theatre ends with a 'do it yourself' diagram of a Molotov cocktail (see Lebel 1968: 378).

30. In relation to this use of Brechtian method, Bertolucci later dismissed the film in its entirety: 'The fear of establishing an adult relationship with the audience made us find shelter in a perverse and childish cinema. From this point of view *Partner* is truly a manifesto for the cinema envisaged around 1968. The notion of alienation that the film invokes is culturally equivocal and is grounded in a misguided reading of Brecht'

(Bertolucci 1987: 59–60). 'In 1968, there were a lot of grand, marvellous and stupid things said: "The camera is like a machine gun". There were a lot of people who said this. Me too, for a moment, I also let myself be swept up by this idea. In fact, it was a romantic, juvenile and blind idea' (quoted in Gili 1998: 133).

31. Lovell, however, argues that the film is an 'exemplary case of Brecht's ideas' through its description of 'a social process' (Lovell 1975/76: 70) – in this case, the workings of the public school. For Anderson himself, the film was 'rather Brechtian' (Sussex 1969: 75) and he claimed that during its making 'we constantly thought of Brecht, and his definition of the "epic" style' (Hedling 1998: 95). Anderson seems to have intended the Brechtian aspect to have been through a use of 'types' – of the caning scene, for example 'The boys are beaten actually for what they are' (Sussex 1969: 84).

32. Anderson distanced himself from Godard's work (Hedling 1998: 103); there is no convergence of ideas between Godard and Anderson as to what constitutes a Brechtian film, and both employed Brechtian strategies for different ends. Hedling sees *The White Bus* as entirely Brechtian, but more by association (that is, Anderson's 'involvement' with Brechtian theory and practice in writing and theatre (quoted in Hedling 1998: 62–69)). For Hedling, Anderson's Verfremdungseffekt comes through the arbitrariness of the interpolation of colour and black and white sequences and moments that go against the documentary impulse of the film (such as an imaginary hanging, in the opening moments of the film). References to surrealist films, or Vigo's films, work in this manner too (Hedling 1998: 70), as do the devices that separate sound from image (Hedling 1998: 71–72).

33. The end of the film is partly homage to Vigo's revolution in a public school in *Zéro de Conduite* (1933). Lovell finds that the film as a whole suggests 'an imaginative form generated by novels like *Tom Brown's Schooldays*' (Lovell 1975/76: 69). But those scenes that present a continuation of such public school traditions (the house 'thump', the canings, cold showers and so forth) speak of their opposite: not tradition and history but the unpleasant reality of such practices and their failure to exist as anything other than institutionalised abuses of power (rather than as the 'benefits' of the public school upbringing). The locating of revolutionism in romanticism as a caricature of student revolutionaries holds more in common with the world of Billy Bunter than Tom Brown.

34. The ambiguities on all levels of the film prompted critics on the Left to question the progressive use of a film open to a variety of interpretations (see Viano 1993: 201). Like *Il Vangelo Secondo Matteo*, the film received the Office Catholique International du Cinéma award at the September 1968 Venice Film Festival. However, *Teorema* was then attacked by the Vatican organ, the Osservatore Romano (which eventually published the directive that the film should not be seen (Schwartz 1995: 524)), and the Office Catholique International du Cinéma was itself attacked by the Italian Right. Pope Paul VI reputedly found the film 'inadmissible' (Greene 1990: 134). Pasolini attributed this controversy to the way in which the film was 'in the centre of

a cyclone which is hitting the Church at the moment, with a clerical left and clerical right and so on' (Stack 1969: 157). Pasolini was prosecuted (unsuccessfully) on a charge of obscenity (Macdonald 1969: 32) (for the charges made against the film, all primarily of a sexual nature, see Pasolini (1999: 51–52)) and the film was temporarily withdrawn on these grounds (Siciliano 1987: 317): an 'offence to decency . . . contrary to every moral, social or family value' (quoted in Schwartz 1995: 525). Pasolini himself withdrew the film from the Venice festival, in protest at the re-emergence of the competition aspect of the festival and the inevitable police presence during sit-ins, something the festival director, Luigi Chiarini, had promised would not happen. Pasolini asked those present at the beginning of the screening to leave the hall in protest (Siciliano 1987: 317). *Teorema* was both film and novel, the latter written during the making of the former (production began in March 1968) but first existed as a 1966 verse play, *Pilade*. The novel, when withdrawn from the competition for the Strega Prize, also aroused controversy (Siciliano 1987: 134–35).

35. Lino Pèroni, in an autumn 1968 interview with Pasolini in *Inquadrature*, compared the film to *La Guerre est Finie* and *La Chinoise* – all films about 'a "crisis in ideology"' (quoted in Stack 1969: 157). Such a sentiment finds a final echo in *Die Artisten in der Zirkuskuppel: Ratlos* with the collapse of the radicalism of the circus experiments – dishearteningly abandoned in favour of a sell-out to popular television.

36. The painter of the revolutionary cell in *La Chinoise* seems to work from a more pessimistic assumption that anti-bourgeois gestures are all that can be achieved, and so commits suicide.

37. Pasolini's relating of such negations of the established order to student revolutionary activity of 1968 is made apparent in the inclusion of an attack on the students of 1968 in the appendix of the novel *Teorema*: 'Sure, what else do young, intelligent / kids from well-off families do except / talk about literature and painting? . . . / What do the kids of 1968 talk about – with their / barbaric hair and Edwardian suits . . . / [nothing] except about literature and painting? And what / does this do except evoke from the darkest / depths of the petit bourgeoisie the / exterminating God, who strokes them once again / for sins even greater than those committed in '38?' (quoted in Schwartz 1992: 528–29). The idea of a dissenting 'Left bourgeoisie' was again attacked in 'Il PCI ai Giovani!' ('The PCI to the Youth!' – headlined, when first published, with 'Vi odio cari studenti', 'Dear students, I hate you'): 'It's sad. The polemics against / that party were all over in the first half / of the last decade. You're late kids . . . / When yesterday in the Valle Giulia you came to / blows / I sympathized with the cops! / Because the cops are the sons of the poor' (quoted in Schwartz 1992: 529). Pasolini accused the student revolutionaries of gesture politics (along with many in the PCI and PCF) and condemned their 'false tolerance' – the whole movement was a sham: 'It is strange, abandoning the revolutionary lan- / guage of the poor, old, Togliattian, official Com- / munist Party . . . / I hope you have understood that making / puritanism is a way of keeping yourselves / from

any real revolutionary action' (quoted in Schwartz 1992: 531). In 1968, and of this 'puritanism', Pasolini talked of 'the fascism of the Left' in the 'the restorers of the revolutionary spirit' with 'a new Zhdanovism' (Pasolini 2005: 162). This class problem of the protests, as soon revealed as 'a revolt not of the oppressed, but the privileged' (Hewison 1986: 276), eventually drove a wedge between Truffaut and Godard, with the former claiming he could be forced to side with the 'proletarian riot police' (quoted in MacCabe 2003: 210).

Fassbinder's reading of 1968 was similar to Pasolini's; a play written for his 'antitheatre' troupe, *Anarchy in Bavaria* (first performed in June 1969), expressed disapproval of the naive nature of 'a revolution "on the run"' via a satire concerning students successfully seizing power and the consequential disastrous results. The play 'passes judgement on the revolutionary romantics of the late sixties' (Thomsen 1997: 58) – whom Fassbinder termed 'these [Leftist] idiots' (Thomsen 1997: 16) – while retaining a measure of sympathy for them. (Indeed, the profits from an earlier play concerning the attempted assassination of Rudi Dutschke, *Axel Caesar Haarmann*, went to the Students for a Democratic Society (SDS) legal rights fund (see Iden and Karsunke et al. 1981: 4, 5).) Pasolini was publicly condemned by students, the PCI, groups on the left of the PCI and Fortini (Schwartz 1992: 533). Pasolini saw 1968 as an internal struggle, within the bourgeoisie, hence the – as the situationist street paper *Arson News* had it – 'middle-class drop-out scene' (quoted in Hewison 1986: 168); in Giuliano Manacorda's terms: 'bourgeois society expressed these oppositions to itself, then reintegrating them into its own category' (quoted in Van Watson 1989: 13). Such a reading formally existed at the time too; with the Kabouters in Holland, for example (Young 1977: 235). This reading of the events of 1968 was to be contextualised in Pasolini's later novel *Petrolio* (left incomplete and existing only in uncorrected manuscript form). Here the 'youths of '68', as he called them (Pasolini 1997: xiv), are only a blip on the progression towards neo-capitalism. Pasolini's overview here addresses the wider evolution of 'la strategia della tensione' rather than placing 1968 as any kind of turning point. Gordon notes that Pasolini was not as intolerant of the students in his articles, even terming the events 'battaglie di retroguardia' (rearguard battles), (Gordon 1996: 65–66).

38. This dichotomy also exists in Pasolini's *Edipo Re* (1967) and *Medea* (1969). The use of Etna – invariably giving rise to a minimalist, two-tone mise en scène (the landscape and the sky) – suggests a return to the bare minimum of actual existence, as if the characters find themselves reborn as cavemen or primitives, and so unencumbered with a super-ego to keep in check their id. *Porcile* also first existed as a play.

39. In and of 1968, Pasolini noted that the bourgeoisie had shifted ground: 'it is assimilating everything to the petit[e]-bourgeoisie: the whole of mankind is becoming petit[e]-bourgeois' – these, for Pasolini, are the 'new problems' of 'Neo-Capitalism' and the reasons for *Teorema*'s radical ambiguity, its 'absence of an answer' (quoted in Stack 1969: 158). The notion of assimilation finds a metaphor in

cannibalism and the consumption of a protagonist by pigs in *Porcile* – for Gian Piero Brunetta, 'the ability of the bourgeois world to absorb and digest any opposition' (quoted in Greene 1990: 143).

40. A slight proof of the undermining nature of the loss of the ontological-real at this juncture is that the same gridlock sequence is effectively remade by Godard in the documentary *British Sounds* (1969) – this time a long take tracking shot of factory workers – and the resultant sequence is often noted as one of the most provocative in its experientialism and exposé of the blue collar working conditions of contemporary industrial society of Godard's work of the late 1960s.

41. In this respect, *Week-end* subverts the idea of the rural commune, returning a sense of horror to the Woodstock-era imaginings of a one-ness with nature (for example, the great claims made for the open-air music festival that date to this moment: 'a rehearsal for the time when basic amenities as we know them have broken down, perhaps, through the running out of natural resources, perhaps through revolution and social eruption, perhaps through nuclear war' (quoted in Sandford and Reid 1974: 5); 'There are many among those who use festivals who believe . . . that this is the way that much of Britain may one day be; that the life style provided and lived at pop festivals may be an indication of the way that society itself may be moving. Future social structures are seen as being more closely linked to the soil, to be more concerned with sharing . . . to contain more tribal togetherness than now' (Sandford and Reid 1974: 119)).

42. Silverman and Farocki also find the collapse of society as portrayed as denoted in the loss of power of the status of the phallus, apparent in the opening monologue in which digits and an egg are also described as penetrating the anus (Silverman and Farocki 1998: 88–89): the phallus has lost its uniqueness now that it has been replaced by 'lesser' objects. Capitalism as anality was to be a concern of Godard's beyond 1968.

43. In Marxist term equivalents, these actions – particularly those of the radicalised son in the film and his artistic experiments – can be termed 'leftist' adventurism: 'basing a revolutionary tactic on revolutionary feelings alone' (Glucksmann 1968: 117).

44. Such a concern with the futility of revolution is also to be found in films associated with, but outside of, the field of this study: the above-mentioned *Easy Rider*; Želimir Žilnik's *Rani Radovi* (released, briefly, in 1969); many of the late 1960s films, all banned at the time, of the Czech New Wave, such as *Ucho*, *Smutečhí Slavnost* (*Funeral Ceremony*, Zdenek Sirový, 1969) and *Sedmy Den, Osmá Noc* (*Seventh Day, Eighth Night*, Evald Schorm, 1969); and Skolimowski's *Ręce do Góry* (*Hands Up!*, 1967, not released until 1981, and then in a modified form).

45. A copy of a Gilles Jacob article on Truffaut from *Sight and Sound* is seen in *Ciné-tract 9*, 'Hollywood sur Seine', with the words 'philosophy' and 'bourgeoisie' scrawled over it, seemingly in Godard's handwriting (the original is Jacob 1967: 162). Truffaut's

Baiser Volés (1968) had begun boldly with a dedication to Langlois in the shot of the locked Cinémathèque Française, but then moved straight into romantic comedy.

46. Such a pronouncement from the New Left's opposition was a gift, to them, from Moscow: 'The Gaullists pointed to a concrete example of what would happen to France if Communists ever seized power. Frenchmen were willing to believe them' (Priaulx and Ungar 1969: 158).

47. The repetition of the rumour in Michael Beloff's red-baiting *Encounter* article (Beloff 1968: 53) illustrates the transformation of such an idea across only half a dozen months – from the promise of an upturning of the hegemony to evidence presented should a pre-emptive use of state force be deemed necessary to defuse such a threat.

48. However, Herzog distanced the film from 1968 altogether and distanced himself from the revolutionary climate of the 1960s (see Cronin 2002: 55–56), claiming the film was attacked (it was termed fascist) because of such an unfashionable stance.

49. His next film, the U.S.-set *Punishment Park*, along with Kubrick's *A Clockwork Orange* (both 1971), in their visions of authoritarian future dystopia, are often read as the epitome of post-1968 films.

50. This was notably so in *Fellini-Roma* (1972), *Amarcord* (1974) and *Fellini-Casanova* (1976).

51. The trilogy consists of: *Il Decameron* (*The Decameron*, 1971), *I Racconti di Canterbury* (*The Canterbury Tales*, 1972) and *Il Fiore delle Mille e una Notte* (*The Thousand and One Nights*, 1974).

52. More generally, Viano identifies new strains of film, which 'sought to fabricate new modes of representation' (Viano 1993: 215), as with Bertolucci's post-1968 films. For Viano, they are: *Le Gai Savoir*, *Antonio das Mortes* (Rocha, 1969), *Katzelmacher* (Fassbinder, 1969), *I Dannati della Terra* (Valentino Orsini, 1967), *Sotto il Segno dello Scorpione* (*Under the Sign of Scorpio*, Taviani brothers, 1969). Moeller adds *Die Artisten in der Zirkuskuppel: Ratlos*, (Moeller 1979: 5). Harvey identifies *Tout va Bien* (Godard and Gorin, 1972) as representing a post-1968 reconsideration of Brecht and film (Harvey 1980: 75), in its attempt to fashion a revised critical discourse (in which Hollywood stars report on a workers' strike, revealing a cross-section – literally – of factory life and relations). And, to a certain extent, the *Screen* conference 'Brecht and Cinema/Film and Politics' at the 1975 Edinburgh International Film Festival was also an attempt to assess the worth of the Brechtian film method before and after 1968.

53. The beginnings of a confiscation of art from the radical/revolutionary left can be discerned in both these areas after 1968. For example, Walker notes the populist conservatism of the BBC's 1969 *Civilisation* series, with Kenneth Clark's 'patrician and patriarchal' reading of the history of art (Walker 2002: 67), which Wyver takes as effectively evidencing 'a profound uncertainty on Clark's part about the future' (Wyver 2014: 131), in the context of the making of the series during May 1968 – an argument fully advanced by Conlin (2009). Direct attacks on the youth culture of

1968, with revolutionary aspirations reworked as cynical sexual opportunism, seem to have occurred in the areas of low comedy produced by establishment figures: *Take a Girl Like You* (Jonathan Miller, 1970) and *The Adventures of Barry McKenzie* (Bruce Beresford, 1972), for example. The idea of sexual opportunism focused on the available hippies by the middle aged bourgeoisie seems a more sympathetic reading of the ideals of free love, as with *Lettera Aperta a un Giornale della Sera, Say Hello to Yesterday* (Alvin Rakoff, 1970) and John Schlesinger's *Darling* (1965), *Midnight Cowboy* (1969) and *Sunday Bloody Sunday* (1971).

54. Smith discusses the work of Jean-Louis Comolli with just such a post-1968 sea change as her principal context (see Smith 2005: 136 and ff). Such a post-1968 sensibility had been anticipated as much in the popular (rather than the ultra- or militant-left) quarter, with *C'era una Volta il West* (*Once Upon A Time in the West*, Sergio Leone, 1968). Revolutionism, for Leone, had informed the reinterpretation of the western rather than given rise to 'direct' expressions of revolutionism within the western. (For this reason, Leone would state: 'I really didn't want to make a eulogy to revolution as was presented for example in *Quién Sabe?* by Damiano Damiani [1966], filmed with a lot of passion but whose ideology suddenly seemed old and formulaic like the prayer of a medieval mystic' (quoted in Frayling 2000: 319)). Thus genre constraints ensured that the intrusion of the ontological-real, and the revolutionary and radical baggage that was attached to the ontological-real in the late 1960s, had no bearing on the spaghetti western. Via a process of intertextual mimesis, the western is regurgitated, in Leone's film, as a form of discourse born of a certain type of society – one that utilises the myths of the West for political ends, so that the western itself is posited, and unmasked, as a system of mythic order. This occurs, in the clearest example, through an inversion of the good and the bad – both in terms of characters (the iconographic casting against type) and imperatives (the capitalisation-marketisation, rather than civilisation, of the West). Thus, from the outset, *C'era una Volta il West* is able to suggest a revision of the system of mythic order, and the semiotic systems that inform the nature of representation in this framework, rather than 'intervene' in found reality. It is the question of the creation of 'meaning' within this populist system of mythic bourgeois order that is continually raised.

55. For *Pravda*, the collective seems to have consisted of Paul Burron, Godard, Jean-Pierre Gorin (previously a member of the editorial board of *Cahiers Marxistes-Léninistes*), Jean-Henri Roger and 'a Czechoslovakian documentary film unit', filming clandestinely. The film was shot between March and August 1969 for West German television, but sources differ (see MacCabe 2003: 413 footnote 38). To a certain extent, these films, as well as Fassbinder's late 1960s theatre work, can also be considered as collective or 'group' work – originating in a desire for democratic systems of artistic creation (see Hayman 1984: 34–35), if not the completely democratic model of the Dziga Vertov Group; films made by mass meeting

(MacCabe 2003: 224). This belated 'death of the auteur', to paraphrase Barthes, resonates, MacCabe notes, with the renewed attacks on the idea of the author (from Barthes and Foucault) in 1967 (MacCabe 2003: 227). The close working relationship of Straub and Huillet and their joint credit for their films also places their work in this category.

56. One declared modus operandi in this respect, for the Group, was the use of Marxist equivalent strategies of film language; Cannon terms such uses (for example 'sometimes the class struggle takes the form of a struggle between image and image or sound and sound . . . is the Marxist notion of surplus value not a useful weapon in the struggle against the bourgeois concept of representation?') as a 'metaphorical use of Marxism in discussing film techniques' (Cannon 2000: 104). The Group's films remain little seen and little discussed (and their roughness certainly dictates against wider dissemination) and, in their convolutions, are 'difficult' – MacCabe identifies a 'wearying political content' (MacCabe 2003: 216) and can only extract limited sense from *British Sounds* (MacCabe 2003: 217). Ali notes the results of Godard's 'ultra-radical view of the world' as 'both a political and aesthetic disaster' (Ali 1987: 253).

57. This provocatively suggests the film is a counterpart to *British Sounds*; irrespective of ideological sphere, the 'bourgeoisie' enslaves workers all the same. The same kind of provocation is true of the film's title too; *Pravda* was the organ of the Soviet Communist Party – that is, a fount of almost anything but the 'truth'. Thus the film, with the ironic reappropriation of the word, suggests the truth of the lies of the Soviet system, as manifest in present-day Prague.

58. A similar reading of late Cold War accommodation is evident in *The Gladiators*, with the military of the East and West united against the working classes.

59. Despite the collective nature of the Group's films, it is possible to trace a line of methodological development from Godard's films. Such a conscious reading of the world plastered with advertisements was first evident in *Deux ou Trois Choses* and the dialectic voice-overs commenting on the film (from 'within' the film) was first evident in Godard's *La Contestation* sketch (*L'Aller et Retour des Enfants Prodigies, Andate e Ritorno dei Figli Prodighi*).

60. The French censor refused to certify the film for public exhibition (Dixon 1997: 99), and the Office de Radio-diffusion et Télévision Française (ORTF), who funded it, refused to show it. Dixon concludes '*Le Gai Savoir* was . . . assiduously suppressed by the French government' (Dixon 1997: 101) although, across 1968, much of ORTF's output, particularly news, was censored or self-censored.

61. It is uncertain if this represents Godard's self-censorship or censorship on the part of ORTF (some English subtitled prints subtitle the inaudible dialogue).

62. The film, often incorrectly (and tellingly) attributed to the Dziga Vertov Group, was shot in May and June and edited in August.

63. The two films seem to have been in production at the same time.

64. Of the haphazardness of *Un Film Comme les Autres*, Dixon notes that Godard was apparently absent for most of the filming and had included an instruction to the projectionist in the film cans to '"flip a coin" . . . to determine which reel of the two-reel film should be shown to the audience first' (Dixon 1997: 95). Roud feels compelled to attack 'legends' about the impenetrability of the film (Roud 1970: 148), and indeed it is far from the only film from this period to contain extended sequences of dialogue: *La Sua Giornata di Gloria* includes a twenty minute group discussion. A further level of negation in operation in *Un Film Comme les Autres*, albeit unintentional, is a near-unintelligible simultaneous English and French soundtrack, which suggests a simultaneous English translation was applied in post-production (and the plummy tone of the English voice could be uncharitably commandeered as evidence of the reading of 1968 as middle class insurrection).

65. The same could be said for Bene. *Capricci* (1969) replaces the rich and delirious aesthetics of his 1968 films with a harsh and naturally lit presentation of straitened circumstances.

66. *British Sounds*, known as *See You at Mao* in the United States, was commissioned by London Weekend Television and then refused transmission.

67. She wanders around in a house, presumably illustrating the lack of such freedom in contemporary industrial society. Her physical appearance, unusual for film nudity, anticipates the notions of 'alternative' beauty that would be espoused by early feminists.

68. Cannon notes that the work of the Group was addressed to an extremely marginal element within society (which is deduced by listing those leftists to whom the films are not addressed) – only those 'both politically revolutionary and impassioned by the aesthetic questions which enthused Godard' (Cannon 2000: 105); (see also Morrey 2005: 95). A reverberation of this sentiment is apparent in Trevor Griffiths' 1974 play *The Party*; one New Left character is modelled on Godard's British *British Sounds* producer, and is roundly trounced by a Trotskyist for his blind romanticism, a mixture of elitism and adventurism.

69. The cycle consists of *Verona* (1967), *Callas Walking Lucia* (1968), *Callas Text mit Doppelbeleuchtung* (1968), *Maria Callas Porträt* (1968), *Mona Lisa* (1968) and *Maria Callas Singt 1957 Rezitativ . . .* (1968), although Callas appears elsewhere in Schroeter's film too.

70. These attacks, as mentioned in (Viano 1993: 56 and ff) and (Orr 1997: 3–5), can be seen to occur in Heath (1973: 110–24).

71. MacCabe notes the point of connection between such an aspirant Maoist analysis and the general undercurrent of structuralism in *Cahiers* (see MacCabe 2003: 205–6).

72. Eco took issue with Pasolini's equating of a semiology of the cinema with a semiology of reality; Pasolini's 1967 letter to Eco, 'The Code of Codes', outlines the theoretical stance from which he rejected Eco's critique (see Pasolini 2005: 276–83).

73. See, for example, Durgnat's consideration of Sirk's *Imitation of Life* (1959), (Durgnat 1976: 78).

74. Originally released as *The Bridegroom, The Actress and the Pimp*. The film, which includes a performance from Fassbinder, was shot between April and May 1968 and premiered October.

75. Auslander, in his history and analysis of 1970s 'glam rock', posits the eradication of the, or a, counterculture as a prerequisite for the next stage of progressive artistic expression (which occurs via the same praxes as those touched upon above – a radical problematisation of representation, albeit, in the 'glam rock' phase, via 'gender bending', a making strange of generic norms and so on); (see Auslander 2006: 10 and ff). Indeed, the very feel, the newness, of the new sensibility is itself understood to be in direct opposition to the counterculture, with an attention paid to the theatrical image (that is, the self-consciously created, or 'mediatised') rather than the 'authentically' live happening, flamboyance over concentration, a subversive intervention from within the system rather than a dismantling of the system, and so forth.

76. This technique became even more pronounced later: 'As Fassbinder has professed himself, his ideal after 1974 includes the blending of "Hollywood" and of Brechtian aesthetics' (Moeller 1979: 6). Erffmeyer notes that assimilation of the un-reality of Hollywood occurred 'while maintaining a decidedly German milieu' (Erffmeyer 1983: 37) and goes on to observe that such a tendency itself illustrates the influence of Godard (Erffmeyer 1983: 38), as do (Elsaesser 1996: 267) and (Kolker 1983: 237). In this context, Fassbinder's later use of transgender and transvestite characters may be seen as an ideal visual 'result' of the mining of semiotic ambiguities and of the muddling of image and representation. Elsewhere, Elsaesser notes that the real influence of Godard was not in the tendency to pastiche Hollywood, but in the approach Godard adopted for *Vivre sa Vie* and the revealing of the notional relationship between capitalism and prostitution (Elsaesser 1976: 27). Thomsen notes that an early Fassbinder short, *Das Kleine Chaos* (*The Little Chaos*, 1967), is a homage to *Vivre sa Vie* (Thomsen 1997: 45), the Godard film with which Fassbinder was most enamoured (see Iden, Karsunke et al. 1981: 61). *Das Kleine Chaos* is a lot like Godard, but the Godard of pastiche, whereas Fassbinder's earlier short *Der Stadtstreicher* (*The City Tramp*, shot in November 1966), in its street filming, documentary realism and arbitrary shifts on the soundtrack (diegetic noise, silence, classical music), is made directly under the sign of Godard's Nouvelle Vague methodology. This illustrates that by the time of *Liebe ist Kälter als der Tod* Fassbinder had made a conscious decision to remove any New Wave stylistic elements – an absence heightened by its dedication to Rohmer and Chabrol, and confirmed by the third dedicatee: Straub. This formally represents a post-New Wave sensibility; it is not just that Fassbinder chronologically began with feature-length films in the '"post-revolutionary" period' as O'Kane puts it (O'Kane 1983: 24).

77. Shattuc notes that Brecht was thought of as an orthodox Leftist in Germany in the 1960s and 1970s (and, it could be added, now): depoliticised and very acceptable to the bourgeoisie – his method was not a pole of radicalism to which to aspire, but one bound up with political compromise (Shattuc 1995: 87–89). While Fassbinder's work must be seen within an evolution of Brechtian alienation, even via Sirk's Hollywood films, he sought to sever any formal connections to the Brechtian tradition associated with Kluge.

78. Such strategies were soon to be relocated to the mores of the specifically contemporary petty bourgeoisie in the documentary-like *Warum Läuft Herr R. Amok? (Why Does Herr R. Run Amok?* Fassbinder and Michael Fengler, 1970). Here the literally inexplicable actions of the 'well adjusted' protagonist (a nihilistic murder spree and suicide) demand answers from that milieu; what is it that is so seriously amiss in society that acting in accordance to society's expectations results in such tragedy?

Seized, Freed, Remade and Deployed

At the outset of this study, the observation was made of the reluctance to outline the 'hardwiring' between the film artefact and its era that characterises much critical/academic writing on the period under scrutiny. This omission is arresting, since, it was noted, it is just such a symbiotic relationship that typifies the nature of the artefacts themselves; a conscious understanding or unconscious acceptance of this relationship can be seen to inform and motivate their praxes. The possibility of revealing this overlooked or missing element in critical/academic writing, here initially identified as an 'unknown quality' and then specified as the 'subterranean connections' between text and context, is seen to arise from the examination of the evolution of a post-Bazinian realism. It is within these shared coordinates of a conceptualisation of film itself that a variety of canon-excluded directions suggest the possibility of a 'total critique' of radical and progressive Western European film of the 1960s. In these terms, the idea of a 'likeness' between text and context is seen as an inadequate critical response to the ontology that links these films and their times. Indeed, it is at the point of the hasty marriage of film form and forms of consciousness-raising and political action that 'likeness' is seen as the least appropriate term for the reconfiguration of an engaged cinema for the 1960s.

This approach results in the two major directions that become apparent in, and so for this study, organise, the area at hand: the intellectual phase, which eventually becomes unstuck in a problematisation of form, to the extent of a routing of post-Bazinian realism; and the revolutionary phase, which assumes so strong an ontological link between the film and its time as to incorporate and further revolutionary praxes into, and via, its post-Bazinian realism. The former concedes and finally defines itself in relation to that which, ultimately, it says it is not: as possessed of a materialist sense of cognition, as derived from found reality that organically arises from a conceptualisation of cinema that exemplifies an ontology of the real, as identified by Bazin. The latter, while a straight continuation of just such a conceptualisation, stumbles at the point at which the imported revolutionary praxes suddenly appear to lack real revolutionary potential. Hence the films' lack of theoretical rigour and historical analysis becomes immediately suspect; the vagueness of a conception of politically radical cinema, which had been accommodated by post-Bazinian realism, meeting and matching the vagueness of a variety of revolutionary gestures and strategies of attempted interjection and/or intervention. While the former tendency, the Late Modernist film, rejects post-Bazinian realism, the latter tendency, the revolutionary cinema of 1968, has it wrenched away (an occurrence apparent in the very newness of many of the directions beyond 1968); yet neither manage to kill the father of the New Waves – a cluster of post-Bazinian realisms, of one sort or orthodoxy or another, as accepted or rejected, remain the centre of this one universe.

Since the two crises of post-Bazinian realism, associated with each major direction, have been discussed in relation to the evident film forms and praxes, it only remains to comment upon the strategies of dissent in radical Western European film in the years 1966 – 1969 in the light of the evolution within the tradition of European film realism.

This study has rejected the historical-methodological connections made between neo-realism and the New Waves on aesthetic, and then philosophical, grounds. It would be possible to extend this historical disjuncture now, and claim that while neo-realism unified audiences (as both a populist and progressive mode of film-making), subsequent 'movements' lost such a unification. Thus the Late Modernist film utilised venerable traditions (a revived modernism) to the ends of a 'high' avant-gardism of predominantly psychological realism for middle-class filmgoers, newly acquainting themselves with the pastime of film-going. And, meanwhile, the cinéma-militant attempted to directly address, galvanise and radicalise cohorts of the discontented proletariat and/or activist-revolutionary vanguard, arriving at the cinema from the streets and university campuses. Therefore, following this line of thought, the progressive directions apparent between 1966 and 1968 reflect the way in which two questionable groups (liberal middle-class connoisseurs of art, middle-class revolutionary adventurists) divide up the spoils of the neo-realist reshaping of cinema between them, for their own particular constituencies.

Yet even such an uncharitable blanket dismissal of the films that fall into this period cannot diminish the nature, aspirational and actual, of the expansion of the 'expanded cinema' that had occurred. In this zone of exploration and experimentation, a sustained capitalisation on contemporary and progressive film-making methodologies, and then, to an extreme degree after 1966, the convergence, synchronisation and/or counterpointing of a number of previously apparent, and often untapped, directions are observable. Herein was untempered phenomenology, the ruptures and materialisation of alienation (in the Marxist and Brechtian senses), unapologetic obscurantism in the frustrating of cognitive mapping, the meta-critique of intertextuality and the auto-critique of 1968, the – or a – situationist discourse, the Reichian contextualisation and reimagining of free love and Artaudian frameworks for consciousness-raising, an unqualified utopianism and, in the background, limitless negations of preconceived norms (i.e., bourgeois-hegemonic) of film language. Film form, as a means of production, had been seized, freed, remade and deployed for emancipatory ends.

What is so shocking in the starkness of Fassbinder, the numbness of Schroeter and the coldness of Straub and Huillet is their necessary rejection of the openness, richness and depth of the 1960s radical film discourse; it is as if the Puritans have fled from this carnival, condemning its jouissance, rejecting its anti-establishment antics, even despising its colour, and in so doing accidentally discover the path to the cinema for the 1970s.

Progressive and radical film, by the end of 1968, had achieved a language in order to survey and critique the rapidly changing contemporary landscape in the area of the Late Modernist film. Any impasse encountered in this process, at the point of the overwhelming burden of unsublimatable alienation, was an impasse presented as a progressive articulation – a generative crisis, born of self-criticism. Elsewhere, film had attempted to approach, interrogate and even advance, albeit sporadically, or even blindly, the objective revolutionary conditions that had seemed to unfold in society at large, and had exemplified a revolutionary subjectivity, collective and individual, that was inextricably intertwined with that moment. Two revolutions had therefore occurred. Firstly, a revolution of film form and film praxis – that is, the revolution of progressive film itself. And, secondly, the counter-revolution of the post-1968 directions in film that arose after the phase of post-Bazinian realism.

Filmography

Additional English language titles included below are the typically or most usually used translations, should the film have initially been released with a translated English title, and one that then stuck. The given year is the year of first release of the film or, failing that, the year of its public circulation.

A Bientôt, J'Espère	Chris Marker	
	Mario Marrett	1967–68
A Bout de Souffle / Breathless	Jean-Luc Godard	1960
Abschied von Gestern / Yesterday Girl	Alexander Kluge	1966
Accattone	Pier Paolo Pasolini	1961
Acéphale	Patrick Deval	1968
Action Stress Test	Werner Schulz	1970
Adieu Philippine	Jacques Rozier	1963
Adventures of Barry McKenzie, The	Bruce Beresford	1972
Age of Consent	Michael Powell	1969
Aggression	Werner Schroeter	1968
Alice's Restaurant	Arthur Penn	1969
Alphaville, Une Étrange Aventure de Lemmy Caution / Alphaville	Jean-Luc Godard	1965
Amant Réguliers, Les / Regular Lovers	Philippe Garrel	2005
Amarcord	Federico Fellini	1974
Amerikanische Soldat, Der / The American Soldier	Rainer Werner Fassbinder	1970
Amore, L'	Roberto Rossellini	1948
Angel Exterminador, El / The Exterminating Angel	Luis Buñuel	1962
Angry Silence, The	Guy Green	1960
Année Dernière à Marienbad, L' / Last Year at Marienbad	Alain Resnais	1961
Antonio das Mortes / The Dragon of Evil Against the Warrior Saint	Glauber Rocha	1969
Apa / Father	István Szabó	1966
Argila	Werner Schroeter	1969
Artisten in der Zirkuskuppel: Ratlos, Die / Artists under the Big Top: Perplexed	Alexander Kluge	1968
Ascenseur pour l'Echafaud / Lift to the Scaffold	Louis Malle	1957

Auch Zwerge Haben Klein Angefangen /		
Even Dwarfs Started Small	Werner Herzog	1970
Avventura, L'	Michelangelo Antonioni	1960
Baiser Volés / Stolen Kisses	François Truffaut	1968
Bande à Part	Jean-Luc Godard	1964
Barbarella	Roger Vadim	1968
Batman	Various; television series	1966–68
Beau Serge, Le	Claude Chabrol	1959
Belle de Jour	Luis Buñuel	1967
Beyond the Valley of the Dolls	Russ Meyer	1970
Biches, Les	Claude Chabrol	1968
Blow-Up	Michelangelo Antonioni	1966
Bodil Joensen "A Summerday" / Bodil	Shinkichi Tajiri	
Joensen – en sommerdag juli 1970	Ole Ege	1970
Bomberpilot, Der	Werner Schroeter	1970
Boucher, Le / The Butcher	Claude Chabrol	1970
Bräutigam, die Komödiantin und der Zuhälter,	Jean-Marie Straub	
Der / The Bridegroom, The Comedienne and		
the Pimp	Danièle Huillet	1968
Breaking of Bumbo, The	Andrew Sinclair	1970
British Sounds / See You at Mao	Dziga Vertov Group	1969
Callas Text mit Doppelbeleuchtung	Werner Schroeter	1968
Callas Walking Lucia	Werner Schroeter	1968
Cannibali, I / The Cannibals	Liliana Cavani	1970
Capricci	Camelo Bene	1969
Castle 1	Malcolm Le Grise	1966
C'era una Volta il West / Once Upon A		
Time in the West	Sergio Leone	1968
Chelsea Girls, The	Andy Warhol	
	Paul Morrissey	1966
Chinoise, ou Plutôt à la Chinoise, La	Jean-Luc Godard	1967
Choses de la Vie, Les / The Things of Life	Claude Sautet	1969
Chronik der Anna Magdalena Bach /	Jean-Marie Straub	
Chronicle of Anna Magdalena Bach	Danièle Huillet	1968
Chronique d'un Été / Chronicle of a Summer	Jean Rouch	
	Edgar Morin	1961
Cina è Vicina, La / China is Near	Marco Bellocchio	1967

Ciné-tracts / some also titled *Film-tracts*	Various, anonymous	1968
Ciociara, La / *Two Women*	Vittorio De Sica	1960
Citizen Kane	Orson Welles	1941
Civilisation: A Personal View by Kenneth Clark	Various; television series	1969
Classe de Lutte	Le Groupe Medvedkine de Besançon	1968
Cléo de 5 à 7	Agnès Varda	1962
Clockwork Orange, A	Stanley Kubrick	1971
Columbia Revolt	New York Newsreel	1968
Committee, The	Peter Sykes	1968
Conformista, Il / *The Conformtist*	Bernardo Bertolucci	1970
Contestation, La / *Vangelo 70* / *Evangile 70* / *Amore e Rabbia*	Carlo Lizzani	
	Bernardo Bertolucci	
	Pier Paolo Pasolini	
	Jean-Luc Godard	
	Marco Bellocchio	
	Elda Tattoli	1970
Cousins, Les	Claude Chabrol	1959
Damned, The / *La Caduta Degli Dei*	Luchino Visconti	1969
Dannati della Terra, I	Valentino Orsini	1967
Darling	John Schlesinger	1965
Decameron, Il / *The Decameron*	Pier Paolo Pasolini	1971
Deep End	Jerzy Skolimowski	1970
Degree of Murder, A / *Mord und Totschlag*	Volker Schlöndorff	1967
Départ, Le / *The Departure*	Jerzy Skolimowski	1967
Deserto Rosso, Il / *The Red Desert*	Michelangelo Antonioni	1964
Détruisez-Vous: Le Fusil Silencieux	Serge Bard	1968
Deux fois	Jackie Raynal	1969
Deux ou Trois Choses que Je Sais d'Elle / *Two or Three Things I Know About Her*	Jean-Luc Godard	1966
Dillinger è Morto / *Dillinger is Dead*	Marco Ferreri	1969
Dolce Vita, La	Federico Fellini	1960
Dragées au Poivre	Jacques Baratier	1963
Dreamers, The	Bernardo Bertolucci	2003
Easy Rider	Dennis Hopper	1969
Eclisse, L' / *The Eclipse*	Michelangelo Antonioni	1962
Eden Miseria	Jacques Baratier	1967
Edipo Re / *Oedipus Rex*	Pier Paolo Pasolini	1967

Eika Katappa	Werner Schroeter	1969
Enfant Sauvage, L' / The Wild Child	François Truffaut	1969
Europa '51	Roberto Rossellini	1951
Faccia a Faccia / Face to Face	Sergio Sollima	1967
Far from the Madding Crowd	John Schlesinger	1967
Fellini-Casanova	Federico Fellini	1976
Fellini-Roma	Federico Fellini	1972
Fellini-Satyricon	Federico Fellini	1969
Femme est une Femme, Une / A Woman is a Woman	Jean-Luc Godard	1961
Femme Infidèle, La / The Unfaithful Wife	Claude Chabrol	1969
Femme Mariée, La / A Married Woman	Jean-Luc Godard	1964
Feu Follet, Le	Louis Malle	1963
Film Comme les Autres, Un	Dziga Vertov Group	1968
Fiore delle Mille e una Notte, Il / The Thousand and One Nights	Pier Paolo Pasolini	1974
Gai Savoir, Le	Jean-Luc Godard	1969
Germania Anno Zero / Germany, Year Zero	Roberto Rossellini	1947
Gladiators, The	Peter Watkins	1969
Götter der Pest / Gods of the Plague	Rainer Werner Fassbinder	1970
Grande Silenzio, Il / The Big Silence	Sergio Corbucci	1968
Grin without a Cat, A / Le Fond de l'Air est Rouge	Chris Marker	1977, 1993
Guerre est Finie, La / The War is Over	Alain Resnais	1966
Hard Day's Night, A	Richard Lester	1964
Harem, L' / The Harem / Her Harem	Marco Ferreri	1967
Head	Bob Rafelson	1968
Hell's Angels on Wheels	Richard Rush	1967
Héraclite l'Obscur	Patrick Deval	1967
Hermitage	Carmelo Bene	1968
Hiroshima, Mon Amour	Alain Resnais	1959
Homme et une Femme, Un / A Man and a Woman	Claude Lelouch	1966
Hora de los Hornos, La / The Hour of the Furnaces	Fernando Solanas	1968
HWY: An American Pastoral	Jim Morrison	
	Frank Lisciandro	
	Paul Ferrara	
	Babe Hill	1970

Loneliness of the Long Distance Runner, The	Tony Richardson	1962
Lotte in Italia / Luttes en Italie	Dziga Vertov Group	1970
Made in USA	Jean-Luc Godard	1966
Mademoiselle	Tony Richardson	1966
Mama und Papa /Mama and Papa	Otto Muehl	
	Kurt Kren	1963–69
Mamma Roma	Pier Paolo Pasolini	1962
Manopsychotik: Otto Muehl / Manopsychotik /		
Manopsychotik Ballet	Otto Muehl	
	Joerg Síegert	1970
Maria Callas Porträt	Werner Schroeter	1968
Maria Callas Singt 1957 Rezitativ . . .	Werner Schroeter	1968
Marie pour Mémoire	Philippe Garrel	1967
Masculin-Féminin	Jean-Luc Godard	1966
Medea	Pier Paolo Pasolini	1969
Medium Cool	Haskell Wexler	1969
Mépris, Le	Jean-Luc Godard	1963
Midnight Cowboy	John Schlesinger	1969
Mona Lisa	Werner Schroeter	1968
More	Barbet Schroeder	1969
Morgan: A Suitable Case for Treatment	Karel Reisz	1966
Nanook of the North	Robert Flaherty	1922
Necropolis	Franco Bracani	1970
Neurasia	Werner Schroeter	1969
Nicht Löschbares Feuer / The Inextinguishable		
Fire	Harun Farocki	1969
Nostra Signora dei Turchi / Our Lady of the		
Turks	Camelo Bene	1968
Notte, La / The Night	Michelangelo Antonioni	1960
Notti di Cabiria, Le / Nights of Cabiria	Federico Fellini	1957
Nuit et Brouillard / Night and Fog	Alain Resnais	1955
One Plus One / Sympathy for the Devil	Jean-Luc Godard	1968
Orfeu Negro	Marcel Camus	1959
O Sensibility	Otto Muehl	1970
Otto e Mezzo / 8½ / Eight and a Half /		
Fellini's Eight and a Half	Federico Fellini	1963
Paisà / Paisan	Roberto Rossellini	1946

Paradise Now	Marty Topp	1968
Parapluies du Cherbourg, Les / The Umbrellas of Cherbourg	Jacques Demy	1964
Paris nous Appartient	Jacques Rivette	1960
Paris vu Par . . .	Jean Douchet	
	Jean Rouch	
	Jean-Daniel Pollet	
	Eric Rohmer	
	Jean-Luc Godard	
	Claude Chabrol	1964
Partner	Bernardo Bertolucci	1968
Peau Douce, La / The Soft Skin	François Truffaut	1964
Performance	Donald Cammell	
	Nicholas Roeg	1970
Persona	Ingmar Bergman	1966
Piège	Jacques Baratier	1970
Pierrot le Fou	Jean-Luc Godard	1965
Porcile / Pigsty	Pier Paolo Pasolini	1969
Posto, Il	Ermanno Olmi	1961
Pravda	Dziga Vertov Group	1969
Prima della Rivoluzione / Before the Revolution	Bernardo Bertolucci	1964
Privilege	Peter Watkins	1967
Psych-Out	Richard Rush	1968
Psychotik-Party	Otto Muehl	1970
Pugni in Tasca, I / Fists in the Pocket	Marco Bellocchio	1965
Punishment Park	Peter Watkins	1971
Quatre Cents Coups, Les / The Four Hundred Blows	François Truffaut	1959
Quemada! / Burn	Gillo Pontecorvo	1969
Quién Sabe? / A Bullet for the General	Damiano Damiani	1966
Racconti di Canterbury, I / The Canterbury Tales	Pier Paolo Pasolini	1972
Rani Radovi / Early Works	Želimir Žilnik	1969
Raz, Dwa, Trzy / The Singing Lesson	Lindsay Anderson	
	Piotr Szulkin	1967
Ręce do Góry / Hands Up!	Jerzy Skolimowski	1967, 1981
Religieuse, La	Jacques Rivette	1966
Repulsion	Roman Polanski	1965
Resa dei Conti, La / The Big Gundown	Sergio Sollima	1966

Rocco e i Suoi Fratelli / Rocco and his Brothers	Luchino Visconti	1960
RoGoPaG / Ro.Go.Pa.G	Roberto Rossellini	
	Jean-Luc Godard	
	Pier Paolo Pasolini	
	Ugo Gregoretti	1963
Roma, Città Aperta / Rome, Open City /		
Open City	Roberto Rossellini	1945
Rote Sonne / Red Sun	Rudolf Thome	1969
Rupture, La	Claude Chabrol	1970
Sailor from Gibraltar, The	Tony Richardson	1966
Salvatore Giuliano	Francesco Rosi	1961
Sang des Bêtes, Le / The Blood of Beasts	George Franju	1949
Saturday Night and Sunday Morning	Karel Reisz	1960
Say Hello to Yesterday	Alvin Rakoff	1970
Scheisskerl	Otto Muehl	
	Hanel Koeck	1969
Sedmikrásky / Daisies	Věra Chytilová	1966
Sedmy Den, Osmá Noc / Seventh Day,		
Eighth Night	Evald Schorm	1969
Servant, The	Joseph Losey	1963
Signe du Lion, Le	Eric Rohmer	1962
Simón del Desierto / Simon of the Desert	Luis Buñuel	1965
Skammen / Shame	Ingmar Bergman	1968
Smutečhí Slavnost / Funeral Ceremony	Zdenek Sirový	1969
Sodoma	Otto Muehl	
	Hanel Koeck	
	Kurt Kren	1968–70
Sorcerers, The	Michael Reeves	1967
Sotto il Segno dello Scorpione / Under the		
Sign of Scorpio	Paolo Taviani	
	Vittorio Taviani	1969
Stadtstreicher, Der / The City Tramp	Rainer Werner Fassbinder	1966
Stille Nacht	H. P. Kochenrath	1969
Strada, La	Federico Fellini	1954
Strategia del Ragno, La / The Spider's		
Strategem	Bernardo Bertolucci	1970
Strawberry Statement, The	Stuart Hagman	1970
Stromboli	Roberto Rossellini	1949
Sua Giornata di Gloria, La	Edoardo Bruno	1969

Sunday Bloody Sunday	John Schlesinger	1971
Sweet Movie	Dušan Makavejev	1974
Sweet Sweetback's Badasssss Song	Melvin Van Peebles	1971
Take a Girl Like You	Jonathan Miller	1970
Teorema / Theorem	Pier Paolo Pasolini	1968
Third Man, The	Carol Reed	1949
This Sporting Life	Lindsay Anderson	1963
Time for ACTION has come, The	Gottfried Schlemmer	1969
Tonite Let's All Make Love in London	Peter Whitehead	1967
Tout va Bien	Jean-Luc Godard	
	Jean-Pierre Gorin	1972
Trans-Europ express	Alain Robbe-Grillet	1966
Trip, The	Roger Corman	1967
Two American Audiences	Mark Woodcock	1968
Uccellacci e Uccellini / Hawks and Sparrows	Pier Paolo Pasolini	1966
Ucho / The Ear	Karel Kachyňa	1970
Vallée, La	Barbet Schroeder	1972
Vampyros Lesbos	Jesús Franco	1970
Vangelo Secondo Matteo, Il / The Gospel According to Saint Matthew	Pier Paolo Pasolini	1964
Vargtimmen / Hour of the Wolf	Ingmar Bergman	1967
Vent d'Est	Dziga Vertov Group	1970
Verona	Werner Schroeter	1967
Viaggio in Italia / Voyage to Italy	Roberto Rossellini	1953
Victim	Basil Dearden	1961
Vie Privée / A Very Private Affair	Louis Malle	1961
Viol du Vampire, Le	Jean Rollin	1967
Virgin and the Gypsy, The	Christopher Miles	1970
Visa de censure	Pierre Clémenti	1968
Vite	Daniel Pommereulle	1969
Vive le Tour	Louis Malle	1962
Vivre sa Vie / My Life to Live	Jean-Luc Godard	1962
Voie Lactée, La / The Milky Way	Luis Buñuel	1969
Warum Läuft Herr R. Amok?/ Why Does Herr R. Run Amok?	Rainer Werner Fassbinder	
	Michael Fengler	1970
We are The Lambeth Boys	Karel Reisz	1958

Week-end / Le Weekend / Weekend	Jean-Luc Godard	1968
Whistle Down the Wind	Bryan Forbes	1961
White Bus, The	Lindsay Anderson	1966
Wife Swappers, The	Derek Ford	1970
Wild in the Streets	Barry Shear	1968
Women in Love	Ken Russell	1969
Wonderwall	Joe Massot	1968
Woodstock	Michael Wadleigh	1970
W.R. – Misterije Organizma / W.R.: Mysteries of the Organism	Dušan Makavejev	1971
Year of the Sex Olympics	Michael Elliott, television drama	1968
Zabriskie Point	Michelangelo Antonioni	1970
Zazie dans le Métro	Louis Malle	1960
Zéro de Conduite	Jean Vigo	1933
Z	Constantin Costa-Gavras	1968
12 Dicembre	Giovanni Bonfanti Pier Paolo Pasolini and others	1972
2001: A Space Odyssey	Stanley Kubrick	1968

References

Adorno, T., W. Benjamin, E. Bloch, B. Brecht and G. Lukács. 1992. *Aesthetics and Politics*. London: Verso.

Ali, T. 1987. *Street Fighting Years: An Autobiography of the Sixties*. London: Collins.

Ali, T. and S. Watkins. 1998. *1968: Marching in the Streets*. London: Bloomsbury.

Althusser, L. 1971. *For Marx*. London: Allen Lane, The Penguin Press.

Anderson, L. 1959. 'Get Out and Push', in T. Maschler (ed.), *Declaration*. London: MacGibbon and Kee, pp. 153–78.

Andrew, D. and H. Joubert-Laurencin. 2011. *Opening Bazin: Postwar Film Theory & its Afterlife*. Oxford, New York: Oxford University Press.

Aranda, F. 1975. *Luis Buñuel: A Critical Biography*. London: Secker and Warburg.

Arendt, H. 1966. *The Origins of Totalitarianism*. New York: Harvest.

Armes, R. 1968. *The Films of Alain Resnais*. London: Zwemmer.

Armes, R. 1976. *French Cinema since 1946: Volume Two – The Personal Style*. London: Tantivy Press.

Arrowsmith, W. and T. Perry (ed.). 1995. *Antonioni: The Poet of Images*. London: Oxford University Press.

Artaud, A. 1999. *Collected Works Volume Three: Scenarios on the Cinema, Interviews, Letters*. London: John Calder.

Auslander, P. 2006. *Performing Glam Rock: Gender & Theatricality in Popular Music*. Ann Arbor: University of Michigan Press.

Austin, J. 2005. 'Rome is Burning (Psychedelic): Traces of the Social and Historical Contexts of Psychedelia', in C. Grunenberg (ed.), *Summer of Love: Art of the Psychedelic Era*. London: Tate Publishing, pp. 189–96.

Bailey, D., and P. Evans. 1970. *Goodbye Baby and Amen: A Saraband for The Sixties*. London: Corgi Books.

Barber, S. 2001. *Artaud: The Screaming Body*. London: Creation Books.

Barber, S. 2004. *The Art of Destruction: The Films of the Vienna Action Group (Persistence of Vision Volume 5)*. New York: Creation Books.

Baumann, B. 1979. *Terror or Love?: The Personal Account of a West German Urban Guerrilla*. London: John Calder.

Bazin, A. 1967. *What is Cinema? Volume I*. London: University of California Press.

Bazin, A. 1971. *What is Cinema? Volume II*. London: University of California Press.

Bazin, A., with B. Cardullo (ed.). 1997. *Bazin at Work: The Major Essays and Reviews from the 1940s and 1950s*. London: Routledge.

Beck, J. 1974. *The Life of the Theatre: The Relation of the Artist to the Struggle of the People*. San Francisco: City Lights Books.

Benayoun, R. 1968. 'The King is Naked', in P. Graham (ed.), *The New Wave: Critical Landmarks Selected by Peter Graham*. London: British Film Institute and Secker and Warburg, pp. 157–80.

Benjamin, W. 1998. *Understanding Brecht*. London: Verso.

Bertolucci, B. 1987. *Bertolucci by Bertolucci*. London: Plexus.

Betti, L. and L. Thovazzi (eds). Undated catalogue. [1989]. *Pier Paolo Pasolini: A Future Life*. Rome: Ministero del Turismo e dello Spettacolo / Associazione "Fondo Pier Paolo Pasolini" / Ente Autonomo Gestione Cinema.

Booker, C. 1992. *The Neophiliacs: The Revolution in English Life in the Fifties and Sixties*. London: Pimlico.

Britton, C. 1989. 'The Representation of Vietnam in French Films before and after 1968', in D.L. Hanley and A.P. Kerr (eds), *May '68: Coming of Age*. London: Macmillan, pp. 163–81.

Brunette, P. 1998. *The Films of Michelangelo Antonioni*. London: Cambridge University Press.

Brunette, P. and D. Wills. 1989. *Screen/Play: Derrida and Film Theory*. New Jersey: Princeton University Press.

Bürger, P. 1996. *Theory of the Avant-garde*. Minneapolis: University of Minnesota Press.

Cameron, I. and R. Wood. 1968. *Antonioni*. London: Studio Vista.

Cameron, I. and J. Chabot, M. Ciment, R. Daundelin, A. Engel, M. Walker, R. Wood. 1970. *Second Wave*. London: Studio Vista.

Cannon, S. 2000. '"When You're Not a Worker Yourself . . .": Godard, the Dziga Vertov Group and the Audience', in D. Holmes and A. Smith (eds), *100 Years of European Cinema: Entertainment or Ideology?* Manchester: Manchester University Press, pp. 100–8.

Cardullo, B. (ed.). 2008. *Michelangelo Antonioni: Interviews (Conversations with Filmmakers)*. Mississippi: University of Mississippi Press.

Carroll, K.E. 1972. 'Film and Revolution: Interview with the Dziga-Vertov Group', in R.S. Brown (ed.), *Focus on Godard*. New Jersey: Prentice-Hall, pp. 50–64.

Cassou, J., M. Ragon, A. Fermigier, G. Lascault, G. Gassiot-Talabot, R. Moulin, P. Gaudibert, R. Micha, A. Jouffroy. 1970. *Art and Confrontation: France and the Arts in an Age of Change*. London: Studio Vista. Caute, D. 1988. *Sixty-eight: The Year of the Barricades*. London: Hamish Hamilton.

Cavell, S. 2005. *Cavell on Film*, W. Rothman (ed.). Albany: State University of New York Press.

Channan, M. (ed.). 1983. *Twenty-five Years of the New Latin American Cinema*. London: Channel Four Television / British Film Institute.

Chatman, S. 1985. *Antonioni, or the Surface of the World*. London: University of California Press.

Cohn-Bendit, D. and G. Cohn-Bendit. 1969. *Obsolete Communism: The Left-wing Alternative*. London: Penguin Books.

Cohn-Bendit, D. and J.-P. Sartre. 1968. 'Daniel Cohn-Bendit interviewed by Jean-Paul Sartre', in H. Bourges (compiler), *The Student Revolt: The Activists Speak*. London: Panther Books, pp. 97–107.

Conlin, J. 2009. *Civilisation: BFI TV Classics*. London: British Film Institute.

Cowie, P. (ed.). 1963. *International Film Guide 1964*. London: Tantivy Press.

Cowie, P. 2004. *Revolution! The Explosion of World Cinema in the 60s*. London: Faber and Faber.

Cronin. P. (ed.). 2002. *Herzog on Herzog*. London: Faber and Faber.

Croyden, M. 1975. *Lunatics, Lovers and Poets: The Contemporary Experimental Theatre*. New York: Delta Books.

Dall'Asta, M. 2011. 'Beyond the Image in Benjamin and Bazin: The Aura of the Event' in D. Andrew, and H. Joubert-Laurencin (eds), *Opening Bazin: Postwar Film Theory & its Afterlife*. Oxford, New York: Oxford University Press, pp. 57–65.

de Baecque, A. 1997. 'The New Wave, or the Power of the Ephemeral', in D.A. Mellor and L. Gervereau (eds), *The Sixties: Britain and France, 1962-1973: The Utopian Years*. London: Philip Wilson, pp. 150–61.

Deleuze, G. 1989. *Cinema 2: The Time-image*. London: Athlone Press.

Deleuze, G. and F. Guattari. 2001. 'May '68 Did Not Take Place', in C. Kraus and S. Lotringer (eds), *Hatred of Capitalism*. Los Angeles and New York: Semiotext(e), pp. 209–11.

Derrida, J. 1993. *Aporias*. California: Stanford University Press.

Derrida, J. and D. Attridge (eds). 1992. *Acts of Literature*. London: Routledge.

Dixon, W.W. 1997. *The Films of Jean-Luc Godard*. New York: State University Press of New York.

Dorléac, L.B. 1997. 'Tomorrow You'll All be Artists: The Art Scene in France, 1960-1973', in D.A. Mellor and L. Gervereau (eds), *The Sixties: Britain and France, 1962-1973: The Utopian Years*. London: Philip Wilson, pp. 30–55.

Douchet, J. with C. Anger. 1999. *French New Wave*. New York: Distributed Art Publishers.

Doyle, M.W. 2002. 'Staging the Revolution: Guerrilla Theatre as a Countercultural Practice, 1965–1968', in P. Braunstein and M.W. Doyle (eds), *Imagine Nation: The American Counterculture of the 1960s and '70s*. London: Routledge, pp. 71–98.

Drake. R. 1989. *The Revolutionary Mystique and Terrorism in Contemporary Italy*. Bloomington and Indianapolis: Indiana University Press.

Durgnat, R. 1968. *Luis Buñuel*. London: Studio Vista.

Durgnat, R. 1972. *Sexual Alienation in the Cinema*. London: Studio Vista.

Durgnat, R. 1976. *Durgnat on Film*. London: Faber and Faber.

Durgnat, R. 1999. *WR – Mysteries of the Organism*. London: British Film Institute.

Eaden, J. and D. Renton. 2002. *The Communist Party of Great Britain since 1920*. London: Palgrave.

Eagleton, T. 2004. *After Theory*. London: Penguin.

Eco, U. 1989. *The Open Work*. Cambridge: Harvard University Press.

Elsaesser, T. 1976. 'A Cinema of Vicious Circles', in T. Rayns (ed.), *Fassbinder*. London: British Film Institute, pp. 24–36.

Elsaesser, T. 1989. *New German Cinema: A History*. New Jersey: Rutgers University Press.

Elsaesser, T. 1996. *Fassbinder's Germany: History, Identity, Subject*. Amsterdam: Amsterdam University Press.

Faber, M. 2005. *Günter Brus: Nervous Stillness on the Horizon*. Barcelona: Actar / Museu d'Art Contemporani de Barcelona.

Farber, M. 1998. *Negative Space: Manny Farber on the Movies*. New York: Da Capo Press.

Farren, M. and E. Barker. 1972. *Watch Out Kids*. London: Open Gate Books.

Fehér, F. and A. Heller. 1983. *Hungary 1956 Revisited: The Message of a Revolution – a Quarter of a Century After*. London: George Allen and Unwin.

Firestone, S. 1988. *The Dialectic of Sex: The Case for Feminist Revolution*. London: The Women's Press.

Foucault, M. 1980. *Power / Knowledge: Selected Interviews and Other Writings, 1972-1977*. Sussex: Harvester Press.

Franklin. J. 1983. *New German Cinema: From Oberhausen to Hamburg*. Boston: Twayne Publishers.

Frayling, C. 1981. *Spaghetti Westerns: Cowboys and Europeans from Earl May to Sergio Leone*. London: Routledge and Kegan Paul.

Frayling, C. 2000. *Sergio Leone: Something To Do With Death*. London: Faber and Faber.

French, P. (ed.). 1993. *Malle on Malle*. London: British Film Institute.

Garner, P. and D.A. Mellor. 2010. *Antonioni's Blow-Up*. Gottingen: Steidl.

Gerard, F.S., T.J. Kline, and B. Sklarew (eds). 2000. *Bernardo Bertolucci: Interviews*. Jackson: University of Mississippi Press.

Gili, J.A. 1998. *Italian Filmmakers Self Portraits: A Selection of Interviews*. Rome: Gremese.

Godard, J.-L. with T. Milne and J. Narboni (eds). 1972. *Godard on Godard: Critical Writings by Jean-Luc Godard*. London: Cinema 2 / Secker and Warburg.

Goddard, M., B. Halligan and N. Spelman (eds). 2013. *Resonances: Noise and Contemporary Music*. London and New York: Bloomsbury.

Goddard, M. and E. Mazierska (eds). 2014. *Polish Cinema in a Transnational Context*. New York: University of Rochester Press.

Gordon, R.S.C. 1996. *Pasolini: Forms of Subjectivity*. Oxford: Clarendon Press.

Graham, P. 1968. *The New Wave: Critical Landmarks Selected by Peter Graham*. London: British Film Institute and Secker and Warburg.

Greene, N. 1970. *Antonin Artaud: Poet without Words*. New York: Simon and Schuster.

Greene, N. 1990. *Pier Paolo Pasolini: Cinema as Heresy*. New Jersey: Princeton University Press.

Grunenberg, C. (ed.). 2005. *Summer of Love: Art of the Psychedelic Era*. London: Tate Publishing.

Hale, J.A. 2002. 'The White Panthers' "Total Assault on the Culture"', in P. Braunstein and M.W. Doyle (eds), *Imagine Nation: The American Counterculture of the 1960s and '70s*. London: Routledge, pp. 125–56.

Hall, S. and C. Critcher, T. Jefferson, J. Clarke, B. Roberts. 1979. *Policing the Crisis: Mugging, the State, and Law and Order*. London: Macmillan Press.

Halligan, B. 2003. *Michael Reeves*. Manchester: Manchester University Press.

Hanley, D.L. and A.P. Kerr (eds). 1989. *May '68: Coming of Age*. London: Macmillan.

Hardt, M. and A. Negri. 2001. *Empire*. London: Harvard University Press.

Harrison, M. 1998. *Young Meteors: British Photojournalism: 1957–1965*. London: Jonathan Cape.

Harvey, S. 1980. *May '68 and Film Culture*. London: British Film Institute.

Hayman, R. 1984. *Fassbinder: Film Maker*. London: Weidenfeld and Nicholson.

Hedling, E. 1998. *Lindsay Anderson: Maverick Film-maker*. London: Cassell.

Henderson, B. 1976a. 'Towards a Non-bourgeois Camera Style', B. Nichols (ed.), *Movies and Methods Volume One: An Anthology*. London: University of California Press, pp. 422–37.

Henderson, B. 1976b. 'Two Types of Film Theory', in B. Nichols (ed.), *Movies and Methods Volume One: An Anthology*. London: University of California Press, pp. 388–400.

Hewison, R. 1981. *In Anger: Culture in the Cold War 1945-60*. London: Weidenfeld and Nicholson.

Hewison, R. 1986. *Too Much: Art and Society in the Sixties 1960-75*. London: Methuen.

Hogenkamp, B. 2000. *Film, Television and the Left in Britain, 1950 to 1970*. London: Lawrence and Wishart.

Home, S. 1991. *The Assault on Culture: Utopian Currents from Lettrisme to Class War*. Stirling: A.K. Press.

Houston, P. 1968. *The Contemporary Cinema*. London: Penguin Books.

Huss, R. (ed.). 1971. *Focus on Blow-Up*. New Jersey: Prentice-Hall.

Iden, P., Y. Karsunke, R. McCormick, H. H. Prinzler, W. Roth, W. Schuette, W. Wiegand. 1981. *Fassbinder*. New York: Tanam Press.

Jameson, F. 1990. *Signatures of the Visible*. London: Routledge.

Jameson, F. 1992. *Late Marxism: Adorno, or, The Persistence of the Dialectic*. London: Verso.

Jameson, F. 1998. *Brecht and Method*. London: Verso.

Jay, M. 1984. *Adorno*. London: Fontana Paperbacks.

Kaiser, R. 1970. 'Letting Go', in Editors of Playboy Press, *From Playboy: The Sexual Revolution*. Chicago: Playboy Press, pp. 4–15.

Kardish, L, in collaboration with J. Lorenz. 1997. *Rainer Werner Fassbinder*. New York: Museum of Modern Art.

Katsiaficas, G. 1987. *The Imagination of the New Left: A Global Analysis of 1968*. Massachusetts: South End Press.

Kline, T.J. 1987. *Bertolucci's Dream Loom: A Psychoanalytical Study of the Cinema*. Amherst: University of Massachusetts Press.

Kline, T.J. 1992. *Screening the Text: Intertextuality in New Wave French Cinema*. London: John Hopkins University Press.

Kolker, R.P. 1983. *The Altering Eye: Contemporary International Cinema*. Oxford: Oxford University Press.

Lacey, S. 1995. *British Realist Theatre: The New Wave in its Context 1956-1965*. London: Routledge.

Lachman, G.V. 2001. *Turn Off Your Mind: The Mystic Sixties and the Dark Side of the Age of Aquarius*. London: Sidgwick & Jackson.

Lambert, G. 2000. *Mainly About Lindsay Anderson*. London: Faber and Faber.

Lascault, G. 1970. 'Contemporary Art and the "Old Mole"', in J. Cassou, M. Ragon, A. Fermigier, G. Lascault, G. Gassiot-Talabot, R. Moulin, P. Gaudibert, R. Micha, A. Jouffroy, *Art and Confrontation: France and the Arts in an Age of Change*. London: Studio Vista, pp. 63–94.

Lebel, J. 1968. *Entretiens avec le Living Theatre*. Paris: Editions Pierre Belfond.

Loshitzky, Y. 1995. *The Radical Faces of Godard and Bertolucci*. Detroit: Wayne State University Press.

Lotringer, S. and D. Morris (eds). 2013. *Schizo-culture: The Event 1975*. London: Semiotext(e) / The MIT Press.

Lovell, A. and J. Hillier. 1972. *Studies in Documentary*. London: Secker and Warburg and British Film Institute.

MacBean, J.R. 1975. *Film and Revolution*. London: Indiana University Press.

MacCabe, C. 1998. *Performance*. London: British Film Institute.

MacCabe, C. 2003. *Godard: A Portrait of the Artist at 70*. London: Bloomsbury.

MacCabe, C. and M. Eaton, L. Mulvey. 1980. *Godard: Images, Sounds, Politics*. London: British Film Institute.

Maisetti, M. 1964. *La Crisi Spirituali del'uomo Moderno nei Film di Ingmar Bergman*. Busto Arsizio: Centro Communitario di Rescaldina.

Marcuse, H. 1969. *An Essay on Liberation*. London: Penguin Press.

Marie, M. 2000. '"It Really Makes You Sick!" Jean-Luc Godard's *A Bout de Souffle* (1959)', in S. Hayward and G. Vincendeau (eds), *French Films: Texts and Contexts*. London: Routledge, pp. 158–73.

Marie, M. 2003. *The French New Wave: An Artistic School*. Oxford: Blackwell Publishing.

Michalka, M. 2004. *X-Screen: Film Installations and Actions in the 1960s and 1970s*. New York: Distributed Art Publishers.

Montagu, I. 1967. *Film World: A Guide to Cinema*. London: Penguin Books.

Morrey, D. 2005. *Jean-Luc Godard*. Manchester: Manchester University Press.

Morrison, B. 1980. *The Movement: English Poetry and Fiction of the 1950s*. London: Methuen.

Murphy, R. 1992. *Sixties British Cinema*. London: British Film Institute.

Neupert, R. 2002. *A History of the French New Wave Cinema*. Wisconsin: University of Wisconsin Press.

Nicholls, D. 1993. *François Truffaut*. London: B.T. Batsford.

Nichols, B. (ed.). 1976. *Movies and Methods Volume One: An Anthology*. London: University of California Press.

Nowell-Smith, G. 1997. *L'Avventura*. London: British Film Institute.

Ollman, B. 1979. *Social and Sexual Revolution: Essays on Marx and Reich*. London: Pluto Press.

Orr, J. 1997. *Contemporary Cinema*. London: Edinburgh University Press.

Pâquet, A. 1972. 'Alternative Cinema' in P. Cowie (ed.), *International Film Guide 1973*. London: Tantivy Press.

Pasolini, P.P. 1997. *Petrolio*. London: Secker and Warburg.

Pasolini, P.P. 1999. *The Savage Father*. Lancaster: Guerica.

Pasolini, P.P. with L.K. Barnett (ed.). 2005. *Heretical Empiricism*. Bloomington: Indiana University Press.

Porton, R. 1999 *Film and the Anarchist Imagination*. London: Verso.

Priaulx, A. and S.J. Ungar. 1969. *The Almost Revolution: France – 1968*. New York: Dell Publishing.

Purdon, N. 1977. 'Pasolini: The Film of Alienation', in P. Willemen (ed.), *Pier Paolo Pasolini*. London: British Film Institute, pp. 43–54.

Reader, K. 2004. 'Godard and Asychrony', in M. Temple, J.S. Williams and M. Witt (eds), *For Ever Godard*. London: Black Dog Publishing, pp. 72–93.

Rees, M.A. (ed.). 1983. *Luis Buñuel: A Symposium*. Leeds: Trinity and All Saints' College.

Richardson, T. 1993. *Long Distance Runner: A Memoir*. London: Faber.

Reich, W. 1997. *The Mass Psychology of Fascism*. London: Souvenir Press.

Rohdie, S. 1990. *Antonioni*. London: British Film Institute.

Rohdie, S. 1995. *The Passion of Pier Paolo Pasolini*. London: British Film Institute.

Rosen, P. 2003. 'History of Image, Image of History: Subject and Ontology in Bazin' in I. Margulies (ed.), *Rites of Realism: Essays on Corporal Cinema*. Durham and London: Duke University Press, pp. 42–79.

Rosenbaum, J. 2000. *Movie Wars: How Hollywood and the Media Limit What Films We Can See*. London: Wallflower.

Roszak, T. 1971. *The Making of a Counter Culture: Reflections on the Technocratic Society and its Youthful Opposition*. London: Faber and Faber.

Roud, R. 1970. *Godard*. London: Thames and Hudson.

Roud, R. 1972. *Straub*. New York: Viking Press.

Roud, R. 1983. *A Passion for Films: Henri Langlois and the Cinémathèque Française*. London: Secker and Warburg.

Rumble, P. 1996. *Allegories of Contamination: Pier Paolo Pasolini's Trilogy of Life*. London: University of Toronto Press.

Rycroft, C. 1971. *Reich*. London: Fontana / Collins.

Sandford, J. and R. Reid. 1974. *Tomorrow's People*. London: Jerome Publishing Company.

Sanjek, D. with B. Halligan. 2013. '"You Can't Always Get What You Want": Riding on The Medicine Ball Caravan' in R. Edgar, K. Fairclough-Isaacs, B. Halligan (eds), *The Music Documentary: Acid Rock to Electropop.* New York and London: Routledge, pp. 100–12.

Sarris, A. 1971. 'Antoniennui', in R. Huss (ed.), *Focus on Blow-Up.* New Jersey: Prentice-Hall, pp. 31–35.

Schwartz, B.D. 1992. *Pasolini Requiem.* New York: Vintage Books.

Shafto, S. 2000. *The Zanzibar Films and the Dandies of May 1968.* New York: Zanzibar USA Publication.

Shattuc, J. 1995. *Television, Tabloids and Tears: Fassbinder and Popular Culture.* London: University of Minnesota Press.

Siciliano, E. 1987. *Pasolini.* London: Bloomsbury.

Silverman, K. and H. Farocki. 1998. *Speaking about Godard.* London: New York University Press.

Sinclair, I. 1997. *Lights Out for the Territory: 9 Excursions in the Secret History of London.* London: Granta.

Sinker, M. 2004. *If. . ..* London: British Film Institute.

Škvorecky, J. 1982. *Jiří Menzel and the History of Closely Watched Trains.* New York: Columbia University Press.

Smith, A. 2005. *French Cinema in the 1970s: The Echoes of May.* Manchester: Manchester University Press.

Sontag, S. 1967. *Against Interpretation and Other Essays.* New York: Farrar, Straus & Giroux.

Sontag, S. 1969. *Styles of a Radical Will.* New York: Farrar, Straus & Giroux.

Stack, O. 1969. *Pasolini on Pasolini: Interviews with Oswald Stack.* London: Thames and Hudson, British Film Institute.

Stam, R. 2000. *Film Theory: An Introduction.* Oxford: Blackwell Publishers.

Stephens, J. 1998. *Anti-disciplinary Protest: Sixties Radicalism and Postmodernism.* Cambridge: Cambridge University Press.

Sussex, E. 1969. *Lindsay Anderson.* London: Studio Vista.

Sussman, E. (ed.). 1989. *On the Passage of a Few People through a Rather Brief Moment in Time: The Situationist International 1957-1972.* Massachusetts, London: MIT Press.

Sweet, F. 1981. *The Film Narratives of Alain Resnais.* Michigan: UMI Research Press.

Taylor, J.R. 1964. *Cinema Eye, Cinema Ear: Some Key Film-makers of the Sixties.* London: Methuen.

Taylor, J.R. 1975. *Directors and Directions: Cinema for the Seventies.* New York: Hill and Wang.

Thoms, A. 1978. *Polemics for a New Cinema.* Sydney: Wild & Woolley.

Thomsen, C.B. 1997. *Fassbinder: The Life and Work of a Provocative Genius.* London: Faber and Faber.

Tyler, P. 1969. *Sex Psyche Etcetera in the Film.* London: Penguin.

Tytell, J. 1997. *The Living Theatre: Art, Exile, and Outrage*. London: Methuen Drama.

UNEF National Executive (Union Nationale des Étudiants de France). 1968. 'UNEF Proposes', in H. Bourges (compiler), *The Student Revolt: The Activists Speak*. London: Panther Books, pp. 109–14.

Van Watson, W. 1989. *Pier Paolo Pasolini and the Theatre of the Word*. London: UMI Research Press.

Viano, M. 1993. *A Certain Realism: Making use of Pasolini's Film Theory and Practice*. London: University of California Press.

Viénet, R. 1992. *Enragés and Situationists in the Occupation Movements, France, May '68*. London: Rebel Press.

Vogel, A. 1974. *Film as a Subversive Art*. London: Weidenfeld and Nicholson.

Walker, J.A. 2002. *Left Shift: Radical Art in 1970s Britain*. London: I.B. Tauris.

Wall, B. 1969. *Headlong into Change: An Autobiography and a Memoir of Ideas since the 1930s*. London: Harvill Press.

Walsh, M. 1981. *The Brechtian Aspect of Radical Cinema*. London: British Film Institute.

Ward, D. 1995. *A Poetics of Resistance: Narrative and the Writings of Pier Paolo Pasolini*. London: Associated University Presses.

Weeks, J. 1994. *Sex, Politics and Society: The Regulation of Sexuality since 1800*. London: Longman.

Wenner, J.S. 2000. *Lennon Remembers*. London: Verso.

Willemen, P. (ed.). 1977. *Pier Paolo Pasolini*. London: British Film Institute.

Willemen, P. 1994. *Looks and Frictions: Essays in Cultural Studies and Film Theory*. London: British Film Institute.

Williams, A. 1992. *Republic of Images: A History of French Filmmaking*. London: Harvard University Press.

Wollen, P. 1982. *Readings and Writings: Semiotic Counter-strategies*. London: Verso.

Wood, R. and M. Walker. 1970. *Claude Chabrol*. London: Studio Vista.

Wyver, A. 2014. 'Television', in C. Stephens and J.-P. Stonard (eds), *Kenneth Clark: Looking for Civilisation*. London: Tate Publishing, pp. 123–31.

Young, N. 1977. *An Infantile Disorder? The Crisis and Decline of the New Left*. London: Routledge & Kegan Paul.

Youngblood, G. 1970. *Expanded Cinema*. New York: P. Dutton.

Žižek, S. 2002. *The Sublime Object of Ideology*. London: Verso.

Žižek, S. 2004. *Iraq: The Borrowed Kettle*. London: Verso.

Articles referred to

Bates, R. 1985. 'Hole in the Sausage of History: May '68 as Absent Center in Three European Films', *Cinema Journal* Spring: 24–42.

Beasley-Murray, J. 1997. 'Whatever Happened to Neorealism? – Bazin, Deleuze, and Tarkovsky's "Long Take"', *Iris* Spring: 37–52.

Beloff, M. 1968. 'October for the Rebels: Student Barricades in Britain?', *Encounter* October: 48–56.

Beloff, M. 1969. 'The L.S.E. Story', *Encounter* May: 66–77.

Belton, J. 1987. 'Bazin is Dead! Long Live Bazin!', *Wide Angle: Film Quarterly of Theory, Criticism and Practice* 9(4): 74–81.

Bertolucci, B. 1967. 'Versus Godard', *Cahiers du Cinéma* January: 29–30.

Bordwell, D. 1984. 'Jump Cuts and Blind Spots', *Wide Angle: Film Quarterly of Theory, Criticism and Practice* 6(1): 4–11.

Coutard, R. 1965/66. 'Light of Day', *Sight and Sound* Winter: 9–11.

Demoriane, H. 1968. 'Jean Luc Godard talks to Hermine Demoriane', *IT* [The International Times] 39, 6–19 September: 4.

DiIorio, S. 2007. 'Total Cinema: *Chronique d'un Été* and the End of Bazinian Film Theory', *Screen* 48(1): 25–43.

Eagle, H. 1991. 'Dada and Structuralism in Chytilova's Daisies', *Cross Currents: Yearbook of Central European Culture* 10: 223–234.

Erffmeyer, T.E. 1983. 'I Only Want You to Love Me: Fassbinder, Melodrama, and Brechtian Form', *Journal of the University Film and Video Association* Winter: 37–43.

Finler, J. 1968. 'L'affaire Godard', *IT* [The International Times] 46, 13–31 December: 24.

Geras, N. 1973. 'Rosa Luxemburg: Barbarism and the Collapse of Capitalism', *New Left Review* November-December: 17–37.

Godard, J.-L. 1966. 'Night, Eclipse, Dawn . . . an Interview with Michelangelo Antonioni by Jean-Luc Godard', *Cahiers du Cinema in English* January: 9–16.

Habermas, J. 1968. 'A Critical Word at "The Court . . . of our Self-appointed Revolutionaries"', *Encounter* September: 58–59.

Hames, P. 1979. 'The Return of Vera Chytilova', *Sight and Sound* Summer: 168–173.

Harris, T. 1987. 'Rear Window and Blow-Up: Hitchcock's Straightforwardness vs. Antonioni's Ambiguity', *Film / Literature Quarterly* 15(1): 60–63.

Hartog. S. 1972/73. 'The Estates General of the French Cinema', *Screen* 13(4): 58–89.

Heath, S. 1973. 'Film/Cinetext/Text', *Screen* 14(1/2): 102–27.

Houston, P. and R. Roud. 1968. 'Cannes 1968' *Sight and Sound*. Summer: 115–117.

Jacob, G. 1964/65. 'Nouvelle Vague or Jeune Cinema', *Sight and Sound* Winter: 4–8.

Jacob. G. 1967. 'Hollywood sur Seine', *Sight and Sound* Autumn: 162–66.

Jameson, F. 1984. 'Periodizing the 60s', *Social Text*, Spring-Summer: 178–209.

Jungk, R. 1968. 'Naked Revolution', *Encounter* September: 93.

Jussawalla, A. and H. Bellville. 1968. 'Eye Witness Reports of the Godard Explosion at the NFT', *The Listener* 12 December: 791–92.

Lebel, J. 1968. 'On the Necessity of Violation', *The Drama Review* Fall: 89–105.

Lovell, A. 1976/76. 'Brecht in Britain – Lindsay Anderson (on *If. . .* and *O Lucky Man!*)', *Screen* 16(4): 62–80.

Lunn, E. 1974. 'Marxism and Art in the Era of Stalin and Hitler', *New German Critique* Fall: 12–44.

MacCabe, C. 1975/76. 'The Politics of Separation', *Screen* 16(4): 46–61.

Macdonald, S. 1969. 'Pasolini: Rebellion, Art and a New Society', *Screen* 10(3): 19–34.

Moeller, H. 1979. 'Brecht and "Epic" Film Medium', *Wide Angle* 3(4): 4–11.

Morgan, D. 2006. 'Rethinking Bazin: Ontology and Realist Aesthetics', *Critical Inquiry* 32 (Spring): 443–81.

Narboni, J. 1987. 'Andre Bazin's Style', *Wide Angle: Film Quarterly of Theory, Criticism and Practice* 9(4): 56–60.

New Left Review. 1968. 'Editorial Introduction' *New Left Review* 52 (November-December): 1–8.

O'Kane, J. 1983. 'Framing the Sixties', *Enclitic* Autumn: 24–34.

Rosen, P. 1987. 'History of Image, Image of History: Subject and Ontology in Bazin', *Wide Angle: Film Quarterly of Theory, Criticism and Practice* 9(4): 7–34.

Slover, G. 1968. 'Blow-up: Medium, Message, Mythos, and Make-believe', *Massachusetts Review* Autumn: 753–70.

Von Moltke, J. 2000. 'Between the Young and the New: Pop Sensibilities and Laconic Style in Rudolf Thome's *Rote Sonne*', *Screen* 41(3): 257–281.

Williams, R. 1973. 'Base and Superstructure in Marxist Cultural Theory', *New Left Review* November-December: 3–16.

Wollen, P. 1995. 'Possession', *Sight and Sound* September: 20–23.

World Wide Web articles referred to

Anon. 1966. 'The Role of Godard', *Internationale Situationniste* #10, March. Retrieved 18 April 2014 from www.bopsecrets.org/SI/10.godard.htm

Index